Haunting the House of Fiction

Haunting the House of Fiction

Feminist Perspectives

on Ghost Stories by American Women

Edited by

Lynette Carpenter and

Wendy K. Kolmar

The University of Tennessee Press   Knoxville

The paper in this book meets the minimum requirements of the
American National Standard for Permanence of Paper for Printed
Library Materials.⊗ The binding materials have been chosen for
strength and durability.

LIBRARY OF CONGRESS CATALOGING IN PUBLICATION DATA
Haunting the house of fiction : feminist perspectives on ghost stories
  by American women / edited by Lynette Carpenter and Wendy K.
  Kolmar. — 1st ed.
      p. cm.
  Includes bibliographical references and index.
  ISBN 0-87049-688-3 (cloth: alk. pa.)
    1. Ghost stories, American—History and criticism.   2. Domestic
fiction, American—History and criticism.   3. American fiction—
Women authors—History and criticism.   4. Feminism and
literature—United States.   5. Women and literature—United
States.
  I. Carpenter, Lynette, 1951–   . II. Kolmar, Wendy K., 1950–   .
  PS374.G45H38   1991
  813' .08733099287—dc20   90-12910   CIP

To

Mary Jane Carpenter

Peg Kolmar

Klaus Kolmar

Anna Rachel Kolmar Muldoon

Casey Carpenter

Acknowledgments

THE AUTHORS GRATEFULLY ACKNOWLEDGE the financial support of the University of Cincinnati, Drew University, and Ohio Wesleyan University.

Special thanks go to our research assistants, Lovelle Clark, Deirdre Kane, Caroline McCall, Laura Nelsen, Martina Nowak, and Elizabeth Smith. We have also appreciated the assistance of University of Cincinnati librarians Sharon Propas and Sally Moffitt.

For advice and counsel we thank Juliann E. Fleenor, Tricia Lootens, Susan Gubar and Ellen Messer-Davidow; and for unflagging support and encouragement, as well as shared information, Alfred Bendixen. Jessica Amanda Salmonson has also generously shared resources with us.

At The University of Tennessee Press, we thank Carol Wallace Orr for her patient encouragement and advice, and Kim Scarbrough, Lee Sioles, and the rest of the Tennessee staff for keeping us on track. We also thank Jean Tyrone for her careful and sensitive editing.

Contents

Illustrations

Haunting the House of Fiction

Lynette Carpenter and Wendy K. Kolmar

Introduction

THIS COLLECTION OF ESSAYS represents one part of a larger
project that began eight years ago with a fortunate coincidence.
In 1982 we proposed and presented a panel called "Subversive Themes in Women's Popular Literature" for the National
Women's Studies Association annual conference, held that year at
Ohio State University. For that panel, one of us wrote a paper on
ghost stories by several nineteenth-century British women writers,
including Vernon Lee and Charlotte Riddell. At the time, the
other had just finished an essay on ghost stories by a twentieth-
century American woman, Ellen Glasgow. Separately, each of us
had observed women writers using the ghost story genre to critique mainstream male culture, values, and tradition, yet neither
of us knew at that point if the works we were considering were
anomalous or if they were evidence of a female tradition of supernatural literature.

With feminist criticism like Ellen Moers's *Literary Women*,
Sandra Gilbert and Susan Gubar's *Madwoman in the Attic*, and
Elaine Showalter's *A Literature of Their Own* already in print to
suggest the existence of a female tradition in literature, we believed that we were likely to find a relatively unexplored body of
women's work in supernatural fiction, and we did. We discovered

that many so-called major women writers as well as many less well-known writers had written ghost stories and that there were women's ghost stories to be found throughout the nineteenth and twentieth centuries in England and America.

Recently, some of these stories have become available, thanks to the publication of collections by Alfred Bendixen, Richard Dalby, Alan Ryan, and Jessica Amanda Salmonson. With these stories as evidence, we believe that women's writing in the ghost story genre does represent a reimagining of this genre not unlike women writers' reinvention of the genres of the Gothic, science fiction, autobiography and bildungsroman.[1] In women's stories, we perceive a set of common reasons for turning to the ghost story, a set of similar perceptions among many women writers of the possibilities of the form for exploring dangerous territory. What we found and wish to outline here is a series of tendencies, not inevitabilities: the works of some men may manifest the characteristics of this tradition; the works of some women will not.

From the beginning of the project, we focused our interest very clearly on ghost stories—stories with an actual, probable, or suspected ghost—or stories like Edith Wharton's "Miss Mary Pask" or Ellen Glasgow's "Dare's Gift," which clearly invoke the ghost story form, though the ghost ultimately turns out to be a living person.[2] We excluded from consideration tales of horror and terror, many of which, like Le Fanu's "Green Tea," are often classed with ghost stories. We also excluded Gothic tales, mysteries, and tales that involved psychic phenomena, clairvoyance, witches, magic, or other unexplained but possibly supernatural occurrences. We made this distinction in part simply to give our project clear boundaries and in part because some other areas, such as the female Gothic, had already received considerable attention from feminist critics, but also, and perhaps most importantly, because we felt that women writers' use of the ghost story was distinctive and deserved separate exploration. We focus in this volume on American women writers (and plan a companion volume on British women writers), but we see strong affinities between British and American women's ghost stories. Though there is certainly evidence in American and British women's stories of their relationship to their own national literatures, we would finally prefer to think of an Anglo-American women's ghost story tradition.

Origins and Development of the Ghost Story

Most historians of the ghost story genre date its emergence from the mid-nineteenth century and trace its roots to the Gothic novel of the late eighteenth century. In his book, *American Gothic*, Donald Ringe has noted the availability of British Gothic novels in the U.S. from the 1790s on, often in Minerva Press reprints; many of these were written by women, including Ann Radcliffe, Clara Reeve, Sophia Lee, Regina Maria Roche, Eliza Parsons, and Eleanor Sleath. Reeve seems a particularly important figure in preparing the way for the ghost story form, since she condemned Horace Walpole's supernatural excess in *The Castle of Otranto* (1764), but she did not reject the supernatural altogether; she includes ghosts in her most famous novel, *The Old English Baron* (1777). Her more realistic haunting seems to be a precursor for nineteenth-century women's stories in which hauntings are tied to domestic gender politics. Ringe further indicates that American supernatural fiction was also probably influenced by the translations of German romances available in this country, including such ghostly tales as Freidrich von Schiller's *The Ghost-Seer* and Karl Grosse's *Horrid Mysteries* (1797).

American Gothic fiction begins with Charles Brockden Brown's *Wieland* (1798), which undertakes to redefine the Gothic in an American setting. Several features of the novel may suggest its significance to American women writers of the ghost story. Not only is its heroine embattled and terrorized in her own home, but she serves as narrator of the story, making her the forebear of later American female narrators. As in earlier Gothic novels and later ghost stories, the source of danger to the women and children of the family in *Wieland* is the patriarch. *Wieland* ushered in a generation of American Gothics. By the early 1920s, Ringe asserts, "Gothic works were so widely read and admired that even those American authors who were more strongly attracted to the quite different fiction of Henry Fielding and Laurence Sterne felt the need to include some kind of Gothic material in their works" (102).

Washington Irving's tales of the 1820s contribute further to the development of the modern ghost story in the U.S. Critics often point to Irving's German sources, yet Ringe argues that Irving had also read two of Ann Radcliffe's novels as early as 1804. Although Irving, like Radcliffe, always explained the supernatural as natural, or allowed for such an explanation, he established in the U.S. some of the elements of the ghost story, in particular the convention of a group of narratives told by different narrators on a social occasion ("Strange Stories by a Nervous Gentleman").

Both Edgar Allan Poe and Nathaniel Hawthorne played prominent roles in the development of the American supernatural tale; their influences on the women's tradition, while significant, were rather more limited. Poe's use of the house in such stories as "William Wilson," discussed in E. Suzanne Owens's essay on Gilman in this volume, and "The Fall of the House of Usher," helped to open for later writers the symbolic possibilities of household politics. Often, however, Poe's stories offered women writers a masculine vision of horrifying otherness against which to define their own vision, a relationship explored by Priscilla Leder in her essay on Jewett. Hawthorne, on the other hand, more often explored gender politics in his works, as indicated by such stories of female victimization as "The Birth-Mark" (1843) and "Rapaccini's Daughter" (1844). However, he was rarely willing in his stories to suggest the reality of the supernatural.

While we do not dispute the influence on American women writers of Irving, Poe, and Hawthorne, representative as they are of what Cathy Davidson calls the "American pantheon" (255), we believe with Davidson that such persistent emphasis on the major male writers can obscure other valid perspectives. We contend that American women writers of the ghost story were more profoundly influenced by British women's traditions than by their American male contemporaries and forebears. Donald Ringe's observation that "Ann Radcliffe remained a major influence on American writing well into the nineteenth century" (102) offers one strong example of the importance of British women's Gothic to American readers. Ellen Moers's observation about Emily Dickinson, herself a ghost writer ("One need not be a chamber to be haunted"), could be applied to other nineteenth-century American women writers as well: her knowledge of her male contemporaries was spotty, but "she read and reread every Anglo-American woman writer of her time" (92). Not only was the work of British women writers available to their American sisters through reprints in American magazines and by American publishers, but until the International Copyright Law of 1891 was passed, the works of foreign writers were actually less expensive than those of U.S. writers.[3] Moreover, as Jane Tompkins has persuasively argued in her book, *Sensational Designs*, the American canon as we know it was not rigidly established in the nineteenth century; women who read Harriet Beecher Stowe, Elizabeth Stuart Phelps, and Harriet Prescott Spofford, in addition to the Brontes, George Eliot, and Mary Elizabeth Braddon, would have felt that they had read some of the major literary figures of their day. Among the most widely published Americans and Britons, social networks supplemented literary networks, as discussions by both Moers and Josephine Donovan seek to demonstrate.[4]

Most critics feel that the ghost story was at its height during the late Victorian and Edwardian periods, though they base this assertion on a rather limited sample of male writers.[5] If we take into account the work of women writers of ghost stories, it seems clear that the ghost story has thrived on both sides of the Atlantic for most of the nineteenth and twentieth centuries.

Even before the beginnings of the Gothic in the 1760s, ghosts appear as literary motifs in many contexts, among them some Greek and Roman texts, Elizabethan drama, medieval romance, and Celtic, Teutonic, and other folk traditions.[6] Stories of supposedly actual hauntings were also popular, particularly in the seventeenth and eighteenth centuries. Collections of tales about "true" hauntings, like Catherine Crowe's *The Night Side of Nature* or Jeanne de Lavigne's *Ghost Stories of Old New Orleans*, persist through the nineteenth and into the twentieth century, as do individual tales that claim to be based in fact; Alice Cary, Lydia Maria Child, and Rose Terry Cooke all published examples of the latter. Publication of such accounts was fueled in the late nineteenth century by popular interest in spiritualism and psychical research. The proliferation of societies for psychical research, which E. F. Bleiler reports thrived in Britain and the U.S. during this period (1977), offers strong evidence of such popular interest. In the twentieth century, interest in parapsychology seems to have sustained interest in allegedly real hauntings.

The emergence of the ghost story genre coincided with the mid-nineteenth-century expansion of both the American and the British publishing industries and the resulting growth in the printing and dissemination of popular literature. In both countries the popularity and certainly the availability of ghost stories seem to have been advanced in the 1850s and 1860s by the proliferation of new periodicals, both middle-class monthlies and cheaper weeklies. Though British periodicals and annuals—particularly those edited by such writers of supernatural tales as Charles Dickens, Mary Braddon, and Charlotte Riddell—are most often noted for increasing the popularity and availability of ghost stories, American periodicals and gift books also welcomed and promoted supernatural tales. Therefore, though Dickens's ghost stories would have been well known to American readers, so would have been those of Fitz-James O'Brien, an Irish American immigrant widely published in American journals. Many British stories were reprinted in American magazines such as *The Eclectic* and *Littell's Living Age*. Other American periodicals, from the high-toned *Atlantic Monthly* and *Harper's New Monthly Magazine* to the more sensational *Frank Leslie's Illustrated Weekly* and *The Flag of Our Union*, nourished native contributions to the genre, many of these by women. Jessica Amanda Salmonson in her introduction to *What Did Miss Darrington See?*, a collection of ghost stories by British and American women, suggests that "as much as seventy percent of the supernatural fiction" in Victorian periodicals, both British and American, "was the work of women" (x).

The growth of a native publishing industry created new opportunities for American women writers. In describing the tenfold increase in American publishing output between 1820 and 1850, Susan M. Coultrap-McQuin asserts that many publishers believed the reading public to be predominantly female, and adds: "Many publishers seemed to see women as the most appropriate authors for the female audience. Women's gains early in the century were amplified in the 1850s by a maturing industry that constantly needed to keep itself profitable" (8). Judith Fetterley's *Provisions* and Nina Baym's *Woman's Fiction* suggest how much work nineteenth-century American women writers were producing for these new markets, and Cathy Davidson has argued that the substantial increase in the literacy of American women generated a fiction focused on women's concerns. In the preface to *What Did Miss Darrington See?*, Salmonson observes: "From the 1830s through the 1920s women were the dominant presence in British and U.S. magazines as poets, essayists, story writers, readers, and often enough as editors; hence women dominated the fashions in literature" (x).

The ghost story was one of several nineteenth-century popular genres dominated by women writers. Women's ghost stories spoke particularly to a female readership and drew their key concerns from women's culture, sometimes crossing with other genres. Local color realism and consolation literature, for example, are closely related to the ghost story. Local color writing was extremely receptive to the supernatural, perhaps in part because of the prominence of ghosts in folklore. More importantly, however, local color realism, as characterized by Josephine Donovan in her book, *New England Local Color Realism: A Women's Tradition*, was dominated by women writers, and its themes were strongly woman-centered as a consequence. Local color writers Alice Cary, Harriet Beecher Stowe, Elizabeth Stuart Phelps, Sarah Orne Jewett, Rose Terry Cooke, Mary Wilkins Freeman, Annie Trumbull Slosson, Charles Craddock (Mary Ann Murfree), and Mildred Haun all wrote ghost stories.

Consolation literature, which claimed a considerable readership by the mid-nineteenth century, also demonstrates clear affinities with the ghost story. As Ann Douglas notes in *The Feminization of American Culture*, the "domestication of death" in the nineteenth-century U.S. encouraged mourners to see heaven as an extension of this world in the most literal terms. The most popular expression of this impulse was Elizabeth Stuart Phelps's *The Gates Ajar*, published in 1868. The novel consists largely of conversations between an aunt and niece concerning the nature of heaven. Their discussions suggest the commonalities between heaven and earth by furnishing heaven's "many mansions" with window boxes and pianofortes. Such literature, ordinarily written by and for women, was like women's ghost stories in further eroding the boundaries between natural and supernatural, life and afterlife.

In general, the supernatural tradition in American literature has been slighted in the past, and histories of the ghost story have tended to focus on British writers. Perhaps, then, it is not surprising that the few sources that examine the American supernatural give little space to women's contributions, which are rarely included in the canon and therefore remain invisible to many critics. For example, in their collection, *The Haunted Dusk*, editors Howard Kerr, John W. Crowley, and Charles Crow describe a tradition in the U.S. dominated by a few men. They see the American supernatural tradition, as embodied early on by Poe and Hawthorne, and later by James and Howells, as "a literature of the unconscious" (5). In *The Haunted Dusk*, Jay Martin's essay, "Ghostly Rentals, Ghostly Purchases: Haunted Imaginations in James, Twain, and Bellamy,"—while crediting Phelps's *The Gates Ajar* (1868) with beginning this trend—sees the work of male writers, chiefly James, Twain, and Bellamy, as "helping to fashion" in their supernatural writing "a modern, psychological version of the romance" (6). Kerr, Crowley, and Crow argue that the development of both sophisticated psychoanalytic theory in the twentieth century and of a physical science revealing a natural world governed more by abstract principles than by benign "anthropocentrism" led to the decline of the supernatural in mainstream literature. "The supernatural tale," they write, "evolved either into the surreal fiction of a Kafka or the psychoanalytical case history" (9).

Most historians of the genre observe a gradual decline in the ghost story over the early decades of the twentieth century, and certainly the record of mainstream periodicals bears out this observation. Salmonson observes a "masculinization" of the mainstream magazine industry in the twentieth century that may account, to some extent, for this decline. However, the twentieth century has provided newer, more specialized outlets for ghost stories in such periodicals as *Weird Tales* and *Amazing Stories* and with publishers such as Arkham House and Strange. Moreover, the prominence of ghosts in other popular genres, especially during the forties, suggests that interest in the supernatural has never entirely faded.[7] More recently, the seventies and eighties have witnessed not only the resurgence of ghosts in popular genres such as film and television, but the reentry of the supernatural into mainstream literature. This is especially true in the case of women writers, and perhaps ascribable in part to the increased publication of women of color by mainstream presses. Among the American women writing novels that one might classify as ghost stories, many now are women of color: Toni Morrison, Gloria Naylor, Toni Cade Bambara, Paule Marshall, Maxine Hong Kingston, and Louise Erdrich.

An American Women's Ghost Story Tradition

We claim, then, the existence of a distinctive women's tradition of ghost story writing in both England and the U.S. from 1850 on. Like work by women in other genres and periods, ghost stories by women challenge the assumptions of men's work in the genre during each period; women often seem to develop their stories in conscious antithesis to men's stories. Though women's stories may have grown out of some of the social concerns and cultural anxieties that critics identify as the sources of men's supernatural stories, women writers often explore different areas of concern, and express their responses differently.

In addition, women are the literary inheritors of key thematic concerns that come to them from substantially female genres, particularly the Gothic. From the Gothic, women ghost story writers inherited a context for describing what Kate Ferguson Ellis calls the "failed home" (ix), and a precedent for addressing issues that could not be confronted openly: "The conventions of the Gothic novel, then, speak of what in the polite world of middle-class culture cannot be spoken" (7). From the female Gothic, they inherited a series of themes and images—of women victimized by violence in their own homes, of women dispossessed of homes and property, of the necessity of understanding female history, and of the bonds between women, living and dead, which help to ensure women's survival. Immensely significant in recasting these themes was Charlotte Bronte's *Jane Eyre*, a novel that influenced not only the ghost story but also that other descendant of the Gothic novel, the modern Gothic romance. *Jane Eyre's* language of captivity and freedom, female empowerment and disempowerment, its images of the ghostlike double who wanders the house at night, and its fiery denouement, in which the woman burns the house where she has been permitted to be mistress: these would all be incorporated into the ghost story tradition as it was practiced by American women, a tradition that remained hidden until recently.

Ghost stories by women writers, then, have often been measured against definitions and standards based on men's stories and have been found anomalous. This seems clear if we look at the major thematic concerns most often identified with men's ghost stories. Critics usually associate the flourishing of the ghost story in the late nineteenth century with two major intellectual/cultural trends: first, the growing preference for scientific rationality rather than Christian faith as a way of explaining the workings of nature; and second, a fin de siecle uncertainty about the stability of the institutions of society and culture, and perhaps also the stability of the human personality, as Freudian ideas about the unconscious gained currency. Writing specifically about nineteenth-century American supernatural fiction, Kerr, Crowley, and Crow observe that "the disorienting effect of the supernatural encounter in fiction seems to reflect some deeper disorientations in the culture at large. The nineteenth century, after all, was the scene of great debates between faith and doubt, religion and science, transcendentalism and positivism" (2–3). The perception of the world as dualistic—defined by "debates" between reason and unreason, science and spirituality, conscious and unconscious, or natural and supernatural—informs both the men's stories of the nineteenth and early twentieth century and the critics' definitions of them. Thus, critics see "ambiguity" in many of these stories that is simply a tension between the poles of these binary oppositions.

Such dualistic thinking, an approach to the supernatural that

seeks to confirm one side of the dichotomy by wholly denying the
other, is not characteristic, we believe, of ghost stories by women.
Women often seem to violate consciously this aspect of the genre
as practiced by male writers. In her introduction to Salmonson's *What Did Miss Darrington See?*, Rosemary Jackson asserts:
"Women writers of the supernatural have overturned many of
these assumptions and definitions [concerning rigid boundaries
between life and death]—not, as with some of their male counterparts, to investigate 'horror' for its own sake, but in order to extend our sense of the human, the real, beyond the blinkered limits
of male science, language, and rationalism" (xviii).

In their ghost stories, women writers seem more likely to portray natural and supernatural experience along a continuum.
Boundaries between the two are not absolute but fluid, so that
the supernatural can be accepted, connected with, reclaimed, and
can often possess a quality of familiarity. For example, in Annie
Trumbull Slosson's "A Dissatisfied Soul" (1904), a woman explains that she was not surprised when her sister-in-law returned
after death, since her relative had always been a restless spirit,
never remaining in the same place for very long: "It appeared
to come about so natural, just in the course of things, as you
might say" (116). Similarly, in Mary Austin's "The Readjustment"
(1908), Emma Jossylin's return from the dead is reported almost
casually in the second sentence of the story: "The sister who had
come to the funeral had taken Emma's child away with her, and
the house was swept and aired; then, when it seemed there was
least occasion for it, Emma came back" (206). Emma's return is
certainly curious, but hardly earth-shattering.

As Wendy Kolmar suggests in her essay, this sense of the continuity between the natural and supernatural is often nurtured
by cultural traditions other than a white Eurocentric one. So,
American women writers with roots in minority cultures seem
even more likely to accept the supernatural. In African-American
and Native American cultures, family ghosts, like living family

members, are simply part of experience. They can be healing and supportive, and can bring information crucial to survival, as they do in Toni Morrison's *Song of Solomon* (1977), Toni Cade Bambara's *The Salt Eaters* (1980), Paule Marshall's *Praisesong for the Widow* (1984), and Gloria Naylor's *Mama Day* (1989). Like the living family, they can also be angry and resentful, as in Maxine Hong Kingston's *The Woman Warrior* (1976) and Morrison's *Beloved* (1988).

One common characteristic of the ghost story as it has been generally defined is the narrators' opening claim to rationality, their attempts to establish their credentials as credible observers. In the British women's tradition, such an opening gambit often signals a critique of the classic ghost story and its espousal of rationality. Some American women also employ this technique; in the first paragraph of Ellen Glasgow's "Dare's Gift," for example, the male narrator wrestles with irrationality: "There are, of course, no haunted houses in this age of science; there are merely hallucinations, neurotic symptoms, and optical illusions. There is—I admit it readily!—a perfectly rational explanation of every mystery" (47). In this case, as Lynette Carpenter observes in her essay, there is a perfectly rational explanation for the events of the story, one which the male narrator, in his arrogant self-assurance, cannot perceive. However, American women writers, who seem more inclined to use female narrators rather than the heavily undercut male narrators preferred by their British sisters, often find other means of challenging the valorization or glorification of reason. Priscilla Leder, in her essay, notes that when a mother's ghost appears at a daughter's deathbed, the narrator remarks, "I never called it beyond reason that I should see the other watcher" (Jewett, *World* 290).

More prevalent than this expansion of "reason" to include the supernatural, however, is the replacement of reason as the key interpretive faculty with another faculty: sympathy. The valuing of the quality of sympathy shows the affinity of these American women's stories with consolation literature, which, in keeping with the feminine ideology promulgated by the Beechers, privileged sentiment and feeling over reason and intellect. Fisken's essay on Freeman, Fedorko's essay on Wharton, and Carpenter's essay on Glasgow all suggest that it is sympathy that allows female characters to encounter the supernatural and, often, to respond appropriately. In Mary Elizabeth Counselman's "The Unwanted" (1950), a woman census taker in the mountains of Alabama sees, through sympathy born of her own motherhood, the ghostly children their mother claims but their father denies.

We emphasize here the appropriateness of the character's sympathetic response because the term "ghost story" has traditionally been used interchangeably with terms such as "tale of horror" or "tale of terror," a practice that further obscures women's contributions to the genre. While ghostly encounters may be horrifying or terrifying in the women's tradition, horror and terror are rarely the most appropriate responses to such visitations. Instead, women characters realize their commonality with the ghostly women and children they encounter and are often called upon to understand and act upon the messages brought by those who haunt their houses. Often, these messages warn of the dangers of domesticity, frequently through connections between the ghost's history and that of the living woman.

That a genre concerning itself so centrally with the haunting of houses should attract women writers is hardly surprising, given the long-standing designation of home as "woman's sphere." But inhabiting a literary tradition, like inhabiting a house, does not guarantee ownership, and women's contributions to the genre even in this area are seldom acknowledged. Women's ghost stories, filled with dispossessed women and children, testify that house keeping is hard work for women. Glasgow's "The Shadowy Third," discussed in the Carpenter essay, and Shirley Jackson's *The Haunting of Hill House*, discussed in the Lootens essay, offer examples of the dangers to women of life in patriarchal houses.

A woman returns to claim her family home, for which she worked herself to death in E. D. E. N. Southworth's *The Haunted Homestead*. Photo by Jay Yocis and Ken Van Dyne from the 1860 edition published by T. B. Peterson.

Gilman's nameless narrator in "The Yellow Wallpaper," discussed by Suzanne Owens, is not even permitted to choose her own room in the family's summer rental.

However, women's attachment to their houses can also be confirmed after death, when they return to reassert their claim, as in E. D. E. N. Southworth's *The Haunted Homestead* (1860), Mary Wilkins Freeman's "The Southwest Chamber" (1903) and Amélie Rives's *The Ghost Garden* (1918).[8] Houses haunted by women provide a powerful image of the house as an embodiment of female tradition. The ghostly claimant in *The Haunted Homestead* worked herself to death trying to save her family farm, only to see it sold by her husband as soon as she died. In Glasgow's "The Shadowy Third," a woman dies when her husband removes her to an asylum from the house in which she was born, a house haunted by her ghostly daughter. Indeed, the madhouse acts as a persistent threat to women's house keeping, since it provides a convenient means of dispossessing female property owners. This is one area of thematic commonality between women's ghost stories and the female Gothic. The young woman imprisoned in a madhouse in Louisa May Alcott's "A Whisper in the Dark" (1863)[9] is virtually haunted by a shadowy figure in the room above; she discovers that it is her mother, not dead as she has been told but defiantly alive and unghostly despite her long confinement in the same house to which her daughter has been brought.

Ghostly visitations often bring characters into contact with their maternal legacies, as in Glasgow's "Whispering Leaves." In Mary Raymond Shipman Andrews's "Through the Ivory Gate" (1905), a poor young man returns to his mother's family home in Kentucky to see it for the last time but receives ghostly guidance that permits him to recover a treasure and save the house. A similar visitation permits a young man to save his mother's house in Jeanne de Lavigne's "Up the Garret Stairs" (1946). In both cases, the actual ghosts are male—an uncle and a grandfather—but their connection to the protagonist is maternal, and their appearances ultimately enable the protagonist to marry and thus perpetuate the female history of the house.

As already suggested, however, the politics of domesticity tends to make that history a violent one. Women and children are the most frequent victims of domestic violence, as many of the essays in this volume attest, and their victimization provides the explanation for numerous hauntings. A woman in Rebecca Harding

A young man receives ghostly guidance to a legacy that will save his maternal home in Mary R. S. Shipman Andrews's "Through the Ivory Gate." Photo by Jay Yocis and Ken Van Dyne from B. West Clinedinst's illustration for *Scribner's Magazine*, 1905.

Davis's "A Story of a Shadow" (1872) thus explains the haunting of her house with "a story that a child was killed here, or a bride" (542). Crimes against women range from neglect and isolation, as in Gertrude Atherton's "The Dead and the Countess" (1905) and Elia Wilkinson Peattie's "The House that Was Not" (1898); to the oppressive silencing in Cynthia Ozick's *The Pagan Rabbi*, discussed here by Ruth Rosenberg; to coercion, seduction, and betrayal, as in Harriet Prescott Spofford's *Sir Rohan's Ghost* (1860); to assault and murder, as in Wharton's "The Lady's Maid's Bell" and Spofford's *Sir Rohan's Ghost*. Children are equally vulnerable. In A. M. Hoyt's "The Ghost of Little Jacques" (1863), the narrator suspects her employer's wife of poisoning a sickly child who cannot contribute to the family income; only after she subsequently marries the supposed widower does she learn the truth: the child was killed by its father, not its mother.[10]

At the same time, women's stories often envision the empowerment of the powerless by death. In Wharton's "Kerfol" (1916), a woman insists that she has been rescued from her violent husband by the ghosts of the pet dogs he has strangled. In *Sir Rohan's Ghost*, an English nobleman is pursued by the ghost of the woman he seduced and attempted to murder, "a Ghost that, sleeping or waking, never left him, a Ghost whose long hair coiled round and stifled the fair creations of his dreams, and whose white garments swept leprously into his sunshine" (11). In Emma Dawson's "A Sworn Statement" (1897), a valet recounts how his master was hounded by a sad but vengeful lady before he disappeared. In Josephine Daskam Bacon's "The Unburied" (1913), a jilted woman secrets her letters behind a brick in the fireplace and effectively corrupts the house after her death until the letters are discovered and burned. And as Ellen Glasgow's "The Shadowy Third" illustrates, children are also given opportunities for revenge.

Not surprisingly, motherhood constitutes a central theme of women's ghost stories, as of much literature by women. Glasgow's

"The Shadowy Third" and Counselman's "The Unwanted" both illustrate a maternal love that transcends the boundaries between life and death. Similarly, in Bacon's "The Children" (1913), a woman's desire for the children she has never had, when nurtured by a sympathetic nurse who has lost children of her own, calls into being two ghostly children. The woman dies of happiness when the children's presence is confirmed by a child witness, just as a mother dies of happiness when reunited with her ghostly daughter in Hildegarde Hawthorne's "A Legend of Sonora" (1891).[11] In Cornelia A. P. Comer's "The Little Gray Ghost" (1912), a ghostly mother hounds a man until he adopts her orphaned daughter.

As Beth Wynne Fisken's essay on Freeman suggests, however, maternity is not always presented as unproblematic in women's ghost stories, which often record anxiety and ambivalence. At the same time, few ghost stories conform to Juliann Fleenor's description of the female Gothic: "Perhaps these dichotomies [between male/female, bad woman/good woman] and subsequent tensions account for the conflict at the heart of the Female Gothic, the conflict with the all-powerful, devouring mother. This maternal figure is also a double, a twin perhaps, to the woman herself" (12). In women's ghost stories, conflicts between mother and daughter, where they appear, are much more ambiguous. As Barbara Rigney notes in her essay on Toni Morrison's *Beloved*, Morrison's protagonist Sethe is a mother who creates as well as kills, and both creation and infanticide are considered expressions of maternal love. Sethe is thrilled when her daughter returns as a ghost, and the ghostly Beloved both loves her passionately and wishes to destroy her. Sethe could hardly be described unequivocally as "the all-powerful, devouring mother." The same can be said of the "Great, Great, Grand, Mother," Sapphira Wade, who haunts the island of Willow Springs in Gloria Naylor's *Mama Day*, and who passes on her power to her granddaughter Mama Day. Sapphira is associated with the great goddess, who sends both life and death. Mama Day feels deeply ambivalent about the powers she has inherited, since she often foresees but cannot divert disaster, and since her special status requires that she be without a mother and childless herself, but her reward is to be claimed at last by the Great Mother herself in a dream: "Daughter. The word comes to cradle what has gone past weariness" (283).

The women's tradition in supernatural fiction, which we have only just sketched here, both historically and conceptually, has had almost no critical attention. Literary historians have frequently associated women writers with the Gothic and Gothic romance genres, but rarely with the ghost story. The anthologists have, for the most part, likewise failed to present women's work. Salmonson observes: "In the United States, it remains accepted practice for 'leading' anthologists, nearly all male, to exclude women altogether" (xii). She adds: "Among British anthologists the exclusion is slightly less severe, perhaps because a larger number of the anthologists are women" (xii).

American women writers of the ghost story have received virtually no critical attention beyond the work of Salmonson and Bendixen. Kerr, Crowley, Crowe, and their nine contributors (only one of whom appears to be a woman) include just one essay focused on a woman writer and include one additional essay that mentions a woman writer as a major source. The present collection, we believe, suggests not only the richness of possibilities for critical work in this genre, but argues for the explanatory power of a range of feminist approaches. Contributors and editors alike have drawn on an array of feminist work in history, philosophy, psychology, anthropology, popular culture, and ethnic and minority studies, as well as feminist literary criticism, genre criticism, and debates regarding canon formation.

The essays in this collection have been arranged more or less chronologically by authors studied, since an arrangement reflecting their thematic commonalities seemed overly complex. Some essays, such as those on Jewett, Ozick, and Kingston, describe attempts to invent or reinvent the genre. Some, such as the essays on

Freeman and Glasgow, use biographical information extensively. The essay on Jackson involves scrutiny of the manuscripts over the various stages of a novel's composition. All of the essays, however, address issues of gender and power that women writers felt were best expressed through use of the supernatural, and all of the essays together argue persuasively that the history of supernatural literature in the U.S. would be understood quite differently if it were written with careful attention to the work of American women writers.

BIBLIOGRAPHIC NOTES and works cited by individual contributors are located at the end of each chapter.

Notes

1. Studies in which feminist critics have explored women writers' re-creation of these genres include: Estelle C. Jellinek, ed. *Women's Autobiography* (Bloomington: Indiana UP, 1980); Elizabeth Abel, Marianne Hirsch, and Elizabeth Langland, eds. *The Voyage In* (Hanover, NH: UP of New England, 1983); Juliann E. Fleenor, ed. *The Female Gothic* (Montreal: Eden, 1983); Ellen Moers, *Literary Women* (New York: Doubleday, 1986); Marlene Barr, ed. *Future Females* (Bowling Green, OH: Bowling Green UP, 1981).

2. We should note here that we have not restricted our use of the term "ghost story" to a narrative of any particular length, though most treatments of the genre do assume that "ghost stories" are short stories. The distinction is not very useful, however, for the nineteenth century, when novels often ran to several volumes, stories to several chapters, and when publishers arbitrarily designated their offerings by a host of names, such as novellas, novelettes, and E. D. E. N. Southworth's "nouvelette" *The Haunted Homestead*.

3. We are grateful for this insight to Vic Doyno, who spoke at the 1989 San Diego Conference on American Literature about Mark Twain's attitude toward the absence of an international copyright.

4. Both Donovan and Moers give examples of trans-Atlantic connections between literary women, like the more frequently discussed connections between male writers like Emerson and Carlyle. Donovan cites George Eliot as a principal source for nineteenth-century local color realism, and although she notes Stowe's emphasis on developing an American tradition that would counter European sentimentalism, she traces Stowe's realism to British women writers Charlotte Lennox and Maria Edgeworth. To the circle of women realists that centered on Annie Adams Fields, wife of publisher James P. Fields, Stowe brought her European connections with Dickens, Eliot, Gaskell, Barrett Browning, and Madame Belloc, *Uncle Tom* translator and grandmother of supernatural writer Marie Belloc Lowndes.

5. Jack Sullivan in *Elegant Nightmares*; Edward Hynes in *The Edwardian Turn of Mind*; Philip Van Doren Stern in his "Introduction" to *Great Ghost Stories*.

6. For surveys of the origins of the transitions see Birkhead, Briggs, Penzoldt, Scarborough, and Sullivan, among others.

7. For a discussion of the persistence of fantasy elements in film and literature of the 1940s, see Peter L. Valenti, "The 'Film Blanc': Suggestions for a Variety of Fantasy, 1940–45," *Journal of Popular Film* 6 (1978):294–304; and Lynette Carpenter, "Benevolent Fantasy and the Imagination in Popular Literature and Film of the Forties," *The Scope of Fantasy—Culture, Biography, Themes, Children's Literature*, ed. Robert A. Collins and Howard Pearce. Westport, CT: Greenwood, 1984. 51–57.

8. Freeman's "The Southwest Chamber" appears in *The Wind in the Rose-Bush* and in the *Collected Ghost Stories*, which are cited in the bibliography at the end of this volume, as are Rives's and Southworth's collections.

9. This story originally appeared in *Frank Leslie's Illustrated Newspaper* in 1863 and was reprinted in *A Modern Mephistopheles and A Whisper in the Dark* in 1889.

10. We have been unable to confirm the sex of the author, but we believe her to be Anna M. Hoyt who published short fiction in *Harper's* during this period.

11. The story originally appeared in *Harper's* in 1891.

Works Cited

Alcott, Louisa May. "A Whisper in the Dark." *Plots and Counter-plots: More Unknown Thrillers of Louisa May Alcott.* Ed. Madeleine B. Stern. New York: Morrow, 1976.

Andrews, Mary Raymond Shipman. "Through the Ivory Gate." *Scribner's* 37 (1905): 698–713.

Austin, Mary. "The Readjustment." *Lost Borders.* New York: Harper, 1909. Rpt. in *What Did Mrs. Darrington See?.* Ed. Jessica Amanda Salmonson. New York: The Feminist Press, 1989: 205–11.

Barr, Marlene, ed. *Future Females: A Critical Anthology.* Bowling Green, OH: Bowling Green UP, 1981.

Baym, Nina. *Woman's Fiction.* Ithaca, NY: Cornell UP, 1978.

Bendixen, Alfred, ed. *Haunted Women.* New York: Ungar, 1985.

Bleiler, E. F. "Mrs. Riddell, Mid-Victorian Ghosts and Christmas Annuals." *The Collected Ghost Stories of Mrs. J. H. Riddell.* New York: Dover, 1977.

Briggs, Julia. *The Rise and Fall of the English Ghost Story.* London: Faber, 1977.

Comer, Cornelia A. P. "The Little Gray Ghost." *Atlantic* 109 (1912): 311–20.

Coultrap-McQuin, Susan M. "Why Their Success? Some Observations on Publishing by Popular Nineteenth-Century Women Writers." *Legacy* 1, 2 (Fall 1984): 1, 8–9.

Counselman, Mary Elizabeth. "The Unwanted." *Weird Tales.* 1950. Rpt. in *Half in Shadow.* Sauk City, WI: Arkham House, 1978.

Crowe, Catherine. *The Night Side of Nature.* London: n.d.

Dalby, Richard. *Victorian Ghost Stories by Eminent Women Writers.* London: Carroll & Graf, 1989.

Davidson, Cathy. *Revolution and the Word: The Rise of the Novel in America.* New York: Oxford UP, 1986.

Davis, Rebecca Harding. "A Story of a Shadow." *Galaxy* 13 (1872): 541–52.

Dawson, Emma Frances. "A Sworn Statement." *An Itinerant House and Other Stories.* San Francisco: Doxey, 1897.

Donovan, Josephine. *New England Local Color Realism: A Women's Tradition*. New York: Ungar, 1983.

Douglas, Ann. *The Feminization of American Culture*. New York: Knopf, 1977.

Ellis, Kate Ferguson. *The Contested Castle: Gothic Novels and the Subversion of Domestic Ideology*. Urbana: U of Illinois P, 1989.

Fetterley, Judith, ed. *Provisions*. Bloomington, IN: Indiana UP, 1985.

Fleenor, Juliann E., ed. *The Female Gothic*. Montreal: Eden, 1983.

Gilbert, Sandra M. and Susan Gubar. *The Madwoman in the Attic: The Woman Writer and the Nineteenth-Century Literary Imagination*. New Haven: Yale UP, 1979.

Glasgow, Ellen. "Dare's Gift." *The Shadowy Third and Other Stories*. Garden City, NY: Doubleday, 1923.

Hawthorne, Hildegarde. "A Legend of Sonora." *Faded Garden: The Collected Ghost Stories of Hildegarde Hawthorne*. Ed. Jessica Amanda Salmonson. Madison, WI: Strange, 1985.

Hoyt, A. M. "The Ghost of Little Jacques." *Atlantic Monthly* 11 (1863): 213–26.

Hynes, Edward. *The Edwardian Turn of Mind*. Princeton, NJ: Princeton UP, 1971.

Jackson, Rosemary. "Introduction." *What Did Miss Darrington See?* Ed. Jessica Amanda Salmonson. New York: Feminist P, 1989.

Kerr, Howard, John W. Crowley, and Charles Crow, eds. *The Haunted Dusk: American Supernatural Fiction, 1820–1920*. Athens: U of Georgia P, 1983.

Lavigne, Jeanne de. "Up the Garret Stairs." *Ghost Stories of Old New Orleans*. New York: Rinehart, 1946.

Martin, Jay. "Ghostly Rentals, Ghostly Purchases: Haunted Imaginations in James, Twain, and Bellamy." *The Haunted Dusk*. Eds. Howard Kerr, John W. Crowley, and Charles Crow. Athens: U of Georgia P, 1983.

Moers, Ellen. *Literary Women*. New York: Doubleday, 1976.

Peattie, Elia Wilkinson. "The House That Was Not." *The Shape of Fear and Other Ghostly Tales*. 1898. Rpt. Freeport, NY: Books for Libraries P, 1969.

Penzoldt, Peter. *The Supernatural in Fiction*. London: Nevill, 1952. Rpt. New York: Humanities P, 1965.

Ringe, Donald. *American Gothic: Imagination and Reason in Nineteenth Century Fiction*. Lexington, KY: UP of Kentucky, 1982.

Ryan, Alan. *Haunting Women*. New York: Avon, 1988.

Salmonson, Jessica Amanda, ed. *What Did Miss Darrington See?*. New York: Feminist Press, 1988.

Scarborough, Dorothy. *The Supernatural in Modern English Fiction*. 1917. Rpt. New York: Octagon, 1967.

Showalter, Elaine. *A Literature of Their Own*. Princeton, NJ: Princeton UP, 1977.

Slosson, Annie Trumbull. "A Dissatisfied Soul." *Atlantic* 94 (1904): 114–24.

Stern, Philip Van Doren. "Introduction." *Great Ghost Stories*. 1942. Rpt. New York: Washington Square, 1948.

Sullivan, Jack. *Elegant Nightmares*. Athens, OH: Ohio UP, 1976.

Tompkins, Jane. *Sensational Designs: The Cultural Work of American Fiction 1790–1860*. New York: Oxford UP, 1985.

Priscilla Leder

Living Ghosts and Women's Religion in Sarah Orne Jewett's *The Country of the Pointed Firs*

LIKE OTHER REALIST WRITERS of her generation and the succeeding one, Sarah Orne Jewett found ghosts to be a fascinating part of real experience and a suitable subject for fiction. Their presence in her fiction, although rare, provides occasions for contrasting male and female perspectives on the nature of reality and for developing a religious vision that is uniquely feminine. In one episode of her novel, *The Country of the Pointed Firs,* Jewett transforms a traditionally male confrontation with an alienating wilderness into a manifestation of continuity within and between this world and the next. The elderly Captain Littlepage's account of the ghostly "shapes" (37) that inhabit a gloomy arctic region "between this world an' the next" (39) has much in common with the tradition in American fiction that features inquisitive male adventurers striking out into unknown territory, only to find themselves confronted with a terrifying realm in which the boundaries of their ordinary experience seem to disappear. On the one hand, by including this adventure in a work dominated by women characters and domestic incidents, Jewett avoids the accusation of narrowness and triviality often leveled at works that focus on female experience. However, Jewett's incorporation of this "male" adventure narrative into a "female" work does more than deflect the disparagement of traditional critics: she resolves a dilemma that haunts American fiction by dissolving the dichotomy between an ordered but confining civilization and a liberating but threatening wilderness, and she thereby transforms alien and terrifying otherness through human significance and use.

In doing so, Jewett resembles some of the pioneer women Annette Kolodny describes in *The Land Before Her*. These women's capacity to withstand the threatening wilderness "often appears directly related to their capacity either to create . . . a garden or at least to project its possibility onto the forested wilderness" (37). Like gardeners, Jewett and her women characters create order and utility out of the threatening and incomprehensible landscape of Captain Littlepage's narrative. By comparing the captain to one of the herbs in Almira Todd's garden, Jewett's narrator affirms Mrs. Todd's ability to "cultivate" even such wild growths as the captain and his ghosts.

In Jewett's writings, ghosts are ambiguous, never firmly identified with this world or the next. Apparitions may turn out to be living people, but that discovery never entirely dissipates their mystery or their power.[1] In fact, the question of their actuality seems unimportant relative to their emotional and moral significance—what they *are* matters less than what they *mean*. The emphasis on significance prevails even in the case of the most substantial of Jewett's ghosts, Mis' Tolland's mother in "The Foreigner." As she watches at the bedside of the dying Mis' Tolland, Almira Todd, like her patient, sees a third woman in the shadowy doorway. In evaluating her experience, Mrs. Todd ignores the question of physical actuality and instead attests to an expanded sense of what is reasonable: " 'I never called it beyond reason I should see the other watcher' " (*World* 290). Mrs. Todd emphasizes her perception of the phenomenon rather than its actuality. To Mrs. Todd, the ghost's appearance is within reason because it performs a recognizable human function—to comfort the dying Mis' Tolland by showing her that she " 'ain't never goin' to feel strange and lonesome no more' " (289). Thus, a visitation from the other world, which might be terrifying in its otherness, finally reveals not distance and strangeness but closeness and familiarity.

In "A Woman's Vision of Transcendence: A New Interpretation of the Works of Sarah Orne Jewett," Josephine Donovan has identified Mrs. Todd with a "women's religion of healing, hospitality, and community" (380), and this religion provides a thematic center for *The Country of the Pointed Firs*. Mrs. Todd's ability to comprehend the ghost's significance is consistent with her function in many works of Jewett's: she draws people and events together by presiding over and participating in domestic rituals—especially rituals that serve to link this world to the next. Elizabeth Ammons writes that Mrs. Todd constitutes one example of Jewett's belief in "a type of therapeutic female psychic energy which could be communicated telepathically and which could operate both to bond individuals and to create a spiritual community—or occult sisterhood—among women in general" (Ammons 168). The narrator of *The Country of the Pointed Firs*, a young woman writer visiting Dunnet Landing for the summer, begins and ends her narrative with Mrs. Todd.

Contained within this larger narrative is another narrative, a ghost story told by Captain Littlepage in an account of his arctic voyage. This account at first evokes much more of the frightening otherness usually associated with ghost stories than does the gentle apparition of "The Foreigner." Captain Littlepage tells the narrator of being shipwrecked north of the Arctic Circle and stranded at a remote mission, where he meets another castaway named Gaffett. The survivor of a polar expedition, Gaffett describes "a strange country 'way up north beyond the ice, and strange folks living in it," and convinces the captain that "it was the next world to this" (35). Altogether, the plot and imagery of the captain's story introduce the alienation, madness, dissolution, and death so often associated with the journey undertaken in traditional nineteenth-century novels by men. Yet despite these elements, Jewett, her narrator, and Mrs. Todd present the captain's story in a way that finally encompasses and, in a sense, redeems a masculine theme in the interests of a "woman's religion" of community.

Many of the best-known critical discussions of the "classic American novel" focus upon the protagonists' flight from civilization into some attractive but perilous unknown territory.[2] Huck Finn on the river, Ishmael at sea, and Natty Bumppo in the forest all abandon the constraints of civilization in favor of a world without boundaries. Such freedom has its dangers, for without geographical boundaries, an explorer can become lost, and outside the social boundaries by which he defines himself, his very identity can be lost. Unable to locate himself, the protagonist feels as if he may be dissolved into the confusion that confronts him. This danger is manifest in the confusing landscapes, threatening encounters, and inconclusive endings of many of the works of American fiction.

The arctic expedition Captain Littlepage recounts contains all the elements of the characteristically American male journey into the unknown: to seek the pole is to travel beyond the boundary of human knowledge in search of some ultimate end. A comparison between Edgar Allan Poe's *The Narrative of Arthur Gordon Pym of Nantucket* and Captain Littlepage's adventures can illuminate the ways in which Jewett reappropriates the classic American encounter with a terrifying wilderness. In *Pym*, Poe provides an account of another fictitious polar exploration that encounters an unearthly presence. Captain Littlepage recounts Gaffett's narrative of an arctic exploration; Pym relates an adventure that takes him to the South Pole. Both adventurers confront confusing, indistinct landscapes and have their expectations violated by unexpected warmth. As Pym approaches the pole, he faces a cataract of white ashes falling silently into a white sea. Nothing is distinct: the top of the cataract cannot be seen; the ashes blend into the water, and the images behind the cataract disappear before they can be classified. In the arctic, Gaffett and his companions see a town that disappears when they approach it, a town peopled by " 'blowing gray figures that would pass along alone, or sometimes gathered in companies as if they were watching' " (37). Like the images behind the cataract, the gray figures are vague in outline and disappear before they can be fully perceived: when the sailors pursue one of the figures, " 'he flit[s] away out 'o sight like a lead the wind takes with it, or a piece of cobweb' " (37).

In both *Pointed Firs* and *Pym*, the loss of perceptual boundaries parallels a loss of metaphysical boundaries: " 'Say what you might,' " Captain Littlepage declares, " 'they all believed 't was a kind of waiting-place between this world an' the next' " (Jewett, *Firs* 39). These ghosts frighten because they cannot be identified with known human experience. When Pym finally penetrates the cataract, he perceives a similarly unaccountable figure: "But there arose in our pathway a shrouded human figure, very far larger in its proportions than any dweller among men. And the hue of the skin of the figure was of the perfect whiteness of the snow" (Poe 198). The word "figure" in each description suggests a disturbing shape that the narrator cannot or will not identify as human.

Confronted with such pervasive uncertainty, Pym and the sailor in Captain Littlepage's narrative, like other explorers in American fiction, become bewildered and disoriented. In the absence of the boundaries they rely upon to orient themselves, they are threatened with loss of identity. In Captain Littlepage's narrative, an attack by the "figures" underscores the danger that the sailors will be engulfed and become undifferentiated from their attackers, who swarm " 'like bats' " in an attempt to " 'drive 'em back to sea' " (38): " 'Sometimes a standing fight, then soaring on main wing tormented all the air' " (38). In *Pym*, the figure makes no such overt threat, but the threat is implicit in the environment: it arises from "the embraces of the cataract, where a chasm threw itself open to receive us" (Poe 198). These voyagers are also in danger of being swallowed up, their identity dissolved.

In their peril, the sailors in Captain Littlepage's account resemble their brothers in American fiction. However, elements of their story serve to distance them from a threat of dissolution. For example, though the figure in *Pym* remains passive, Pym and his companions seem more in peril because they are being drawn into something "with hideous velocity" (197) rather than being driven away as are the sailors in Littlepage's narrative. Similarly, in that narrative the sailors take conscious fright and are able to flee, while in *Pym* the characters experience a kind of dissolution of will: "And now, indeed, it would seem reasonable that we would experience some alarm at the turn events were taking— but we felt none. . . . I felt a *numbness* of body and mind— a dreaminess of sensation—but this was all" (196). Apparently, Pym experiences a kind of paralysis of will that prevents him from differentiating himself from the fearful external reality he confronts. Thus, Poe's characters participate in a dissolution that Jewett's characters escape altogether.

Similarly, Jewett's narrative strategy serves to distance her readers from that confrontation while Poe's attempts to involve them in it. Poe suggests that his account is somehow literal; Jewett assures the reader that hers is literary and should be judged as literature. *The Narrative of Arthur Gordon Pym of Nantucket* was published as Poe's retelling of an actual adventure, with a preface by the "real" Pym. This elaborate strategy does more than simply suggest veracity; it confuses the distinction between truth and fiction. Edward H. Davidson classifies *Pym* as a hoax: "The special trick would be to fool the readers and then let them know they had been fooled. The problem was, therefore, 'scientific': how to create an illusion so lifelike that no one would be sure of the line separating truth from fantasy" (xxiii). Like Pym and his companions, then, those who read his account experience the blurring of an essential psychological distinction. "Pym's" narrative breaks off just as he sees the white figure, and despite the editorial note indicating that the subsequent chapters were lost, the impression is one of the inadequacy of language itself in the face of unstructured, unclassifiable experience. The figure recalls the whiteness of the whale in *Moby-Dick*, which terrifies because it reveals the arbitrariness and fragility of the means by which experience is classified.[3] In a sense, Poe's readers themselves are confronted with the dissolution of boundaries that accompanies the penetration of unknown territory in classic American male adventure novels.

Although *Pointed Firs* depicts that dissolution, Jewett places the experience at a distance from the reader. Poe's adventurer narrates his own story; Jewett's narrator recounts a story told her by Captain Littlepage, who was told it by Gaffett. Furthermore, whereas Poe tries to suggest that this narrator is both real and reliable, Jewett's characters call Captain Littlepage's sanity into question. Yet by treating the tale as a literary work rather than a literal account, Jewett's narrator and Mrs. Todd in effect dismiss the question of the tale's foundation in truth and the disturbing question of the captain's sanity. In a sense, the captain himself reinforces their attitude: he intersperses his story with comments about his reading and about his admiration for Shakespeare and Milton, and he casts his description of the "attack" of the gray figures in the language of Milton: "They stood thick at the edge o' the water like the ridges o'grim war; no thought o' flight, none of retreat. Sometimes a standing fight, then soaring on main wing tormented all the air" (38). Even the captain's name suggests the significance of his adventure tale by labeling him a "little page" to be read with interest and pleasure. Louis Renza suggests that he is "little" in comparison with his literary counterparts Captain Ahab and the Ancient Mariner (171). Similarly, the captain's account presents a miniaturized version of those large-scale confrontations with the oceanic wilderness—a version which reduces its dangers to manageable scale without denying them.

Though Captain Littlepage's tale may be "little" to its auditors and readers, it seems overwhelming to him.[4] He is driven by the need to demonstrate the reality of the ghosts to himself and to others and profoundly disturbed by the impossibility of doing so. Captain Littlepage yearns for the security of direct knowledge. As he and the narrator discuss the death of a neighbor, he declares, " 'It may be found out some o' these days. . . . We may know it all, the next step; where Mrs. Begg is now, for instance. Certainty, not conjecture, is what we all desire' " (23). Those blowing gray figures can never yield that certainty. Gaffett and the captain are mistaken not in their belief that the ghost city exists but in their conviction that its existence can be measured, verified, and used as objective proof of life after death. This conviction, more than his tale itself, makes the captain seem "overset" (21).

Because Captain Littlepage and his male counterparts in American fiction demand objective knowledge, experiences that defy scientific verification disorient and terrify them. However, as women, Mrs. Todd and the narrator ultimately judge the captain's tale by its human usefulness rather than by its status as truth. For example, they seem to respond to the captain's tale as literature, a human creation that can afford entertainment and insight, rather than as a perception whose reality must be validated. Their reflections on it are more concerned with its artistry than with its actuality. For the narrator, "Gaffett with his good bunk and the bird-skins, the story of the wreck of the Minerva, the human-shaped creatures of fog and cobweb, and the great words of Milton with which he described their onslaught upon the crew, all this moving tale had such an air of truth that I could not argue with Captain Littlepage" (42). She seems to praise the captain's literary artistry by calling his account a "moving tale," and she skirts the issue of whether Gaffett's experiences are hallucinatory, or the captain's memory faulty, by commenting not upon the story's veracity but upon its verisimilitude: she will not argue with the captain because his narrative has the *air* of truth, not necessarily because it *is* true. Verisimilitude is essentially a literary convention—a consideration of a reader's idea of reality rather than of reality itself.[5] Because that story is cast in the language of Milton and because the captain's "overset" mind is attributed to too much reading, the tale seems a product of his literary imagination. Similarly, the mysterious forms appear as "human-shaped creatures of fog and cobweb," which intimates that they have been formed by the captain out of indistinct perceptions and blurred memories—shaped *by* a human as well as having human shape.

Like the narrator, Almira Todd seems to view the captain's tales as literature, although she displays a critical concern with internal consistency: " 'Some o' them tales hangs together toler'ble well,' she added, with a sharper look than before. 'An' he's been a great reader all his seafarin' day. Some thinks he overdid, and affected his head, but for a man o' his years he's amazin' now when he's at his best' " (44). Though she does not explain just how the captain is "amazin'," the context of her adjective suggests that he is literally amazing, a teller of wonderful tales.

By considering the captain's story as literature, valuing it for its capacity to serve the community as entertainment, Mrs. Todd and the narrator begin to redeem this gloomy, disturbing tale. Yet it is something more than entertainment in that it addresses the possibility of what the narrator calls "the world beyond this which some believe to be so near" (45)—a realm very much present in *The Country of the Pointed Firs*. Through her presentation of Captain Littlepage's account and her women characters' response to it, Jewett reveals that that other realm is not the chaotic antithesis of this one, but that a natural order extends through both. In confronting the other world, Captain Littlepage and other male adventurers make the mistake of failing to recognize its true relationship to this world.

The ghost city, like other unknown territories in American fiction, fails to yield to objective verification because it lies outside the social structures which serve to order and classify our experience. As Josephine Donovan observes, the "timeless realm beyond history" evoked by Captain Littlepage's story is connected to the domestic sanctuaries of *The Country of the Pointed Firs* (Jewett 105). However, the two spaces extend "beyond history" in different senses. The ghost city, like the unexplored territory of the American male adventure narrative, lies outside of history, immune to the cause-effect explanations we employ to order human experience. The dangers inherent in such spaces embody the dangers inherent in viewing human experience as progress—the end and the beginning of the process remain inaccessible. Polar expeditions provide particularly apt metaphors, since the search for the ultimate, the end, reveals only nothingness. By drawing the captain's "timeless realm" into the natural cycles that run through *Pointed Firs*, Jewett begins to transform the linear progress of traditional "masculine" history into the circle of natural "feminine" history, a transformation described by Ann Douglas in *The Feminization of American Culture*: "American women of Melville's generation were trying to replace the masculine vision of history as a series of political and economic facts enacted and marshaled by men with a feminine view of social and biological process" (Douglas 313). In presenting the captain and his story, Jewett begins to resolve the dilemma inherent in classic American novels by men, by incorporating its central themes into the feminine themes of natural cycles and community.

Though beyond history, Jewett's ghost city lies in a realm that is neither static, nor dead, nor disordered. Donovan and other critics have drawn a connection between Captain Littlepage's ghost city and Green Island,[6] which Mrs. Todd points out to the narrator at the end of their discussion of Captain Littlepage: "The sunburst upon that outermost island [Green Island] made it seem like a sudden revelation of the world beyond this which some believe to be so near. 'That's where mother lives,' said Mrs. Todd.

'Can't we see it plain?'" (45). The narrator's language compares the island to heaven—a "world beyond this" which is radiant, not dim, celestial, not terrestrial. Similarly, Mrs. Todd's age, sixty-seven, invites the inference that her mother has gone to heaven, yet Green Island is a real place where Mrs. Todd's real mother actually dwells. Heaven and earth become one place, life and death part of one process. The place that the narrator associates with the end of life, perhaps recalling the funeral procession she has just witnessed, is in actuality the home of the mother, the beginning of life. The image describes a circle, evoking the cycle of birth and death that transcends the linear progress of history.

Throughout *Pointed Firs*, Jewett draws together mean and extreme, past and present, this world and the next, in such a way as to make them part of one entity. She effects this partly by emphasizing universal domestic human experience—especially marriage; parenthood; the gathering, preparation, and sharing of food; sickness and healing; death and bereavement. She also imparts a certain universality to the life of Dunnet Landing by comparing it to other places and times. Mrs. Todd, for example, seems to embody the archetype of the mysterious nature goddess whose losses and sufferings generate her wisdom and power: she appears to the narrator as "an enchantress" (47) and "a huge sybil" (10). Jewett frequently evokes mythology, especially that of the Greeks, who seem to signify an origin, a kind of prototype of western culture. Often, the language of Jewett's comparisons suggests not merely similarity but actual contiguity. Mrs. Todd "might have been Antigone alone on the Theban plain . . . an absolute, archaic grief possessed this countrywoman; she seemed like a renewal of some historic soul, with her sorrows and the remoteness of a daily life busied with rustic simplicities and the scents of primeval herbs" (78). Although Mrs. Todd only "might have been" Antigone, the grief which possesses her is "absolute" and "archaic"—continuous with Antigone's, almost a Platonic form. Like the emotion that possesses her, she seems a reincarnation of someone from the past; and her herbs are "primeval," as if she were tending not individual plants but the very species themselves. Altogether, life in Dunnet Landing is a life that has been lived forever, or for as long as humans have inhabited the earth.

Just as ancient Greece seems a remote and magical region that nevertheless opens onto the world of Dunnet Landing, the ghost city seems distant yet contiguous. When Mrs. Todd gives the narrator an herb beer and informs her, " 'I don't give that to everybody,' " the narrator feels "for a moment as if it were part of a spell and incantation, and as if [her] enchantress would now begin to look like the cobweb shapes of the arctic town" (47). Mrs. Todd seems part of the other world of the ghost city in the act of using her wisdom to refresh and nourish the narrator: the same gesture that binds women to each other draws the next world into this. In an earlier passage, the captain himself seems a part of Mrs. Todd's magic: "Mrs. Todd . . . seemed to class [Captain Littlepage] with her other secrets. He might have belonged with a simple which grew in a certain slug-haunted corner of the garden, whose use she could never be betrayed into telling me, though I saw her cutting the tops by moonlight once, as if it were a charm, and not a medicine" (17). For those who can perceive and participate in the unifying natural cycle that runs through this world and the next, even the captain and his alienating tale of the breakdown of the boundaries of human knowledge can be put to use.

Although Mrs. Todd can never be betrayed into telling Captain Littlepage's use, her conversations with the narrator as well as the narrator's perceptions themselves reveal that he provides both entertainment and yet another reminder that the other world lies just beyond this one. Less obviously, he constitutes both an acknowledgment of the fascination of the limits of verifiable knowledge and a warning against the perils of attempting to exceed those limits.

The "masculine" theme is thus neither denied nor made preeminent. In a sense, Captain Littlepage's story enables Jewett to escape what Gilbert and Gubar have called the woman writer's "double bind": "She had to choose between admitting she was 'only a woman' or protesting that she was 'as good as a man'" (64). The woman writer who admits to being "only a woman" by taking domesticity as her subject exposes herself to criticism for neglecting the "important"; the woman writer who implicitly protests that she is as "good as a man" by trying to write about the extreme, "important" experience exposes herself to criticism for her ignorance of her subject matter or the inappropriateness—the "unladylikeness"—of her choice. By developing the theme of the exploration of unknown territory in the context of community, Jewett manages to have it both ways.

Critic Warner Berthoff acknowledges this achievement from a decidedly male perspective when he writes that Captain Littlepage makes that "reference to the life of male action and encounter without which the narrator's sympathy for backwater Dunnet Landing would seem myopic, sentimental" (44). From a masculine perspective like Berthoff's, the inclusion of the "important" story of a potentially destructive journey beyond known boundaries redeems an otherwise "unimportant" celebration of continuity and community. From a feminist perspective, that context of continuity and community redeems the alienation and discontinuity inherent in that typically American theme.

Notes

1. In "A Sorrowful Guest," for example, the "ghost," Henry Dunster, turns out to have been alive when he first appears to the protagonist, but his later appearances defy probability. Similarly, in "Lady Ferry," the woman who appears doomed to live forever finally dies, but not after much evidence that she has lived before in another century, and is, therefore, a ghost. Both stories appear in Sarah Orne

Jewett, *Old Friends and New* (Freeport, NY: Books for Libraries Press, 1969).

2. I refer here to a group of works, most of which appeared in the 1950s and early '60s, and all of which attempted to identify characteristic American preoccupations, especially in literature. See especially: Richard Chase, *The American Novel and Its Tradition* (Garden City, NY: Doubleday, 1957); Charles Feidelson, Jr., *Symbolism and American Literature* (Chicago: U of Chicago P, 1953); Leslie Fiedler, *Love and Death in the American Novel* (New York: Stein, 1960); Daniel Hoffman, *Form and Fable in American Fiction* (New York: Oxford UP, 1961); Richard Poirier, *A World Elsewhere: The Place of Style in American Literature* (New York: Oxford UP, 1966); and Richard Slotkin, *Regeneration Through Violence: The Mythology of the American Frontier, 1600–1800* (Middletown, CT: Wesleyan UP, 1973). For a penetrating discussion of the "masculinity" of the "classic American novel," see Nina Baym, "Melodramas of Beset Manhood: How Theories of American Fiction Exclude Women Authors," *American Quarterly*, 33:2 (Summer 1981), 123–39.

3. "Or is it," Ishmael asks, "that as in essence whiteness is not so much a color as the visible absence of color, and at the same time the concrete of all colors; is it for these reasons that there is such a dumb blankness, full of meaning, in a wide landscape of snows—a colorless, all-color of atheism from which we shrink?" Herman Melville, *Moby-Dick* (New York: Norton, 1979), 169.

4. The narrator indicates that just after the captain located the ghost city "between this world and the next," he sprang "to his feet in his excitement, and made excited gestures, but he still whispered huskily" (30). The narrator's response suggests that the captain is losing control: " 'Sit down, sir,' I said as quietly as I could" (31).

5. Nancy K. Miller makes this point cogently in "Emphasis Added: Plots and Plausibilities in Women's Fiction," *PMLA*, 96 (January 1981), 36–48.

6. See especially Robin MacGowan, "The Outer Island Sequence in *Pointed Firs*," *Colby Library Quarterly*, Ser. 6, no. 19 (1964), 421.

Works Cited

Ammons, Elizabeth. "Jewett's Witches." *Critical Essays on Sarah Orne Jewett*. Ed. Gwen L. Nagel. Boston: Hall, 1984. 165–83.

Berthoff, Warner. "The Art of Jewett's 'Pointed Firs.'" *The New England Quarterly* 32 (March 1959), 31–53.

Davidson, Edward H., "Introduction" to *Selected Writings of Edgar Allan Poe*. Boston: Riverside, 1956.

Donovan, Josephine. *Sarah Orne Jewett*. New York: Ungar, 1980.

———. "A Woman's Vision of Transcendence: A New Interpretation of the Works of Sarah Orne Jewett." *The Massachusetts Review* 21 (1980), 365–80.

Douglas, Ann. *The Feminization of American Culture*. New York: Knopf, 1977.

Gilbert, Sandra M. and Susan Gubar. *The Madwoman in the Attic: The Woman Writer and the Nineteenth-Century Literary Imagination*. New Haven: Yale UP, 1979.

Jewett, Sarah Orne. *The Country of the Pointed Firs*. Boston: Houghton, 1896.

MacGowan, Robin. "The Outer Island Sequence in *Pointed Firs*." *Colby Library Quarterly*. Ser. 6, no. 19 (1964).

Miller, Nancy K. "Emphasis Added: Plots and Plausibilities in Women's Fiction." *PMLA* 96 (1981), 36–48.

Poe, Edgar Allan. *The Narrative of Arthur Gordon Pym of Nantucket*. New York: Harper, 1838.

Renza, Louis. *"A White Heron" and the Question of a Minor Literature*. Madison: U of Wisconsin P, 1984.

Beth Wynne Fisken

The "Faces of Children That Had Never Been"

Ghost Stories by Mary Wilkins Freeman

ON AUGUST 12, 1889, AFTER Sarah Orne Jewett wrote to Mary Wilkins[1] praising "A Gentle Ghost," her earliest printed ghost story, Wilkins made two different responses to that praise in a single day. To her friend, Kate Upson Clark, she wrote dismissively: "I do not care much about that story, and do not approve of this mystical vein I am apt to slide into if I don't take care" (*Infant Sphinx* 96), while to Jewett she replied hesitantly: "You don't know how glad I am that you do like my Gentle Ghost, for I have felt somewhat uncertain as to how it would be liked. It is in some respects a departure from my usual vein, and I have made a little lapse into the mystical and romantic one for which I have a strong inclination, but do not generally yield to" (97). Wilkins liked to tell ghost stories around an open fire. She was unsure, however, as to how she felt about having such stories printed. Twenty years after her letter to Jewett on the subject, in a letter to Fred Lewis Pattee dated September 5, 1919, she confessed: "Most of my own work, is not really the kind I myself like. I want more symbolism, more mysticism. I left that out, because it struck me people did not want it, and I was forced to consider selling qualities" (*Infant Sphinx* 382). Evidently, the mining of that "mystical vein" was an issue of artistic integrity that troubled her throughout her career.[2]

Mary Wilkins Freeman undertook the most sustained quarrying of that vein in the years 1900 to 1903, when she wrote the stories included in the volumes *Understudies* (1901), *Six Trees* (1903), and *The Wind in the Rose-bush* (1903). In *Understudies* and *Six Trees*, which explored the spiritual correspondences between her characters and their natural prototypes, she could anchor her stories securely in Emersonian transcendentalism.[3] For her ghost stories, however, there was no such respectable cloak of literary tradition, which surely accounts for some of her discomfort with the use of that form. The fact that three twentieth-century critics who wrote extensively about Freeman, Edward Foster, Perry Westbrook, and Marjorie Pryse, chose not to include these stories in their discussions demonstrates, perhaps, that the ghost story is still viewed as a minor subgenre.[4]

Yet Wilkins Freeman's ambivalence about her ghost stories goes beyond this issue of literary respectability; it appears also to be a reaction to a particularly troublesome and unmanageable personal element that haunts some of these stories and evidently haunted her as well. In describing to Jewett the circumstances that led her to write "A Gentle Ghost," she said: "I believe I rather laugh at myself for writing it, but that forlorn little girl had been in my head a matter of a dozen years, and I had put her in a poem with poor success once. I felt that she must be disposed of, so about two years ago, I put her in the Gentle Ghost" (*Infant Sphinx* 97). Apparently, that solitary and unloved little girl refused to be "disposed of," however, as we see further manifestations of her lost spirit in "The Little Maid at the Door," "The Wind in the Rose-bush," and "The Lost Ghost," each version of the story more disturbing than the last.[5]

The increased sensationalism in these successive retellings of the story of "that forlorn little girl" might have been a conscious strategy on Mary Wilkins Freeman's part to sell these stories to a jaded public by soft-pedaling the obvious repetitions in basic plot structure, as well as by shocking her readers with an increased voltage of thrills; yet there is an obsessive quality to the repetition of that little girl's story which bears examination. Even in her more usual vein of realistic fiction, Wilkins Freeman returned again and again to the plight of an orphaned and neglected child, badly in need of safe harbor and a surrogate parent.[6]

In her ghost stories, the specter of a little girl who is starved, abused, and/or abandoned, whether deliberately or involuntarily by those who should love and care for her, haunts the women who are most vulnerable to her claims—women who have lost children of their own or childless women with strong maternal feelings. Who is this lost child, this "forlorn little girl"? If, as Wilkins said, this character had been in her head for a dozen years before the writing of "A Gentle Ghost" in 1887 (*Infant Sphinx* 97), then her source may have been her own sister, Anna (Nan) Holbrook Wilkins, who died in 1876 at the age of 17; indeed, in "A Gentle Ghost," a family mistakes the crying of an orphan for that of the frightened ghost of the sixteen-year-old daughter they lost three months before. Nan was born the year that Mary first went to school, an entrance that had been delayed until she was seven, due to poor health.[7] The guilt that surrounds the manifestation of this ghostly little girl may derive from the natural jealousy felt by an older child whose secure status in the family was threatened by the appearance of a rival at a particularly stressful time. Nan grew up to be pretty, outgoing, and talented as a musician, and at the age of sixteen, she became engaged to an organist. The twenty-four-year-old Mary was still unattached, despite her fascination with the handsome and rakish Ensign Hanson Tyler. There may have been some ongoing rivalry, at least on Mary's part, suggested in a comment by her father; comparing the two sisters, Wilkins once said: "Nan . . . is a good musician and will be able to take care of herself. But Mary—she has no talent, and I don't know what she will do to make a living" (qtd. from Wilkins Freeman's cousin, Mrs. E. K. Belcher, in Foster 32). Nan had given public performances of piano and vocal solos, and she was elected pianist of the Brattleboro choral union. Mary may have begun to write poetry as early as 1873, but she had received no public recognition, and, in fact, in 1880 was listed by the United States Census as a "music teacher." Any understandable jealousy that Mary felt, the natural sense of loss at having been supplanted as the favored child, might have shamed and tortured her after Nan's premature death.

Yet the details of Mary Wilkins Freeman's biography also strongly suggest that this lost and abandoned little girl was she as well as her sister—first, psychologically abandoned in the mind of young Mary, eclipsed by an engaging and talented sister, and then, abandoned in earnest, as the years 1876 through 1883 saw the deaths of her sister, her mother, and her father. At the age of thirty, just after the publication of her first story in *Harper's Bazaar*, she found herself alone. The connection could hardly have escaped her, and her conflicting feelings about childhood and adulthood are evident throughout her adult life. Wilkins entered the adult, masculine world of publication as a talented and committed professional writer with a flair for business,[8] yet chose to remain a retiring and even childlike woman who prized and honored the traditional trappings of femininity perpetuated by her society, trappings that manifested themselves in a private vanity and coquetry as well as a public reticence and emphasis on propriety.

Mary Wilkins Freeman seemed to strike a bargain with those closest to her in order to perpetuate a kind of childhood. After her father's death and her initial success as a writer, she moved to the home of her friend, Mary Wales, where she became a part of the Wales household and contributed some much needed financial support. In return, the Waleses supplied her with a home, a family, and emotional security; Mary Wales managed the household, leaving Wilkins free to concentrate on her career. When she needed an audience for a story, Mary listened. When she woke up with a nightmare, Mary comforted her. Throughout her life, Wilkins Freeman emphasized the child in herself, signing the names "Pussy Willow" and "Dolly" to close friends, creating an imaginary circle of family and friends with her pets and, even after marriage, depending on her housekeeper to keep her purse and engagement book, buy her tickets, and get her on the right train. The power of the money earned through her career, traditionally a power known only to men in her society, enabled Wilkins Freeman to manufacture a sustained psychological childhood nurtured by surrogate parents of her own choosing. Wilkins Freeman wrote several collections of children's stories, and as late as 1914 she wrote stories from the perspective of children (*The Copy-Cat and Other Stories*), suggesting that she could easily tap the child in herself and that it was important to her to give that child expression.[9]

The first apparition of that abandoned and "forlorn little girl," "A Gentle Ghost," was written in the summer of 1887 when Wilkins was nearly thirty-five years old. The ghost in this story turns out not to be a ghost at all, but rather a lonely and frightened orphan, Nancy Wren, who cries herself to sleep every night at the poorhouse, frightening the Dunns, the family who live next door, because they mistake her crying for that of their dead daughter. Having read on a family tombstone in the graveyard across the street the words "Our Father" and "Our Mother," the lonely child fantasizes that the people buried there were her family, filling "her empty childish world with ghostly kindred, which had led into it an angel playmate in white robe and crown" (*New England Nun* 251). The power of these fantasies, fueled by loss and loneliness, is matched by the nervous and neurotic intensity of Mrs. Dunn and her daughter, Flora; for the past three months, since the death

of sixteen-year-old Jenny Dunn, they have convinced themselves
that Nancy's sobs are nightly manifestations of Jenny's loneliness
and grief. Wilkins suggests that the mother and daughter, who are
described as "intense and nervous" (242), have willed this apparition into being with their grief and their need, their inability to
let go of the dead child, and she suggests that they will continue
to perpetuate the delusion that they need so badly.

Jenny's death and the subsequent "haunting" have destroyed
the harmony and balance of the relationships in the household.
The two women conceal their distress from Mr. Dunn, who never
hears the crying: "He dealt with the simple, broad lights of life;
the shadows were beyond his speculation. For his consciousness
his daughter Jenny had died and gone to heaven; he was not
capable of listening for her ghostly moans in her little chamber
overhead, much less hearing them with any credulity" (244). The
father, who has come to terms with the death of his daughter,
does not listen for the crying, and the mother is bitter about
his inability to hear it. Consequently, she turns to her surviving
daughter, "who was after her own kind, was all the one to whom
she could look for sympathy and understanding in this subtle
perplexity which had come upon her" (244).

Eventually, they discover that the sounds come from Nancy,
whose crying is ignored by Mrs. Gregg, the pragmatic and un-
sympathetic overseer of the poorhouse, because she does not want
to encourage the child or spoil her with affection. The Dunns
adopt Nancy, who then forgets about her ghostly family in the
graveyard. They fill the void left by Jenny in their own family,
heal their wounds, and exorcise the ghosts of their own dead. The
description of the meadow the family walks through at the end of
the story symbolizes their newfound buoyancy: "The buttercups
in the meadows had blossomed out, but the dandelions had lost
their yellow crowns, and their filmy skulls appeared. They stood
like ghosts among crowds of golden buttercups; but none of the
family thought of that; their ghosts were laid in peace" (252).

That this is a mock ghost story populated only with the ghosts of the characters' grief and loneliness indicates, perhaps, that Wilkins was a bit uncomfortable with the sensationalistic conventions of the genre; however, the circumstances of the plot underscore the main theme of the story, which is the adjustment made by the living, rather than the supposed suffering of the dead. This is a tale of bereavement, concerned with the healthy and unhealthy ways by which survivors cope with loss, a subject that Wilkins knew a good deal about from her own experiences. In this story a part of Wilkins was projected onto the lonely orphan who creates what family she can with the materials available to her and the sheer force of her imagination. At the time of writing this story, Wilkins had been living with her own surrogate family, the Waleses, for about three years. Yet she also could have identified with the driven and guilty sister who rushes in with her light to allay her lost sister's unhappiness.

The plight of the bereft mother is a reflection of Wilkins's situation as well. This story was written at a crucial period in her life. As Foster points out, at thirty-five, within her social milieu, Wilkins was presumably confirmed in her single status, and thus at an age when a woman might anxiously review her life and wonder if she would ever marry and have children. It was at this age that Wilkins created her first version of this ghost of a lost and neglected little girl, searching for a family, who seems also to represent the child that she never had.

During Mary Wilkins Freeman's time, an unmarried woman was frequently viewed as unnatural and pitiful, and an unmarried woman who wrote was an especially monstrous phenomenon. Sandra Gilbert and Susan Gubar have remarked: "The female freak is and has been a powerfully coercive and monitory image for women secretly desiring to attempt the pen. . . . If becoming an *author* meant mistaking one's 'sex and way,' if it meant becoming an 'unsexed' or perversely sexed female, then it meant becoming a monster or freak" (34). As Barbara Welter points out, in the late nineteenth century, even as the status of single women improved with the gradual replacement of the ideal of "True Womanhood" with the more varied and adventurous possibilities of the "New Woman," "yet the stereotype, 'the mystique' if you will, of what woman was and ought to be persisted, bringing guilt and confusion in the midst of opportunity" (174). A fragment from an unpublished story suggests the ambivalence Wilkins may have felt about not having married. Its uncharacteristic use of the first person narrative voice allows Wilkins to enter fully into the tortured mind of her protagonist, Jane Lenox, who sees herself as "a monster," "a hybrid," "a graft on the tree of human womanhood" because she has been deprived of the "character of the usual woman," which would enable her to attain her "birthright" of "a real home of her own with a husband and children in it" (Foster 142–43). Yet Jane Lenox also embraces her exile from the promised land of "usual women" because she attains "power" through her rebellion: "I am a power against the Whole, perhaps only through my antagonism toward the part" (Foster 142). In this fragment, Wilkins gives a painfully intimate portrait of how a woman can come to internalize the standards of her society and use them to punish herself for her difference. Jane Lenox was not Wilkins, yet the societal definitions and expectations that torture this woman surely afflicted Wilkins as well. The fact that this story remained stillborn, incomplete and unpublished, suggests that the material was too disturbing for fictional expression, too personal to be exposed to an audience.

In the years following the publication of "A Gentle Ghost," Wilkins clearly decided to dedicate herself wholeheartedly to her career, writing first a play, *Giles Corey, Yeoman* (1893), and then a novel, *Jane Field* (1891); the latter was especially significant, since she had once told Hamlin Garland that she felt that only "a really great novel" could ensure her serious recognition as a writer, that "a few short stories" were not sufficient (*Infant Sphinx* 84). Nevertheless, she still believed such ambitions to be incompatible with the traditional nurturing roles of women. When in December at the age of 37 she had announced to Kate Upson Clark, half-facetiously, that she was devoting herself to "the great American Drama," she had also firmly rejected marriage: "I suppose the first thing you'll want me to tell you is that I am *not* going to get married, and as far as the signs of the time go, I do not see any reason to apprehend that I ever shall be married. I simply cannot support a family yet. . . . It is so much trouble to run one's self in all the departments! Talk about getting married! If I had to see to a man's collar and stockings, besides the drama and the story and Christmas and the new dress, in the next three weeks, I should be crazy" (*Infant Sphinx* 100). Although to some extent this might be an after-the-fact rationalization of her single state, Wilkins seemed to be marshaling her energy and consciously shutting the door on that life of the "usual woman" that had been denied to her so far. That Wilkins felt some guilt and ambivalence concerning her professional ambitions is suggested by the severe headaches that often kept her from writing at all during the early part of her career, and the laryngitis that prevented her from reading her stories aloud in public. That guilt and confusion, that ambivalence toward the traditional role of wife and mother that Wilkins was openly rejecting, became crystallized in the image of "that forlorn little girl" who would never be hers, an image that haunted both her mind and her fiction.

Wilkins dramatized this conflict between genius and nurturing in such early stories as "A Village Singer" and "An Old Arithmetician,"[10] but it is "The Poetess" that gives the version of this dilemma of domestic tradition versus individual talent that is most directly related to Wilkins's own gifts.[11] Betsey Dole, the main character, is asked to write an elegy for a young boy in order to comfort the bereaved mother. While composing it, she remembers the woman's reproach that she cannot truly understand such a loss because she has no children of her own, musing to herself: "I s'pose it *would* have come home to me different" (*New*

England Nun 147). The story implies, however, that the anguish of such an experience, rather than leading her to write about it differently, would have prevented her from writing at all. While composing, Betsey is circled by poetic muses, "smiling with the faces of children that had never been" (147), faces that enable her to empathize with that woman's grief yet maintain sufficient emotional distance to write about it. These "faces of children that had never been" haunt the ghost stories of Mary Wilkins Free-man, who at the height of her career deliberately decided not to seek her "birthright" of husband, home, and family, ensuring that she would remain childless even after her eventual marriage at the age of forty-nine.

Written at the height of this period of single-minded dedica-tion to her career, "A Little Maid at the Door" dramatizes the elements of this haunting. In this story, set in Salem during the witchcraft hysteria, Ann and Joseph Bayley, a couple who have recently lost their child, pass the home of a family that has been arrested for witchcraft, where the youngest child has been aban-doned to fend for herself. Despite her fears, Ann Bayley aids and comforts the child, then leaves, telling the little girl to watch in the doorway for her return. Although the child dies from neglect in the meantime, her ghost appears in the doorway when Ann rides by again several days later, thereby fulfilling her promise to the woman who had been kind to her.

Like Mrs. Dunn, Flora, and Nancy Wren in "A Gentle Ghost," Joseph and Ann Bayley in "The Little Maid at the Door" have created their own ghosts as "gigantic projections which eclipsed the sweet show of the spring and almost their own personalities" (*Silence* 226). The Bayleys' depression in reaction to the death of their daughter is magnified by their morbid fears of witchcraft. Like little children frightening themselves by telling ghost stories, they blunder through a forest that symbolizes the tangled under-growth of their own neurotic dread, a forest in which a stray black cow becomes the devil and a yellow bird a witch's minion. The cycle of terror is broken for Ann, however, when she spies the little girl, who reminds her of her dead daughter, in the doorway of the deserted house; she refuses to listen to her husband, who claims the child is an evil spirit, and responds naturally and spontaneously to the child's needs, giving her food and water.

The suffering of the deserted child is told from her own point of view in eloquent and painful detail. First her mother and father, and then her sister and brother were arrested, and the child was "left alone in the desolate Proctor house in the midst of woods said to be full of evil spirits and witches, to die of fright and starvation as she might" (239). Ironically (and very naturally) she has internalized the superstitions of her society, and terrified by the night sounds around her, she first flees into the woods and then locks herself in the house, sobbing through the night. Townspeople rob the house of all food, and she is left with nothing.

After Ann Bayley leaves her, the little girl goes about reconstructing, in her own childish and pathetic way, a home and substitute family to give her an illusion of security. To replace the favorite doll that had been thrown down a well, she makes a corncob doll. She gathers together her family's old clothes and creates a fairy ring of safety out of them, creeping inside and nuzzling them like an infant at her mother's breast. When she is no longer strong enough to stand in the doorway to watch for Ann's return, she pulls her little chair over to keep her vigil. Even after her sister returns to care for her, she insists on sleeping in her magic circle and then dreams she is still watching in the doorway for the woman who had acted like a mother to her, after the incomprehensible disappearance of her own mother several months before. It is too late to save the child, but her ghost returns to stand in the doorway as Ann Bayley passes it again on her way back, exclaiming: "Nay, but she stands there. I never saw aught shine like her hair and her white gown; the sunlight lies full in the door. See! See! She is smiling! I trow all her griefs be well over" (254). Ann's blithe unawareness of the child's true fate and of her own role in it underscores the painful irony of this image.

This child is abused; her literal starvation is caused by her metaphoric starvation for love, and this physical dimension makes hers a more disturbing portrayal than that of Nancy Wren in "A Gentle Ghost." The horror of her plight is deepened by the ambiguous position of Ann Bayley, who like Mrs. Dunn in "A Gentle Ghost" offers care and affection, yet puts strict limitations on what she gives for fear of her husband's disapproval. Ann Bayley is complicit in the witchcraft persecution that is the direct cause of the child's suffering; she is accompanied by Cotton Mather when she sees the ghost of the child in the doorway on her return. In this story, the pure image of maternal love as found in Mrs. Dunn's character has been transformed into the complex personality of Ann Bayley, who is mother and persecutor, nurturer and abandoner. The neurotic tendencies of Mrs. Dunn, who strove to deny the death of her child, have metastasized in this story into a "disease of the mind which deafened and blinded to all save its own pains" (226), a disease that wastes and ultimately kills what is young and quick, bright and hopeful. Perhaps the orphaned child in Wilkins entered fully and sympathetically into the suffering of this abandoned little girl, who like Nancy Wren makes shift to create an imaginary family to love and care for her. Yet the neurotic and ambiguous Ann Bayley seems to be a guilty projection of the adult Wilkins as well, who had chosen to suppress her nurturing impulses and lead what her society often judged to be a selfish alternative life. Ann Bayley's guilty if indirect collusion in the circumstances leading to the neglect, starvation, and ultimate death of that child may reflect Wilkins's internalized guilt at having, according to her society's standards, starved and thwarted her own maternal feelings. In "A Gentle Ghost," the possibility of a child is miraculously realized when the haunting resolves itself into a flesh-and-blood child who will bring new life to a bereft household. A few years later in "The Little Maid at the Door," this possibility is rejected, however, as a little girl in desperate need of help and comfort pines and fades to a mere ghost, the help coming too little and too late from a woman who leaves the child

behind, gazing pitifully in the doorway. In her own life, Wilkins
seems at this point to have turned her back on the possibility of a
husband and family and traveled on.

Mary Wilkins Freeman wrote two more versions of the story of
that "forlorn little girl" late in her career; they were first published
just months after her marriage in 1902, at the age of forty-nine,
to Dr. Charles Manning Freeman. Apparently the author's doubts
about marriage persisted throughout their courtship. The length
of their engagement, which lasted about five years, was due in
part to her concern about his heavy drinking, to her conscien-
tiousness about her professional obligations, and, one suspects,
to her desire to avoid the issue of childbearing.[12]

During the early stages of this marriage, which would end in
estrangement in 1921 after Dr. Freeman's institutionalization for
alcoholism, Wilkins Freeman was able to fulfill at least part of her
socially defined role without sacrificing her own needs. Despite
the fears expressed to her close friend Harriet Randolph Hyatt
Mayor that marriage might "swallow" her up and change her
basic personality (*Infant Sphinx* 243), her life after marriage, at
least in the early years, was arranged much as it had been before,
with her husband and her housekeeper taking over Mary Wales's
role. Dr. Freeman undertook to arrange her household and her
schedule to enable her to focus on her writing, even going so far
as to direct her reading and limit her social engagements to pre-
serve her writing edge. If occasionally she felt overwhelmed by
the details of managing a house as "actually doing a man's work
and a woman's work at once" (*Infant Sphinx* 287), still the bulk
of the work fell on the servants. Another letter reveals her attitude
toward housekeeping, in which she expressed the wish for "a little
toy house, in which [she] could do just as [she] pleased, cook a
meal if [she] wanted to, and fuss about generally" (326). Wilkins
Freeman also inherited a ready-made family by way of marriage,
four unmarried sisters-in-law ranging in age from twenty-nine to
thirty-eight, who shared her tastes and interests. In the beginning,

her marriage gave her respectability in the eyes of society without interfering with her career; in fact, her husband and staff joined in coddling and nurturing her so that she could concentrate on her writing. The needy child and the dedicated professional in her were both appeased.

One thing was missing, of course, and that was a child of her own. Although the available letters reveal her ambivalent views on marriage, they seldom mention children at all. At the age of sixty-three she would laugh about an essay she wrote entitled "How Much and What to Tell Daughters," saying, "Lots I know about that . . ." (352), but during her fertile years, she was silent; she simply did not talk about it. Yet Wilkins Freeman could not help but make comparisons. Her close friend, Harriet R. H. Mayor, to whom she expressed most freely her doubts about marriage, was a sculptor and a painter who married at the age of thirty-two, a year and a half before Wilkins Freeman did, and then had a son a year later. As Wilkins Freeman said in a rare but characteristically facetious admission: "You have lovely children, and as for me not even a cat" (339).

If Wilkins Freeman's emotions about her childlessness are never directly expressed in the available letters, hints of them animate two stories collected in her volume of ghost tales published in 1903, the title story, "The Wind in the Rose-bush," and the last story, "The Lost Ghost." The reappearance of "that forlorn little girl" takes on the quality of a recurrent nightmare.[13] These two stories are more intensely horrifying than "A Gentle Ghost" and "Little Maid at the Door" because the children in them are criminally neglected by those who should love and care for them. The neglect of a stranger in "Little Maid at the Door" becomes the neglect of an aunt and the direct abuse of a stepmother in "The Wind in the Rose-bush," and the abuse and abandonment of a mother in "The Lost Ghost." It is intriguing to note that while the women who were haunted by these apparitions in "A Gentle Ghost" and "Little Maid at the Door" were married, the women in these two stories are single, in what is perhaps a strategy on Wilkins Freeman's part to maintain a clear and recognizable public separation between her protagonists and herself.

In "The Wind in the Rose-bush," the ghost of a child, Agnes, who died neglected and abused by her stepmother, haunts her aunt, Rebecca, who comes too late to claim and care for the girl. Throughout the story, the stepmother guiltily attempts to conceal from Rebecca the fact that the child is dead. In the course of the story, the suffering of Agnes, as well as her apparition, are kept offstage. We are informed at the end, in a brief telegram, that her stepmother treated her cruelly after her father died, refusing to give her medicine when she was sick and thereby contributing directly to her death, but the abuse is never portrayed directly. We are not shown her ghost, but rather through the testimony of Rebecca, we hear of shadows flitting across a window, a rose moving where there is no breeze, the same rose then subsequently appearing and disappearing from the upstairs bedroom where her aunt is staying. Rebecca also hears someone playing the piano in the middle of the night. The effect of this strategy is to focus on the personality and predicament of the child's aunt, who is the object of these manifestations. And, indeed, the central tragedy of this story is that of the aunt, Rebecca, rather than the niece, Agnes (meek sacrificial lamb though she might be, as her name suggests).

Gradually we come to know a good deal about Rebecca's hard life—that she was the responsible one and her sister the attractive one, how she had to sacrifice her own "chances" to teach school and take care of her mother, while her sister had the life of the "usual woman," caring for husband, home, and family. Rebecca's understandable envy of her sister's life is apparent when she hears that the second wife has refurnished the house: " 'You got all the things new?' said Rebecca hesitatingly, with a jealous memory of her dead sister's bridal furnishings. . . . 'I suppose you saved some for Agnes. She'll want some of her poor mother's things when she is grown up,' said Rebecca with some indignation" (*Wind* 15). Her emotions are complicated; on the simplest level, she is jealous for her dead sister and her niece and the imagined neglect of their property, but on a deeper level she is jealous for herself; these bridal furnishings are a concrete representation of the life allowed her sister and denied to her, and being able to admire them would enable her to savor that life vicariously.

The tragic irony of Rebecca's situation is that now that her mother is dead and she has been left a little property from her uncle, she is able to take over for her sister, to raise Agnes and share in the "birthright" previously denied to her, but now that she is able to take the child, the child is dead, taken from her. At the beginning of the story, Rebecca is described as "tall and spare and pale, the type of a spinster, yet with rudimentary lines and expressions of matronhood. She all unconsciously held her shawl, rolled up in a canvas bag on her left hip, as if it had been a child. She wore a settled frown of dissent at life, but it was the frown of a mother who regarded life as a forward child, rather than as an overwhelming fate" (4). The accumulation of maternal references suggests that her single life has been at odds with the needs of her nature; it is not surprising that the spirit of the neglected child is drawn to her as if to a surrogate mother.

The story centers on Rebecca's inability to confront the fact that there is no longer a child; her collusion with the stepmother's feeble and increasingly farfetched evasions demonstrates the tenacity of her dream that she will now finally be able to take the child home and raise her as her own. Throughout the story, she grasps at the slightest evidence as a sign of the girl's appearance. When she sees a shadow flit across the window, she exclaims "in a trembling, exultant voice, 'There she is!'", and stares longingly at the door, "waiting for it to open" (17). After the stepmother tells her Agnes is at a party, Rebecca lies "awake a long time listening for the sound of girlish laughter and a boy's voice under her window" (20). When the stepmother says, "Be you gone crazy over

that girl" (28), on one level she is manipulating Rebecca to keep
from having to confess her stepdaughter's death, yet on a deeper
level she speaks the truth. "The Wind in the Rose-bush" is a story
of frustrated maternity, the unhappy situation of a woman whose
circumstances are finally such that she can care for a child, but
for whom that opportunity has come too late, just as marriage
and a home had come too late for Mary Wilkins Freeman. The
ghost that haunts Rebecca is the ghost of the child that had never
been in her life and that now would never be; she is haunted by
her own unfulfilled needs.

In "The Lost Ghost," this symbiosis between the needs of the
abused and abandoned child and those of the motherless woman
is portrayed as even more dangerous, and ultimately, destructive.
Of all the avatars of that "forlorn little girl," this is the most
physical, the most unpleasant, and the most pathetic. The little
girl in this story was maltreated by her own mother, who forced
her to do most of the housework, scolded her continually, and before running away with a married man, locked her up in a room
to starve and freeze to death. The pitiful ghost of that little girl,
who haunts the newly reoccupied house, is blue and pinched with
cold and carries an aura of deathly chill around her. Just as she
was in life, the little ghost is starved for love and frozen for the
lack of it; she washes dishes and does odd chores in an attempt to
win the love and approval of those around her, crying piteously
all the while, "I can't find my mother" (*Wind* 214).[14]

The actual ghost story is told by a former boarder in the
haunted house, many years later, in the context of a debate concerning the reality of ghosts. The sisters haunted by the ghost,
Mrs. Dennison and Mrs. Bird, are maternal women, responsive
to the ghost's demands. Both widows without children, they have
recently bought the house and decide to rent a room in it to the
narrator, a young woman recently orphaned, because, as they tell
her, "We wanted the young company in the house; we were lonesome, and we both of us took a great liking to you the minute we

set eyes on you" (221). On one occasion, when Mrs. Dennison nearly faints, she is careful not to use as a waterglass a tumbler that was painted by the children in a Sunday school class she teaches because she cannot bear to have their present spoiled. Mrs. Bird is even more motherly. As her sister points out: "[She] had coddled her husband within an inch of his life"; she adds, "It's lucky Abby never had any children . . . for she would have spoilt them" (212).

The little ghost that gravitates to them, seeking her mother, is grotesque because she is at once beautiful and "dreadful." The cold "was clinging to her as if she had come out of some deadly cold place" and she had "a dreadful little face with something about it which made it different from any other face on earth, but it was so pitiful that somehow it did away a good deal with the dreadfulness" (214). This pitiful child is also dangerous, and the pity that she evokes, which overcomes dread, is her greatest threat, particularly to Mrs. Bird, who was never "so scared by that poor little ghost, as much as she pitied it, and she was 'most heartbroken because she couldn't do anything for it, as she could have done for a live child" (235). Mrs. Bird exclaims, "It seems to me sometimes as if I should die if I can't get that awful little white robe off that child and get her in some clothes and feed her and stop her looking for her mother" (235). Soon after saying this, Mrs. Bird gets her wish; the other women see her walking off hand in hand with the ghost of the little girl—and then find her dead with her hand outstretched.

The portrayal of this little girl as both "pitiful" and "dreadful" is Mary Wilkins Freeman's most direct fictional expression of ambivalence toward motherhood. In the Afterword to his edition of *The Wind in the Rose-bush*, Alfred Bendixen refers to this ambivalence, observing: "Thus in this tale we find a strong sympathy for the deprived child combined with the suggestion that motherhood may require self-sacrifice to the point of sacrifice of self" (249). In "The Lost Ghost," fragments of Wilkins Freeman's

The ghost of Mary Wilkins Freeman's abandoned child in "A Little Maid at the Door." Photo by Ken Van Dyne from H. Pyle's illustration for *Harper's New Monthly Magazine*, 1892.

complex personality are projected onto the child who is abused, the mother who abuses, and the surrogate mother who must die to nurture. The demands of this last incarnation of that "forlorn little girl" are particularly powerful; they match the demands of the lonely child in Wilkins Freeman that cried out for constant attention and fostering. This relentless tale of child abuse, however, might also be a projection of Wilkins Freeman's guilt at having starved and frozen her nurturing impulses. In spite of or even because of the intensity of its demands, this child is a threat; the woman can only die to appease it, and perhaps this last tale actualizes Wilkins Freeman's own fears of what essential needs as a woman and ambitions as a writer she would have to sacrifice to take on the care and responsibility of a child. After all, to have a child, one must give up one's primary image of oneself as a child.

Despite Mary Wilkins Freeman's ambivalence toward the ghost story form, she seems to have turned to it at regular intervals as a means of addressing some particularly problematic subject matter. The conventions of ghost fiction as a less "serious" literary form, the supernatural machinery, melodramatic episode, and exaggerated emotion that defined the genre, enabled Wilkins Freeman to give oblique expression to disturbing personal issues without fear of exposure.[15] In these stories she laid to rest the ghosts of the favored sister who died, the jealous and guilt-ridden sister who survived, the bereaved mother, and the orphaned daughter she always felt herself to be. She exorcised the ghost of the woman in her who mourned the child she never had because of both deliberate choice and external circumstance, as well as the woman in her who feared maternity as a kind of psychic death. The ghosts in these stories are manifestations of the mingled emotions of regret, relief, and guilt that Wilkins Freeman felt at refusing motherhood; these "faces of children that had never been" image what might have been, what must not be, and what could no longer be in the life of Mary Wilkins Freeman.

Notes

1. As this essay discusses, Mary Wilkins Freeman did not marry until late in life, when she had already established her reputation as Mary E. Wilkins. Although she is now known to scholars and critics by her married name, Mary Wilkins Freeman or Freeman, I have maintained historical accuracy in referring to her as Wilkins before her marriage, and as Wilkins Freeman afterward.

2. In still another letter to Pattee, dated 25 Sept. 1919, she said: "I am convinced that the form of expression I have used, is not the best for me, but it was forced upon me by my New England conscience, which is about all of New England I own" (*Infant Sphinx* 383–84).

3. Her animal, flower, and tree portraits in these two collections are fictional expressions of the ideas voiced in Emerson's "Nature." They encourage the reader to learn the language of Nature as a paradigm for the human soul.

4. Fred Lewis Pattee, however, in *The Development of the American Short Story*, praised Mary Wilkins Freeman's ghost stories as "among the best New England has ever produced" (322), an assessment echoed, recently, by Alfred Bendixen in his "Afterword" to his edition of *The Wind in the Rose-bush*. Bendixen claims that Freeman's ghost fiction dissects "the nature of fear itself," as the "supernatural provides a symbol for the repressed natural" (246). For him, the disturbing effect of these stories results from their "perversion of the home" and "distortion of normal family relationships" (247).

5. "A Gentle Ghost" was first published in *Harper's*, 79 (July 1889) and was reprinted in *A New England Nun* (New York: Harper, 1891). "The Little Maid at the Door" was first published in *Harper's*, 84 (Feb. 1892) and was reprinted in *Silence and Other Stories* (New York: Harper, 1898). "The Wind in the Rose-bush" and "The Lost Ghost" appeared in *Everybody's Magazine* in February and May, respectively, of 1902. Subsequently, both stories were reprinted in *The Wind in the Rose-bush and Other Stories of the Supernatural* (New York: Doubleday, 1903).

6. See, for example, "A Gatherer of Simples," "Christmas Jenny," "Old Woman Magoun," and "The Flowering Bush." See also Marjorie Pryse's discussion of the "search for mother" in her "Afterword" to *Selected Stories* (320, 322, 335).

7. An older sister, Mary Clara, had died in infancy, and a younger brother, Edward, had died at the age of three.

8. To the amazement of her heirs and executors, her estate was worth over $100,000 (see Kendrick's comments in *Infant Sphinx* 377).

9. Freeman's collections of children's stories include *The Cow with the Golden Horns*, 1884; *The Adventures of Ann*, 1886; *The*

Pot of Gold, 1892; *Young Lucretia*, 1892; *Comfort Pease and Her Gold Ring*, 1895; and *In Colonial Times*, 1899.

10. In "A Village Singer" (*A New England Nun*, 1891), Candace Whitcomb, the main character, has been supplanted by the younger Alma Way as soloist in the church choir. It is suggested that the fire and passion in Candace's voice come from the "smouldering fires of ambition and resolution" (30) that are fanned by the frustration and limitations of her single life. The mild Alma, engaged to marry Candace's nephew, will know the domestic life of "a usual woman" but will always lack a little "soul" (36). In "An Old Arithmetician" (*A Humble Romance*, New York: Harper, 1887), Mrs. Torry, a mathematical prodigy, neglects her granddaughter while working on a particularly difficult problem. After the disappearance of her granddaughter, she chastises herself for putting her "faculty" above "the love that's betwixt human beings an' the help that's betwixt 'em" (337), but is unable to keep herself from working the problem. Such a gift cannot be denied or suppressed, even though it overshadows domestic responsibilities and relationships. As Mrs. Torry advises her granddaughter: "I'd rather have a man who hadn't any special faculty, if I was goin' to get married" (381). The story implies that the same advice holds true for gifted women.

11. This story was first published in *Harper's*, 81 (July 1890) and was reprinted in *A New England Nun*, 1891. All references are to the latter text.

12. See Kendrick's account in *Infant Sphinx* for a more detailed discussion of Freeman's marriage.

13. Freeman was plagued by nightmares to such an extent that she became addicted to sedatives.

14. Edward Wagenknecht remarks in his "Introduction" to *Collected Ghost Stories by Mary E. Wilkins Freeman* that the realistic kind of ghost story, "in which we cling closely to our own firesides but are chilled every now and then by a mysterious wind which blows in upon us from beyond," is made more terrifying by the accuracy of its domestic details because "if the kind of unimaginative people Mrs. Freeman writes about are not safe in their own New England kitchens, then where in this world can safety be sought?" (viii).

15. Leah Glasser makes a similar point about Freeman's story, "The Hall Bedroom" (39–40).

Works Cited

Bendixen, Alfred. Afterword. *The Wind in the Rose-bush and Other Stories of the Supernatural*. Chicago: Academy Chicago, 1986.

Foster, Edward. *Mary E. Wilkins Freeman*. New York: Hendricks House, 1956.

Freeman, Mary Wilkins. *A New England Nun and Other Stories*. New York: Harper, 1891.

———. *The Infant Sphinx: Collected Letters of Mary E. Wilkins Freeman*. Ed. Brent L. Kendrick. Metuchen, NJ: Scarecrow, 1985.

———. *Silence and Other Stories*. New York: Harper, 1898.

———. *The Wind in the Rose-bush and Other Stories of the Supernatural*. New York: Doubleday, 1903.

Gilbert, Sandra M. and Susan Gubar. *The Madwoman in the Attic*. New Haven: Yale UP, 1979.

Glasser, Leah Blatt. " 'In a Closet Hidden': The Life and Work of Mary Wilkins Freeman." Diss. Brown University, 1983.

Pattee, Fred Lewis. *The Development of the American Short Story*. New York: Harper, 1923.

Pryse, Marjorie. Afterword. *Selected Stories of Mary E. Wilkins Freeman*. New York: Norton, 1983.

Wagenknecht, Edward. Introduction. *Collected Ghost Stories by Mary E. Wilkins Freeman*. Sauk City, WI: Arkham House, 1974.

Welter, Barbara. "The Cult of True Womanhood: 1820–1860." *American Quarterly* 18 (1966), 151–74.

E. Suzanne Owens

The Ghostly Double behind the Wallpaper in Charlotte Perkins Gilman's "The Yellow Wallpaper"

IN 1885, CHARLOTTE PERKINS GILMAN suffered severe post partum depression followed by complete emotional breakdown. By 1890, she had been treated for her condition by the leading specialist in women's "hysteria," Dr. Silas Weir Mitchell. She had also divorced her husband, moved alone to California, and begun a writing career. Soon after, she transformed her personal experience into fiction as the brilliant short story, "The Yellow Wallpaper," published in 1892. In the Afterword to the Feminist Press reissue of the story in 1973, Elaine Hedges calls attention to Gilman's neglected masterpiece as "one of the rare pieces of literature we have by a nineteenth-century woman which directly confronts the sexual politics of the male-female, husband-wife relationship" (*Wallpaper* 39). Predating Kate Chopin's novel *The Awakening* by three years, "The Yellow Wallpaper" evidences Gilman's early critique of "the crippling social pressures imposed on women in the nineteenth century and the sufferings they thereby endured" (55), a theme later writers, including Edith Wharton, would address.

Gilman's tale is acknowledged by feminist critics as a study of psychology and sexual politics grounded in autobiographical realism. It is a significant work in nineteenth-century literature because of these features. But a second story exists beside the story of repression and madness we read today—a supernatural tale drawn from the best nineteenth-century Gothic conventions, particularly from Edgar Allan Poe and Charlotte Bronte. Recently, Eugenia C. Delamotte has noted the story's Gothic elements, yet Gilman's first readers reacted to "The Yellow Wallpaper" as a ghost story, a narrative combining the supernatural with aberrant psychology framed by sexual politics.

Gilman's response to the events of her own life mirrors her narrator's confused assessment of her situation in the story. In a 1935 autobiography, Gilman traced the events of her first marriage to painter Walter Stetson in 1884, a period of genuine happiness mixed with increasing depression that Gilman could neither understand nor dispel. Her diary for 1884 recorded bouts of sleeplessness, sinking spirits and "hysteria" preceding her daughter's birth in March of 1885:

> We had attributed all my increasing weakness and depression to pregnancy, and looked forward to prompt recovery now. All was normal and ordinary enough, but I was plunged into an extreme of nervous exhaustion which no one observed or understood in the least. Of all angelic babies that darling was the best, a heavenly baby. My nurse, Maria Pease of Boston, was a joy while she lasted, and remained a lifelong friend. But after her month was up and I was left alone with the child I broke so fast that we sent for my mother. . . . and that baby-worshiping grandmother came to take care of the darling, I being incapable of doing that—or anything else, a mental wreck. (*Living* 88–89)

Even after moving to "a better home" and securing the help of a servant to assist her mother and her "loving and devoted husband," Gilman "lay all day on the lounge and cried" (89).

Like the narrator she would later create, Gilman found the cure for her condition to be worse than the condition itself. A family friend intervened with money to allow Gilman to visit nerve specialist S. Weir Mitchell in Philadelphia. The "rest cure" prescribed included a prohibition of prolonged intellectual stimulation or writing, a regimen that exacerbated Gilman's condition. Her return to family life under these restrictions cost her her sanity: "The mental agony grew so unbearable that I would sit blankly moving my head from side to side—to get out from under the pain. Not physical pain, not the least 'headache' even, just mental torment, and so heavy in its nightmare gloom that it seemed real enough to dodge. . . . I would crawl into remote closets and under beds—to hide from the grinding pressures of that profound distress . . ." (96). Gilman felt she had no choice but to separate from her husband and daughter, allowing him to remarry and arranging for his new wife to take custody of the child. As she began life over in California, she regained her health, but her bouts with depression continued on and off for nearly forty years.

"The Yellow Wallpaper" was produced during a burst of creative energy in 1890, along with numerous articles and poems. Gilman considered the story "a description of a case of nervous breakdown beginning something as mine did, and treated as Dr. S. Weir Mitchell treated me with what I considered the inevitable result, progressive insanity" (*Living* 119). She had received from William Dean Howells a letter of appreciation for a poem and article she had published that year, so she forwarded the short story to him, hoping that Howells could get it published in the *Atlantic Monthly*. The *Atlantic*'s editor, Horace E. Scudder, rejected the piece with the stunning reply, "I could not forgive myself if I made others as miserable as I have made myself!" (119). Gilman thought his reaction was "funny" because she intended for her tale to be "dreadful"; she comments in her autobiography: "I suppose he would have sent back one of Poe's on the same ground" (119). "The Yellow Wallpaper" was eventually published in the *New England Magazine* in January of 1892, to immediate reader reaction. A letter of protest was sent to the *Boston Transcript* recommending the "severest censure" of such a graphic depiction of "mental derangement," but a physician in Kansas City wrote to praise Gilman for offering the first "account of incipient insanity" he had found in literature, speculating that her tale followed some experience with opium addiction (120–21). Gilman had hoped the story would influence Mitchell and his colleagues in their treatment of other women's "cases"; she discovered some years later that he had, in fact, read it and changed his consideration of women's hysteria.

"The Yellow Wallpaper" was published again in 1920 as part of Howells's collection, *The Great American Short Stories*, although, as Elaine Hedges points out in her Afterword to the recent Feminist Press edition, it was the "chilling" quality of the tale to which Howells apparently responded. Even in 1920, Hedges claims, "no one seems to have made the connection between insanity and the sex, or sexual role, of the victim, no one explored the story's implications for male-female relationships in the nineteenth century" (*Wallpaper* 41). In keeping with Howells's characterization of the tale as a story that would "freeze our . . . blood," Hedges summarizes the work's initial reception: "In its time . . . the story was read essentially as a Poe-esque tale of chilling horror—and as a story of mental aberration" (*Wallpaper* 39). That is, the horror story is what Gilman's first readers reacted to, apart from evidence that at least a few physicians, including Mitchell, learned from it something of the sexual politics that framed Gilman's own experience and that of her fictional character. Gilman's implied comparison of the story to one of Poe's, together with her expressed hope for its impact on physicians, indicate the complexity of her intentions for this story. A close reading of the story in the context of nineteenth-century Gothic conventions illuminates its dual nature.

Gilman's unnamed narrator begins her tale not with descriptions of the story's setting—a colonial house—but with her impressions and expectations about such a setting. A series of questions and suppositions begins the story, an opening that indicates the troubled mood of the woman who spins her own tale and establishes the disturbed aura of her surroundings. She and her husband, John, are "mere ordinary people" in a "hereditary estate," a structure of indeterminate history, but speculates: "I would say a haunted house and reach the height of romantic felicity—but that would be asking too much of fate!" (*Wallpaper* 9).[1] The narrator's expressed desire to find the house haunted may serve to put the reader on notice that subsequent events are to be mediated by a heightened or unstable imagination, but we cannot immediately say whether the narrator's gleeful expectancy reflects mental illness or that lesser condition ascribed to so many women—an imagination excited by overindulgence in novel reading. She goes on, in fact, to "proudly declare that there is something queer about it" (9), and is led to ask two questions concerning the house which commonly appear in ghost stories: "Else why should it be let so cheaply? And why have stood so long untenanted?" (9). To readers familiar with the ghost story genre, the questions affirm the narrator's rationality, since characters in ghost stories usually turn out to have good reason to wonder about these very conditions.

The narrator's husband, John, laughs when she reports her impressions, but she calls him "practical in the extreme" (9). In fact, the reader is given an important clue for judging the validity of the narrator's speculations when she claims that John has "an intense horror of superstition, and . . . scoffs openly at any talk of things not to be felt and seen" (9). The opening of the story draws attention to ambiguous circumstances viewed by one character as queer if "romantic" and appealing, and by the other character, a man of extremes in practicality and a horror of the intangible, as laughably trivial.

This estate is isolated three miles from the closest village and commands a view across an expanse of landscape towards a river.

The house itself is never clearly described in layout or scale, but its grounds are sketched. The narrator notes the garden more than once, "large and shady, full of box-bordered paths, and lined with long grape-covered arbors with seats under them" (11). And she responds to this setting by comparing it to "English places that you read about" (11), a reference that will become clearer later in the story. Although the narrator generally refrains from evaluating the setting outside the house, her descriptive details speak for themselves: "There are hedges and walls and gates that lock, and lots of separate little houses for the gardeners and people" (11). The maze-like garden is at once "*delicious*" (11) and foreboding. Walls and hedges are cells that enclose and partition, while the "gates that lock" add an odd detail that reinforces a sense of the garden as prison. And despite the attraction of "grape-covered arbors," the grounds are in disrepair with greenhouses that, the narrator says, "are all broken now" (11). The narrator repeats the explanation that "the place has been vacant for years" (11) because of what she had heard—but never verified—was "some legal trouble . . . about the heirs and co-heirs" (11), all evidence, she claims, that "spoils my ghostliness" (11).[2] That evidence is far from convincing, however.

Again, the reader is confronted by a mixture of impressions and suggestions. First, the narrator holds to an initial feeling for the queerness of the estate: "There is something strange about the house—I can feel it" (11). Second, she attempts to rationalize her first impressions, to accept John's practicality over her own intuition. This clash between her own propensities and John's is depicted in a brief incident when the narrator apparently tries once more to describe her uneasiness to John "one moonlight evening": "but he said what I felt was a *draught*, and shut the window" (11).

This pattern of details creates a conventionally Gothic setting. Gilman begins with an isolated estate of uncertain but troubled history and surrounds it with extensive shaded, labyrinthine grounds in decay. Even rumored trouble among the heirs is a stock situation. Before Gilman's narrator ever begins her description of the fateful yellow-papered room at the top of the house, she, an emotionally charged woman, has entered what the reader should understand as recognizable territory for ghosts, hauntings, and possessions. Furthermore, the tale has barely begun when the moon rises and a character's uneasiness is dismissed as "a draught": the stage is set for supernatural manifestations in accordance with ghost story conventions. Understandably, the narrator is unable to dispel the "ghostliness" she feels.

If she is psychologically unstable, these signs alone might indicate projections of the woman's deterioration from the moment she enters the scene. When she tries to describe the bedroom, she cannot escape a sense of her own peculiarity, confessing, "I used to lie awake as a child and get more entertainment and terror out of blank walls and plain furniture than most children could find in a toy-store" (17). The reader is supposed to understand that she has always been highly imaginative and perhaps predisposed to terror: "I remember what a kindly wink the knobs of our big, old bureau used to have, and there was one chair that always seemed like a strong friend. . . . I used to feel that if any of the other things looked too fierce I could always hop into that chair and be safe" (17). She checks her "fancy" throughout the tale, however, for John "says that with [her] imaginative power and habit of story-making, a nervous weakness like [hers] is sure to lead to all manner of excited fancies" (15–16). Are her intuitions and perceptions, then, mere manifestations of personality rather than reliable clues to the strangeness of the estate?

But this imaginative predisposition, too, follows conventions of the Gothic tale. For example, Edgar Allan Poe's classic tale of doubling, "William Wilson," published in 1839 and already a classic American tale by Gilman's time, introduces the narrator on the first page: "I am the descendant of a race whose imaginative and easily excitable temperament has at all times rendered

them remarkable; and, in my earliest infancy, I gave evidence of
having fully inherited the family character" (Poe 626). Gilman's
narrator is, in turn, a literary descendant of a race of highly
imaginative Gothic narrators. Gilman's setting would also have
sounded familiar to readers of "William Wilson," with its sug-
gestive description of a boys' school: "The house, as I have said,
was old and irregular. The grounds were extensive, and a high and
solid brick wall, topped with a bed of mortar and broken glass
encompassed the whole. . . . At an angle of the ponderous wall
frowned a more ponderous gate. It was riveted and studded with
iron bolts, and surmounted with jagged iron spikes" (Poe 627).
Here is another walled and imprisoning landscape, yet despite its
frightening appearance, Poe's narrator expresses his pleasure in
the place: "To me how veritably a place of enchantment!" (628).

   In addition to the American Gothic tradition that Poe represented, Gilman drew upon British tradition as well, and in particular from a masterpiece of Gothic terror framed by sexual
politics, *Jane Eyre* (1847). Charlotte Bronte's Thornfield Hall—
literally one of those "English places that you read about"—is
isolated approximately six miles from the village of Millcote, a
distance noted by Jane Eyre as she records her first impressions of
her new home: "About ten minutes after [passing a church] the
driver got down and opened a pair of gates; we passed through,
and they closed behind us" (92). Like Gilman's narrator, Jane
Eyre passes from familiar ground into isolation and enclosure, an
enclosure symbolized by the gates that close behind her. Housekeeper Mrs. Fairfax greets Jane with a brief description of the
estate, noting, "Thornfield is a fine old hall, rather neglected of
late years perhaps, but still a respectable place" (94). Jane will discover that Thornfield has, like the house in Gilman's story, been
virtually "untenanted" for years due to Mr. Rochester's frequent
absences. The foreboding setting has been established.

   The focus of Gilman's story is, of course, the bedroom at the
top of the house where her narrator reluctantly retreats for "rest"

and solitude. She had preferred a room "downstairs that opened onto the piazza and had roses all over the window" (*Wallpaper* 12), but is not permitted a choice in the matter: "John would not hear of it" (12). She enters, instead, a peculiar room that, at first impression, belies its history: "It is a big, airy room, the whole floor nearly, with windows that look all ways, and air and sunshine galore. It was nursery first and then playroom and gymnasium, I should judge, for the windows are barred for little children, and there are rings and things in the walls" (12). Indeed, her judgment is mere speculation. Added to the barred windows and rings are the shredded wallpaper, a "heavy bedstead," which the reader later learns is nailed to the floor, and a "gate at the head of the stairs" (14). The narrator's first reference to the wallpaper suggests another reference to Poe's "William Wilson": "The paint and paper look as if a boys' school had used it" (12). But more specifically, Gilman's attic-level room recreates the symbolic spaces of *Jane Eyre*: Jane's second-floor room and its third-floor counterpart, the prison-room for the madwoman, Bertha Mason Rochester. Gilman's room is no nursery, but a cell designed for physical and psychological restraint.

Sandra Gilbert and Susan Gubar's study of nineteenth-century women's literature takes its title, of course, from Bronte's Bertha: *The Madwoman in the Attic*. They too emphasize the Gothic conventions evident in Bronte's setting, including the ambiguous architecture of Thornfield itself. And Jane Eyre, while not physically confined either to her bed chamber or the house, as Gilman's narrator is through the strictures of her husband's "rest cure," moves, nevertheless, within ambiguous enclosures. Gilbert and Gubar note: "These upper regions [Thornfield's second and third stories], in other words, symbolically miniaturize one crucial aspect of the world in which [Jane Eyre] finds herself. Heavily enigmatic, ancestral relics wall her in; inexplicable locked rooms guard a secret which may have something to do with *her*" (348). Gilman's narrator is denied the smaller piazza room with "such pretty old-fashioned chintz hangings" (12) and moves instead to the isolation of the large yellow-papered, barred-windowed room at the top of the house. Jane Eyre is led to her room by Mrs. Fairfax past a central staircase window which was "high and latticed" (Bronte 94), a variation of the barred window, and into a smaller enclosure on the upper floor: "A very chill and vaultlike air pervaded the stairs and gallery, suggesting cheerless ideas of space and solitude; and I was glad when I was finally ushered into my chamber to find it of small dimensions, and furnished in ordinary modern style" (94).

Jane associates the smaller space with comfort, as Gilman's narrator does by implication when she calls the larger room "as airy and comfortable a room as anyone need wish" (*Wallpaper* 15), after expressing her own wish for the smaller one. The two rooms Gilman's narrator describes suggest Jane's room in other ways as well; when she first sees her room in the light of day, Jane says, "The chamber looked such a bright little place to me as the sun shone in between the gay blue chintz window curtains, showing papered walls and a carpeted floor, so unlike the bare planks and stained plaster of Lowood [Jane's boarding school] that my spirits rose at the view" (Bronte 95). Jane is given a room like the one Gilman's narrator longs for, with chintz curtains and walls presumably papered in something more appealing than the yellow wallpaper, but Jane is also drawn to the mysterious third floor, where Bertha Rochester lives in a room like Gilman's narrator's, a room large enough to have areas of "deep shade" (Bronte 278), a room not barred but "without a window" (278). Nor is Jane's small room secure against encroachment: it is in this room that Jane Eyre receives the nocturnal visits of Bertha Rochester. So, too, Gilman's narrator will be "visited" nightly by a figure (or figures) in the wallpaper, a woman who eventually "breaks out" and, the narrator claims, steals beyond the confines of the imprisoning bedroom. On the night of Bertha's attack on Mason, Jane will be locked in the third-floor room adjoining Bertha's, imprisoned as Bertha is imprisoned. On Gilman's narrator's last day in the house, she will lock herself in her room in order to claim the space as her own.

Gilman's narrator passes most of her days alone in the bedroom, writing secretly. Gradually, she introduces the yellow wallpaper that becomes her ultimate obsession, and its significance for her changes as she claims its appearance changes: "[It is] one of those sprawling flamboyant patterns committing every artistic sin" (*Wallpaper* 13). She describes the color as "repellent, almost revolting; a smouldering unclean yellow, strangely faded by the slow-turning sunlight" (13), and then "hideous," "infuriating," and "torturing" (25). Her attempts to describe the pattern itself fail each time to form a coherent picture, for the pattern is "pointless," with "bloated curves and flourishes—a kind of 'debased Romanesque' with *delirium tremens*" (20). Moreover, she says of the paper that it "changes as the light changes" (25), and finds it most disturbing by moonlight: "I kept still and watched the moonlight on the undulating wall-paper till I felt creepy" (23), a curiously appropriate choice of terms for a character who will end the story by "creeping."

The wallpaper frightens her, and she tries to convince John that they should leave the estate:

> There are things in that paper that nobody knows about but me, or ever will.
>
> Behind that outside pattern the dim shapes get clearer every day.
>
> It is always the same shape, only very numerous.
>
> And it is like a woman stooping down and creeping about behind that pattern. I don't like it a bit. I wonder—I begin to think—I wish John would take me away from here! (22)

What does she think? She had sensed "strangeness" from the beginning and had tried to reason away the "ghostliness" of this place. Now she sees movement across the patterns on the wall, a movement confined to nighttime until the end of the story: "at night in any kind of light, in twilight, candlelight, lamplight, and worst of all by moonlight" (26). In daylight, she adds, the figure she sees in the paper is still: "By daylight she is subdued, quiet" (26). The narrator's perceptions of the strangeness of the place, combined with her perception of nocturnal movements, suggest that what she fears is a ghost, and like sensitive characters in many ghost stories, she asks to be taken away from the haunted house. As she discovers, it is one thing to wish for a ghost; it is quite another to be haunted by one.

As the visitations continue and, in fact, increase, Gilman's narrator begins to pick up a penetrating odor in the bedroom, a smell that she assumes comes from the wallpaper although it follows her throughout the house and even outside:

> But there is something else about that paper—the smell! I noticed it the moment we came into the room, but with so much air and sun it was not bad. Now we have had a week of fog and rain, and whether the windows are open or not, the smell is here.
>
> It creeps all over the house.
> . . . .
> Even when I go to ride, if I turn my head suddenly and surprise it—there is that smell!
> Such a peculiar odor, too! . . .
> . . . .
> In this damp weather it is awful. I wake up in the night and find it hanging over me. (28–29)

Readers familiar with ghostly conventions will recognize in this odor a conventional indicator of a ghostly visitation. The narrator's fear of that presence in her bedroom and her suspicion that she is confronted by the supernatural frame her description. Her response at this point in the story comes during a period of relative composure and control, yet it identifies her with Bronte's madwoman, who burns down Thornfield Hall: "I thought seriously of burning the house—to reach the smell" (29). If the break in the narrator's sentence signals an unwillingness to associate the smell with the supernatural, it may also prevent her from revealing motives more closely aligned with Bertha's: revenge and liberation from captivity.

Like many of her predecessors in ghost stories, what the narrator resists is her own identification with the haunting presence, the woman or women trapped behind the wallpaper. But if she is, in fact, suffering from the gradual and cumulative effects of a haunting, her final deterioration comes with the ghost's possession of her body, thus leading her to "creep" by daylight. The narrator reports seeing the woman from the wallpaper "on that long road under the trees" just before the narrator admits that she locks her bedroom door and creeps by daylight around the room (31). To a reader familiar with the Gothic, the events of the story suggest possession as much as they do hallucination: the narrator watches a figure appear in the pattern of the wallpaper, witnesses increased agitation in the menacing rattling of the pattern's "bars," follows this figure's movements as it appears to break loose from the bars on the wall, and finally takes on that figure's form as she begins to crawl about the bedroom floor. As Gilbert and Gubar note: "Eventually, as the narrator sinks more deeply into what the world calls madness, the terrifying implications of both the paper and the figure imprisoned behind the paper begin to permeate—that is, to *haunt* the rented ancestral mansion" (90). By the end of the story, the narrator can do nothing *but* "creep," a verb she uses six times in the last thirty lines. Her identification with the woman in the wallpaper is explicit and complete; she worries, "I suppose I shall have to get back behind the pattern when it comes night" (*Wallpaper* 35).

The narrator's cry of triumph has puzzled many critics: "I've got out at last . . . in spite of you and Jane" (36). Elaine Hedges suggests that the intrusion of the name could be a result of a printer's error, a misprint of either "Julia" or "Jennie," the housekeeper and sister-in-law residing in the house, or a reference to the narrator's real name. In the latter case, Hedges takes the line as an indication of "the narrator's sense that she has gotten free of both her husband and her 'Jane' self: free, that is, of herself as defined by marriage and society" (63). Alternatively, if we assume that the narrator's madness accounts for the events, "Jane" is the rational self giving way to the irrational. But if this is an account of supernatural possession, the voice speaking that sentence is the voice of a ghost announcing its victory over the narrator/victim, now revealed to be "Jane."

In any case, the connection to Jane Eyre is inevitable. Gilbert and Gubar read Bronte's novel as a tale of splitting psyches personified by Jane and Bertha, acknowledging the supernatural frame of the story: "In view of [the] frightening series of separations within the self—Jane Eyre splitting off from Jane Rochester, the child Jane splitting off from the adult Jane, and the image of Jane weirdly separating from the body of Jane— it is not surprising that another and most mysterious specter, a sort of 'vampyre,' should appear in the middle of the night to rend and trample the wedding veil of that unknown person, Jane Rochester" (359). Furthermore Jane Eyre's "splitting" is incited, as is Gilman's Jane's, by a scene in which she looks out across the grounds surrounding the house. Jane Eyre's fragmentation is complicated by her doubling with Bertha, whom Gilbert and Gubar call "Jane's truest and darkest double," "the angry aspect of the orphan child, the ferocious secret self Jane has been trying to repress ever since her days at Gateshead" (359–60). Like the ghostly double that finally possesses Gilman's narrator, Bertha is an angry captive, intent upon breaking free. She is finally revealed as a wild, though indistinguishable, figure running back and forth in the attic cell, where, "[she] grovelled, seemingly, on all fours" (Bronte 278), just as Gilman's narrator does at the end.

Gilman's narrator vents her destructive rage only on the wallpaper in her room, while Bertha burns Thornfield Hall to the ground. Whereas Bertha dies and Rochester lives on, however, the ending may be reversed in Gilman's story. John is said to have "fainted" at the end, as the narrator says: "so that I had to creep over him every time!" (*Wallpaper* 36). Perhaps, however, he has died from shock, a classic consequence of confronting a ghost—a fitting end for the disbeliever. The ambiguity of the ending suits the ambiguity of the story as a whole. Has the narrator merely succumbed to madness, or has something more uncanny occurred? Clearly, late nineteenth- and early twentieth-century readers, who were more familiar with the ghost story tradition, read it in those terms. But if "The Yellow Wallpaper" is truly a story of ghostly possession, are we to rejoice in the ghost's victory, or only to lament the limitations of the combined force of female worldly and otherworldly power, which can only be expressed by creeping?

Notes

1. Although the Feminist Press edition is the most widely known text of the story, Alfred Bendixen has argued that it conforms accurately neither to the *New England Magazine* version nor Gilman's original manuscript. Readers might wish to consult the version that appears in Bendixen's *Haunted Women*, included in the bibliography at the end of this volume. —Eds.

2. Here, for example, the Bendixen text reads: "the place has been empty for years." —Eds.

Works Cited

Bronte, Charlotte. *Jane Eyre*. 1847. Boston: Houghton, 1959.

Delamotte, Eugenia C. "Male and Female Mysteries in 'The Yellow Wallpaper.'" *Legacy* 5 (1988): 3–14.

Gilbert, Sandra M. and Susan Gubar. *The Madwoman in the Attic*. New Haven: Yale UP, 1979.

Gilman, Charlotte Perkins. *The Living of Charlotte Perkins Gilman.* Eds. Annette K. Baxter and Leon Stein. New York: Arno, 1972.
———. *The Yellow Wallpaper.* 1892. Ed. Elaine Hedges. New York: Feminist Press, 1973.
Poe, Edgar Allan. "William Wilson." *The Complete Tales and Poems of Edgar Allan Poe.* New York: Modern Library, 1938, 626–41.

Kathy A. Fedorko

Edith Wharton's Haunted Fiction

"The Lady's Maid's Bell"
and *The House of Mirth*

EDITH WHARTON'S 1903 NOVEL *Sanctuary* seethes with anger about her society's moral timidity, its concealment of "undesirable" emotions and deeds. As she describes it, families try to suppress domestic ills much the same way the nervous killer in Poe's "The Tell-Tale Heart" tries to conceal his murder victim under the floorboards: "The best way of repairing the fault was to hide it: to tear up the floor and bury the victim at night. Above all, no coroner and no autopsy" (109). Other comments about the social "house" are as sinister: "The blinds were drawn on the ugly side of things, and life was resumed on the usual assumption that no such side existed" (88); and "[the heroine] had begun to perceive that the fair surface of life was honeycombed by a vast system of moral sewage. Every respectable household had its special arrangements for the private disposal of family scandals; it was only among the reckless and improvident that such hygienic precautions were neglected" (110).

Wharton is not usually compared to Poe, for she is best known as an astute, ironic portrayer of social behavior. One critic speaks of "her ardent observation and analysis of life at the daily level" (Lindberg 9), and another speaks of her "tough-minded analysis, argument and debate on the subject of women" (Ammons 189). Above all she is recognized and praised as a consummate realist, even, in Cynthia Griffin Wolff's words, "a profoundly anti-Romantic realist" (9).

Like Poe, however, Wharton was intrigued by mystery, ghosts, secret misdeeds, haunted houses, simmering eroticism. In *The Writing of Fiction* she comments that the best Poe stories are those in "that peculiar category of the eerie which lies outside the classic tradition" (34). Indeed, the Gothic, Poe's specialty, became the ideal vehicle for Wharton's perception that hidden within social structures—families, friendships, marriages—are ugly secrets. Wharton uses the Gothic, not only in short stories but in her realistic novels as well, to portray one "secret" in particular: that traditional society and the traditional home, with their traditional roles, are dangerous places for women. Female exuberance, ambition, and eroticism are suspect and therefore constrained. Women are made ill and ghostly because of their suppression. The Gothic tells the secret, disallowed story at the same time that it faces fears, an experience that therefore yields both dread and pleasure when the fears are dramatized.[1] As Wharton writes in *A Motor-Flight Through France*, "the Gothic spirit, pushed to its logical conclusion" strives for "the utterance of the unutterable" (17).

Wharton's Gothic stories immerse the reader in suffocating interiors, haunted by sexual suspicions and impending violence as well as by ghosts.[2] In the stories, villainous men tyrannize trapped young women and their potential rescuers. In the novels in which the Gothic is enmeshed, such as *The House of Mirth*, *Summer*, and *The Age of Innocence*, it is transformed. Imprisonment, ghosts, and tyrants are metaphors rather than literal events or beings. Seeing specters is an internal rather than an external act. Most importantly, the novel heroines, unlike their sisters in the Gothic stories, recognize the restraints of their society and try to escape entrapment, try to avoid becoming Gothic heroines. The tapestry of Gothic imagery in these novels creates an alternative text, the other side of the social pattern. Wharton thereby creates what Gilbert and Gubar call palimpsestic literary works, "whose surface designs conceal or obscure deeper, less accessible (and less socially acceptable) levels of meaning" (73). The Gothic enriches the realistic text by haunting it with fear, anger, bewilderment, and suppressed sexuality, but also with the struggle to resist silence and enclosure. The mute claustrophobia in the Gothic stories is revised and complicated in the novels. Thus, although Lily Bart becomes overwhelmed by her Gothic experience and finally stops resisting, her struggle is a revision of the female acquiescence in Wharton's early Gothic stories.

The Gothic mode suits Wharton's motivation to tell the suppressed, unsocial story. Like a dream, it is both uncannily realistic and strange, "the familiar rendered bizarre" (Day 43), not an escape from the real but a deconstruction of it (Punter 97). The taboo is the traditional Gothic content, fear and dread its cardinal emotions, and repression, particularly of sexuality, its theme. William Day writes that the central emotion underlying Gothic fantasy is the fear welling up from the "deformation of identity and family" caused by "the unresolved problem of sexuality in modern society" (84). Respectability, and the silence and constraint it entails for women, becomes the impetus for female passivity and victimization by men. In the Gothic, reflecting this deformation, human nature is fragmentarily portrayed as the archetypal passive woman and aggressive man who mirror a society with rigid gender roles. In the Gothic world, magnifying the "real" one, pleasure is impossible. Female sexuality is monstrous and is therefore imprisoned (Day 81–86). These were constraints familiar to Wharton, making the Gothic a useful way to respond to her Old New York society. As she wrote in her 1937 preface to *Ghosts*, all that ghosts need in order to exist are "not echoing passages and hidden doors behind tapestry, but only continuity and silence" (xii). Ghosts appear with their silent stories when form, tradition, convention—all those structures that maintain continuity—keep things that should be revealed from being acknowledged and spoken about.[3]

Society's fear of female energy and articulateness in turn generates women's internal conflict between their "monstrous" hidden drives and their "nice" socially acceptable selves (Stein 125). When a woman is immersed in a Gothic experience, as Alice Hartley is in "The Lady's Maid's Bell" and Lily Bart is in *The House of Mirth*, that world gives "visual form to the fear of self," the monstrous knowing self (Moers 163). Therefore both Alice and Lily meet a fearful dark double, "a mirror image who is both self and other" (Kahàne 337) and who knows the secret of the house, a secret each fearfully and ambivalently confronts. So Wharton's women who enter the Gothic world—whether haunted house or haunted society—usually do so fearfully, half-willingly, both attracted and filled with dread.

The discovery process is key to Wharton's Gothic. Her very use of the genre emphasizes that confronting the secret in the house, whether of a woman's suppression or other domestic ill, takes courage but is essential to social and personal well-being. Often Wharton depends on the reader to fit the mysterious pieces of the Gothic story together because the characters who discover them are too afraid to understand what they have found out. Nonetheless Wharton's message remains insistent: facing ghosts is fearful, but it is crucial to knowing the full story of life.

"The Lady's Maid's Bell," published in 1904, was Wharton's first ghost story and *The House of Mirth*, published in 1905, her first unqualified commercial success. Their Gothic qualities reflect not only Wharton's perspective of social realities but her personal horrors. Only a few years before, in 1902, she had suffered a nervous breakdown, one of several during her socially correct but physically and emotionally miserable marriage to Teddy Wharton. The wealthy Bostonian Edward Wharton, though handsome and amiable, was no match for his wife's powerful intellect and omnivorous desire for a stimulating life. Sexual compatibility between them was apparently nonexistent. Psychological and physical distress haunted her marriage, six years of intermittent depression, asthma, exhaustion, and constant nausea as well as almost two years of breakdown.[4] In 1908 Wharton wrote in her diary about her marriage, " 'I heard the key turn in my prison-lock. That is the answer to everything worth while! Oh, Gods of derision! And you've given me over twenty years of it' " (Wolff 51). How appropriate, then, that Wharton should refer to her bouts of sickness as an " 'occult and unget-at-able nausea' " (Lewis, *Biography* 74). For while maintaining an active social and artistic life during these years, she was at the same time experiencing the Gothic firsthand, the dark, fearful, otherworld of isolation and despair, the dreadfulness of suppressed sexuality, the entrapment in marriage.

Both the story and the novel portray enclosure in a fearful Gothic world. Alice Hartley, in "The Lady's Maid's Bell," encounters cruelty, suppression, and gloom inside a haunted house and marriage, while Lily Bart gradually realizes that the "house of mirth" is haunted by loneliness, deceit, and sexual manipulation. Both women find *themselves* haunted as well. Pale Alice meets her dark double in a ghost who knows the sexual secret of the house; pale Lily meets her dark double in a ghostly, sexually promiscuous woman. Both Alice and Lily are intensely aware of their surroundings and are fixated by what terrorizes them yet are unwilling to fully face those terrors. Both prefer to keep the closed doors closed rather than swinging them open to face the horrors that lurk there in the dark. Thus Alice only partially understands the mysterious secret of the haunted house; Lily dies more aware than she was but too helplessly weak to act on her knowledge of the horror she has been forced to face. For Wharton's Gothic is also about this nightmarish inability to acknowledge one's knowledge, to face the secret, to claim one's darker self.

Silence rules in "The Lady's Maid's Bell." Knowledge is given and gained by suggestion, innuendo, clues. Alice Hartley, or Hartley, as she is known in the story, is the narrator and a good girl who asks few questions and keeps her fears to herself, even though her acute sensitivity to her environment riddles her with both questions and fears. We know nothing of her past except that she is self-supporting, near penniless, and ghostly white from a bout with typhoid, which makes people afraid to hire her. "I pretty nearly lost heart" from fretting, she tells us (*Descent* 243). Hartley's physical whiteness and her near loss of "heart," with that phrase's play on her name, are manifestations of her precarious existence, making her susceptible to Gothic influence. The woman she finds work with is also a victim of heart trouble, figuratively and literally. Mrs. Brympton is a young semi-invalid living in her country house on the Hudson. The description of her situation provided to Hartley by Mrs. Brympton's aunt is notable for its elliptical Gothic quality: " 'The house is big and gloomy; my niece is nervous, vaporish; her husband—well, he's generally away; and the two children are dead' " (244). Hartley's working there, she admits, is akin to being shut inside a " 'vault' " (244), but the country air and wholesome food might do her good. And besides, her niece is " 'an angel,' " whose former maid of twenty years " 'worshipped the ground she walked on' " (244). What Hartley gets herself into is a Gothic version of the life of the angel in the house.

Her approach to Brympton Place is a toned-down version of the arrival of Poe's narrator at the house of Usher; the echo prepares the reader for an equally unsettling encounter with the house's inhabitants and its "inner life": "It was a dull October day, with rain hanging close overhead, and by the time we turned into Brympton Place the daylight was almost gone. The drive wound through the woods for a mile or two, and came out on a gravel court shut in with thickets of tall black-looking shrubs. There were no lights in the windows, and the house did look a bit gloomy" (245).[5]

Sure enough, as soon as Hartley is shown to her room in the dark upper part of the house, she sees a "thin woman with a white face, and a dark gown and apron" (246) standing in a doorway, silently staring at her as she passes. Other "queer things" immediately start happening. When Mrs. Brympton asks Hartley if she is afraid of feeling lonely in the country, she answers spontaneously, " 'Not with you I wouldn't be, madam,' " but she admits to herself, "The words surprised me when I'd spoken them, for I'm not an impulsive person; but it was just as if I'd thought them aloud" (248). Hartley makes other unsettling observations: apparently only she has seen the thin white-faced woman in the doorway; the locked room across from hers once belonged to Emma Saxon, the former maid; Mrs. Brympton has Hartley fetched rather than using the lady's maid's bell. When Hartley asks a few questions about Emma Saxon she receives such angry retorts from the other servants that she makes up her mind to question no more. The cook, appropriately named Mrs. Blinder, gives Hartley an angry stare when she tries to find out what Emma looked like. Yet knowledge of Emma is crucial to Hartley. Emma is the precursor, the much-missed female helpmate to Mrs. Brympton, the former inhabitant of the now-locked room across the hall.

The arrival of Mr. Brympton from one of his frequent trips adds more tension and eeriness to the house. He is, in Hartley's opinion, "a big fair bull-necked man, with a red face and little bad-tempered blue eyes: the kind of man a young simpleton might have thought handsome, and would have been like to pay dear for thinking it" (252). Her astuteness extends to reading her own position in relation to him. When he looks Hartley up and down, she understands what the look means: "I was not the kind of morsel he was after. The typhoid had served me well enough in one way: it kept that kind of gentleman at arm's length" (252).

When he leaves, she notices that his wife is "white, and chill to the touch" (252). In spite of the difference in their status, the women share the common fate of possible sexual victimization by a common villain.

Hartley's suspicions of Brympton's aggressiveness are strengthened when, on subsequent returns home, he curses the dullness and drinks heavily. She draws her own conclusions concerning his wife's fate: "Once, when I was leaving my mistress's room rather later than usual, I met him coming up the stairs in such a state that I turned sick to think of what some ladies have to endure and hold their tongues about" (254). These stark male and female stereotypes, the mean-tempered, sexually aggressive man and the victimized woman, are common to the Gothic. What is particular to Wharton's Gothic is her emphasis on the silent terrors in marriage, usually "an unhappy match from the beginning" that brings women victimization they "have to endure and hold their tongues about" (254). Wharton also modifies the form by suggesting that the women, especially in the early stories, collaborate in their own restraint. In their timidity and vulnerability, they internalize social prohibitions against self-revelation and risk-taking.

The alternative to the villain who bullies women is the gentle-spirited man who provides companionship and the possibility of rescue to the heroine. In "The Lady's Maid's Bell," he is Mr. Ranford, a neighbor and Mrs. Brympton's only winter visitor, with whom she reads aloud and shares books. Of course her husband notes all this angrily, faulting his wife for his own frequent absence because she makes the place " 'about as lively as the family vault' " and commenting on Ranford's frequent visits (259). Ranford's failure as a rescuer is appropriate. Another man is not the answer to Mrs. Brympton's problems.

Brympton Place has a debilitating effect on Hartley, although she mutes her reaction. She realizes that when she returns from walks, the very sight of the house disturbs her: "The moment I caught sight of the house again my heart dropped down like a

Alice Hartley shrinks from the dark knowledge borne by her ghostly predecessor in Edith Wharton's "The Lady's Maid's Bell." Photo by Jay Yocis from Walter Appleton Clark's illustration for *Scribner's Magazine*, 1902.

stone in a well. It was not a gloomy house exactly, yet I never
entered it but a feeling of gloom came over me" (255). The constant January rain makes her jumpy and she begins hearing noises
from the locked room across the hall. "Somehow, the thought
of that locked room across the passage began to weigh on me,"
Hartley admits. The locked room holds the secret of the house,
the secret of the marriage, which Hartley both wants and does not
want to know, and which Emma, its former inhabitant, probably
does know.

Then one night Hartley is awakened by the sound of her bell
ringing, the bell that Mrs. Brympton refuses to ring. When she
looks at the bell, she sees "the little hammer still quivering" (260).
As Hartley dresses, the door across the hall opens, and she hears
footsteps in the passage. Instinctively Hartley is piecing the mystery together—that the locked door has been unlocked, that the
unrung bell has rung, that she must follow the footsteps of a
ghost into a threatening situation. The yonic imagery of the bell
suggests that its ringing has to do with a sexual incident, but
Hartley does not consider this possibility. She is astonished when
Mr. Brympton answers her knock on her mistress's door, his face
"red and savage" (261), and blurts, " '*You?* . . . *How many of
you are there, in God's name?*' " When Hartley asks if she may
go to Mrs. Brympton, he retorts, as he pushes by her, " 'You may
all go in, for what I care.' " When the wife calls out " '*Emma*' "
as she reaches for Hartley's hand, it is clear that both she and her
husband have seen what Hartley has heard, the ghost of the dead
maid (261). Emma has already come to the rescue of her mistress,
who is under sexual attack.

What also becomes clearer to the reader by this point is that
Emma is Hartley's dark double, the first name to her last, the
one whose words Hartley spoke involuntarily when she first arrived, the woman for whom she is mistaken by her mistress and
whose role she must fill, the ghost who knows the sexual secret
of the house and the marriage. Rather than just creating an effect,

Emma's ghost serves to tell us that a wrong has been committed, and her appearance is an appeal for justice or a preventive against its recurrence. The clues tell us that the wrong has to do with the tyrant's sexual assault on the weakened woman.

This ghost story portrays not only women's constraint but also the nascent companionship among them, hampered by a reticence that prevents them from truly helping one another. In this sense the ghost of Emma Saxon speaks about the silenced, isolated state of women in their society. Hartley and Mrs. Brympton, like Nettie Struther and Lily Bart at the end of *The House of Mirth*, are pale and vulnerable from physical and mental sickness, and all are beset at some point by sexual dilemmas that they cannot control. Yet though Hartley and Emma want to help Mrs. Brympton, and Nettie wishes to help Lily, they all fail. Months after the bell ringing incident Mrs. Brympton's strength and spirits continue to wane and Hartley's affection for her mistress grows, but the young woman admits, "After all there was little I could do to help her" (269). The response echoes Nettie's wistful comment to Lily, "'I only wish I could help *you*, but I suppose there's nothing on earth I could do'" (*House of Mirth* 510). In frustration at her sense of powerlessness, Hartley considers approaching the other servants: "But I had a feeling that if I questioned them they would deny everything, and that I might learn more by holding my tongue and keeping my eyes open" (*Descent* 265). Hers is the response of the isolated observer, the Gothic heroine, whose plight in this case, however, concerns not a danger to herself but to another woman—a danger she can neither comprehend nor articulate. She, like Mrs. Brympton, holds her tongue.

Hartley's sense of powerlessness is accentuated when she sees Emma again in a doorway, looking at her "long and long," her face "just one dumb prayer to me" (270). "How in the world was I to help her?" (270) she asks of the ghost, her response echoing what she says of her mistress and linking them all in a common bond of helpless silence. As Emma leads Hartley to Ranford's house and then disappears, Hartley feels desolate that the ghost "had left me all alone to carry the weight of the secret I couldn't guess" (273). Then she faints. The mystery is too overwhelming to be probed, particularly by a cautious young woman afraid to ask questions.

That it is the weighty secret of female sexuality that Emma leaves with Hartley becomes clear to the reader when Emma appears to her twice more, at the head of the stairs, "peering dreadfully down into the darkness" into which she disappears and then "on the threshold" of Mrs. Brympton's dressing room with the darkness behind her (275, 277). Fraught with connotations of sexuality, the threshold on which Emma stands leads into the darkness of the underworld, the unconscious, the female (see Rabuzzi 88–89).

Emma has a story to tell, possibly about an affair between Mrs. Brympton and Mr. Ranford, possibly about the Brympton marriage, possibly about her own death or her own relationship with Mr. or Mrs. Brympton. That she does not tell her story, but instead stares helplessly, leaves an emptiness where a resource should be. Her disembodiment and muteness make her the ideal symbol for the untold female story.

Alice is no help either in clarifying the mystery. Sensitive to the menace in her situation, she is not courageous enough to ask questions and probe for the secret of the house. Through her, Wharton is portraying female ambivalence, to see the horror of one's situation and not speak, to be afraid of one's more aware self. The pale, bodiless Emma, whose eyes have "an asking look" and who silently stares, is an exaggerated version of the pale, thin Hartley, who asks no questions, and her pale, thin mistress, who suffers silently. Given that blood is, as Susan Gubar has written, a central symbol furnished by the female body, these women seem bled of their femaleness, made sick by their silence (Gubar 83). The unspeakable domestic horror they are experiencing without sharing has made ghosts of them all. Their ghostliness is a visual representation of their story, wisps of which are known, while the rest is only suggested.

Lily's situation in *House of Mirth* is little more secure than Hartley's, in spite of their class difference. Like Hartley, she is an outsider. Although at times she is mothered by Judy Trenor, Lily is essentially Judy's maid, bound to Judy for favors, invitations, and cast-off dresses. She must come when Judy calls, write her notes, commiserate with her about the guests at her house parties. Lily is keenly aware that she is "in bondage to other people's pleasure" (*House* 43), becoming "a mere pensioner on the splendour which had once seemed to belong to her" (40).

From the start there are metaphorical hints that Lily is part of the Gothic text of the novel, created by a pattern of imagery that tells the secret story of the nether world beyond social propriety. Lily is a ghostly "other" who becomes more ghostly as the novel proceeds, just as pale Hartley becomes more like ghostly Emma. Lily is of a "different race" from the social class she mingles with, an observation made first by Selden and then by Lily herself (6, 76). Lily describes herself appreciatively as an "unwonted apparition" when confronted by the charwoman on Selden's stairs (20), but the image takes on ominous overtones when, worried about her bills, Lily sees her "hollow and pale" face in the mirror and is frightened by two tiny lines near her mouth (43)—a foreshadowing of the ghostly figure she will become in Book 2. As she peers at herself between the candle flames, "The white oval of her face swam out waveringly from a background of shadows, the uncertain light blurring it like a haze; but the two lines about the mouth remained" (43). Her fluid, pliant sense of herself and her future, both directly related to her outward beauty, are here palpably portrayed in a nightmarish image. Her only certainty about herself is her beauty, her ability to dazzle in a suitable setting; without this assurance she is a wan being, drained of her substance.

Lily's father was a nonentity, but her mother was a kind of

Gothic villain, pruning and cultivating her daughter as a commodity. When she contemplated her daughter's beauty, Mrs. Bart "studied it with a kind of passion, as though it were some weapon she had slowly fashioned for her vengeance. It was the last asset in their fortunes. . . . She watched it jealously, as though it were her own property and Lily its mere custodian; and she tried to instil into the latter a sense of the responsibility that such a charge involved" (53). It is the lesson Lily will learn best, that her beauty is all of her, that it is an asset to be used for financial gain and that it is hers only until it is owned by a husband. In truth, "beauty" is a euphemism for "sexuality," as Lily will discover most dramatically in her climactic confrontation with Gus Trenor.

On one hand, Lily wants to become the prized possession of a man, who will then lavish money on her maintenance. On the other, she intuitively senses the fearful consequences of such a role, and resists. Selling her sexuality and individuality for financial security in a proper marriage frightens Lily, for she senses it will mean being a captive in a house and a tradition—being, indeed, a Gothic heroine. The family house of Percy Gryce, Lily's latest prospective husband when the novel begins, is "an appalling house, all brown stone without and black walnut within, with the Gryce library in a fire-proof annex that looked like a mausoleum" (33). The family fortunes have, fittingly, flourished from "a patent device for excluding fresh air from hotels" (34). The prospect of a lifetime of boredom shut up in a tomblike house fills Lily with dread: "It was a hateful fate—but how escape from it?" (39).

Another option is her aunt's house, which, in its "state of unnatural immaculateness and order," is "as dreary as a tomb" (160), and Lily's room "as dreary as a prison" (176). It too represents the kind of life Lily fears having to live, her abundant energy "restricted by the necessity of adapting herself to her aunt's habits" (59). In order to gain her aunt's money she must become what her aunt wants her to be, but she feels "as if she were being buried alive in the stifling limits of Mrs. Penniston's existence"

(160). Yet living on her own is equally frightening. Gerty Farish's drab little apartment represents a claustrophobic existence to the more ambitious and energetic Lily, whose propensity for knocking over tables in the apartment's narrow confines is analogous to her struggle to avoid restriction.

The most Gothic house in the novel is the Trenors' dark town house, to which Gus lures Lily. Trenor, "red and massive" (128), with a "heavy carnivorous head" and a "broad expanse of cheek and neck" (87), is the consummate Gothic villain, recalling Mr. Brympton in "The Lady's Maid's Bell." When Lily arrives to find the house empty and the drawingroom shrouded, Trenor comments, " 'Doesn't this room look as if it was waiting for the body to be brought down?' " (227).

The comment is an apt allusion not only to the Gothic aura of the house but also to the Gothic secret it reveals: Lily's awareness of her own sexuality and the use to which she has put it. Unlike Mrs. Brympton, Lily is implicated in her own victimization since she has manipulated Trenor through sexual appeal, but she has refused to admit to herself what she has done, for "in her own mind there were certain closed doors she did not open" (131). In confronting her own sexual complicity, she confronts a secret as frightening as the one Alice fears behind the locked door in "The Lady's Maid's Bell."

The division that appears in the short story between a ghost who knows and a ghost seer who both seeks and avoids knowledge is duplicated in the novel when Lily begins to feel that she is divided into two selves, "the one she had always known, and a new abhorrent being to which it found itself chained" (238). She is "alone in a place of darkness and pollution" (239), pursued by the Furies, horrified by her awareness of what she has encouraged with her sexuality while at the same time disowning that awareness, making it another self—the monstrous knowing self—to which her accustomed self is chained. To Gerty, she confesses, "Can you imagine looking into your glass some morning and seeing a disfigurement—some hideous change that has come to you while you slept? Well, I seem to myself like that—I can't bear to see myself in my own thoughts" (265). As Ellen Moers has said, to give visual form to self-hatred, "to hold anxiety up to the Gothic mirror of the imagination" (163), is women's particular compulsion.

Yet because Lily "had never learned to live with her own thoughts" (288), she flees this confrontation—first to Gerty's, and then to the Mediterranean on a two-month cruise with Bertha and George Dorset. She hopes to forget the trauma that awareness has brought, the knowledge of her darker, ghostly self, as one might try to suppress a nightmare. Book 2, which begins in this new setting, has been called uncentered and wandering compared to Book 1, a change linked to the moral deterioration of the society being described and to Lily's increasingly dilapidated lodgings and declining fortunes.[6] Reading the Gothic text in the novel—the pattern of metaphorical ghosts, sexual malfeasance, constraint, and secrecy—allows the reader to see Book 2 as the ruin of the house of mirth, as a structural representation of crumbling social appearances. For throughout it, Lily becomes ghostlier and her experiences in her society more Gothic as she spirals down into death.

The emphatic Gothic quality of Book 2 makes clear that Bertha Dorset, the woman who has been Lily's dangerous rival, is not simply a rival but Lily's living dark double, the assertive, sexually manipulative "bad" woman who stays married for the money but has one affair after another.[7] Bertha is a metaphorical ghost, as menacing, intriguing, and bewildering to Lily as Emma is to Alice Hartley. For both Bertha and Emma represent knowledge, especially sexual knowledge, which Lily and Alice fear facing. Bertha's small pale face "seemed the mere setting of a pair of dark exaggerated eyes, of which the visionary gaze contrasted curiously with her self-assertive tone and gestures; so that, as one of her friends observed, she was like a disembodied spirit who took

up a great deal of room" (36). Bertha is the ghostly representation of all that is wrong with a social system in which women
can only make money by marrying it and can only be sexual on
the sly. She is all that Lily could be, Lily's dark potential, but that
which Lily keeps preventing herself from becoming by scaring off
one wealthy potential husband after another. Bertha is "dangerous," in Judy Trenor's words, nasty while Lily is not (69). Bertha
has a "reckless disregard for appearances," while Lily struggles to
maintain them (335). Bertha is the temptress who lures all the men
Lily tries to charm with her grace and beauty—George, Percy,
Gus, Selden. Bertha writes passionate love letters to Selden while
Lily's love for him goes unvoiced. Nevertheless, the charwoman
mistakes Lily for Bertha when she attempts to sell the letters, and
Lily's role as distraction for George on the Mediterranean cruise
makes her complicit in Bertha's infidelities.

The letters represent the female sexuality that the novel's society refuses to acknowledge, the secret it tries to keep, "the vol-
canic nether side of the surface over which conjecture and innuendo slide so lightly till the first fissure turns their whisper to
a shriek" (167). The intensity of the language accentuates how
dangerous this repressed passion is to the status quo.[8] For Lily,
possessing the letters is an experience of great anxiety, a confrontation with dark sexual knowledge but also with the alternative
between self-saving action and a larger moral good. The "horror"
of Rosedale's idea to use them as blackmail holds her momentarily "spell-bound" (416). When she refuses, the letters become
the catalyst for Lily's moral decision to give up her last opportunity to be deceitful in order to marry money.[9] Lily flirts with
the role Bertha enacts, and finally refrains from adopting it. But
the many parallels between Bertha and Lily, which become overt
in Lily's implication in the Dorsets' marital imbroglio, emphasize
how much Bertha represents Lily's alter-ego, the evil spirit she
might be were she to fulfill society's expectations.

After the disorienting trauma of the Monte Carlo experience,

Lily becomes inextricably immersed in the Gothic, an otherworld
of ghostly women who float in and out of Lily's perception as
she drifts from one blurry experience to another, debilitated by
psychic and physical pain. After her disinheritance, she begins to
disappear literally, becoming frail and ghastly pale, just as she
is metaphorically disappearing from society. Both conjoin in the
surreal scenes in which Lily goes to work, first for Mrs. Hatch—
a tawdry, newly rich social climber—and then in the hatmak-
ing shop.

Through the "pallid world" of Mrs. Hatch, the "stifling in-
ertia" of the Emporium Hotel, move "wan beings" who "drift"
and "float" in a life "outside the bounds of time and space." Lily
has indeed entered the land of ghosts. Although at first pleased
by "the sense of being once more lapped and folded in ease, as
in some dense mild medium impenetrable to discomfort," Lily
quickly realizes that she has entered a disorienting "dimly-lit
region" peopled by beings with "no more real existence than
the poet's shades in limbo" (440–42). Her disquietude increases
when she suspects a sexual/financial trap being set for one of
society's young heirs. The experience is a metaphorical version
of Alice Hartley's when her satisfaction with Brympton Place
turns to uneasiness about its ghost and suspicion about the sexual
wrongdoing the house secrets.

Lily's interaction with working-class women after she leaves
Mrs. Hatch's has been pointed to as an indication of her "growing
awareness and finally her merger with a community of working women" (Showalter 143). Reading the Gothic text in the
novel reveals that, instead, these women are as ghostly as those
wan beings at Mrs. Hatch's, and as discomforting to Lily. In
"this underworld of toilers" (*House* 461), all are equally sallow-
faced: "The youngest among them was as dull and colourless as
the middle-aged" (455). In fact, "in the whole work-room there
was only one skin beneath which the blood still visibly played,"
and that is Lily's flushed face as she attempts to become one of

these ghostly workers (455). In the claustrophobic workroom, the women's talk of men and illness has "the incoherence of a dream" for Lily, except when society names from the past "[float] to the surface" and show her "the fragmentary and distorted image of the world she had lived in reflected in the mirror of the working-girls' minds" (461). The ghostly denizens of this "underworld of toilers" represent what the ghost Emma does in "The Lady's Maid's Bell" or even what the ghostly Bertha does, the untold story of sexuality, of unspoken experience beyond the pale of social acceptability.

Nettie Struther, the sickly young woman Lily had once helped through her charity work at the Girls' Club, had been such a ghost, with a hidden story of sexual impropriety.[10] What has saved her from thinking "it was the end of everything" is that her story was heard and accepted by a childhood friend whom she marries and who, as Nettie puts it, " 'knew about me' " but who " 'cared for me enough to have me as I was' " (509). Now Nettie is "alive with hope and energy" and Lily is the pale, weak figure whose appearance startles Nettie in Bryant Park one dark evening years after their first meeting. Her sympathy and her warm kitchen, which temporarily comfort Lily, seem to achieve the intimacy missing between Alice and Mrs. Brympton in "The Lady's Maid's Bell." Yet the warmth is deceptive, for Nettie cannot hear Lily's plea for help. " 'I have been unhappy—in great trouble,' " Lily confesses, but the young woman invalidates Lily's words: " '*You* in trouble? I've always thought of you as being so high up, where everything was just grand' " (505). She never asks for Lily's story, but instead, oblivious to the irony, gushes to Lily about her baby daughter, " 'Wouldn't it be too lovely for anything if she could grow up to be just like you?' " (511).

That baby daughter whom Lily holds in Nettie's kitchen and later imagines she holds as she dies has been called by one critic the symbol of Lily's "potential rebirth" (Wershoven 42); by another, a symbol of the future "New Woman," a blend of leisure and working-class (Ammons 43); and by a third, more accurately, the "emblem" of Lily herself, infantilized by society's image of women (Wolff 130). Indeed, what appears at first to be a positive experience, the baby thrilling Lily with "a sense of warmth and returning life," becomes ominous, threatening: "At first the burden in her arms seemed as light as a pink cloud or a heap of down, but as she continued to hold it the weight increased, sinking deeper, and penetrating her with a strange sense of weakness, as though the child entered into her and became a part of herself" (*House* 510). This is not rebirth, but a kind of death, the phallic verb "penetrating" suggesting the sexual violation that overcomes Lily because she is defined in purely sexual terms. The life force that the baby represents also has, because of Lily's desperation and emptiness, the destructive potential to overwhelm her.

Overwhelmingness has been called crucial to the Gothic, a genre that communicates the "special understanding of how much this fact matters, for the individual, the race, even the species of man—that the deep truth of life is overwhelming, that it cannot be managed or fully assimilated" (Wilt 118). However much Lily has grown in self-awareness since the beginning of the novel, she is not strong enough to survive overwhelmingness. She feels herself "rootless and ephemeral, mere spin-drift on the whirling surface of existence, without anything to which the poor little tentacles of self could cling before the awful flood submerged them" (515–16). Horror, fear, dread, the primary emotions of the Gothic, all permeate Lily's last days. Like the ghost Emma Saxon "peering dreadfully down into the darkness," Lily looks down into the "dim abysses of unconsciousness" (521). She chooses to lose herself in the darkness rather than learn from it: "Her mind shrank from the glare of thought as instinctively as eyes contract in a blaze of light—darkness, darkness was what she must have at any cost" (521). In the end, she embraces the darkness of death.

Lily has tried to be other than the artistically created sexual object that her family and society have made her, but she is too weak and limited to create a new self and a new story. When, after Lily returns from the Mediterranean, Gerty urges her to tell her friends the whole truth about the Dorset incident, Lily responds, " 'What is truth? Where a woman is concerned, it's the story that's the easiest to believe' " (363). Gerty presses her, " 'But what is your story, Lily? I don't believe anyone knows it yet' " (363). Lily frankly admits, " 'My story?—I don't believe I know it myself' " (363). On one level, this is a discussion about a particular event, but it is also Lily's acknowledgment that she has no story to replace the Gothic one in which she is enmeshed. As for the "truth" Gerty wants to hear, " 'the truth about any girl is that once she's talked about she's done for' " (364). Lily is recognizing that to be talked about rather than to talk, to be a character in someone else's story rather than to create one's own story, is to be powerless. The story Lily would tell, that she loves pleasure, that she shuns the "homely virtues" of Old New York, is not one that her society can hear (363). Though Lily rejects the "happy marriage" of the traditional Gothic heroine, her attempt to write/right the story of her life is stymied by her narcissism, her weariness, her loneliness, her lack of courage.[11]

Lily rouses herself for one attempt to tell her own story when her "passionate desire to be understood" induces her to dispel "the cloud of misunderstanding" between her and Selden (494). Lily speaks frankly and directly to Selden about her situation and his role in helping to keep her from becoming what others have thought her to be, but when he resorts to lightness she muses, "It seemed incredible that any one should think it necessary to linger in the conventional outskirts of word-play and evasion" (494). Lily is attempting to break through the Gothic horror of silence, to tell her story rather than to hold her tongue like the ghostly Alice and Mrs. Brympton. Yet Selden is hardly a sympathetic or perceptive listener because he is too self-engrossed. Susan Gubar points out that "the word which made all clear" as Selden kneels beside "the semblance of Lily Bart" is "Lily's dead body" (81): "For she is now converted completely into a script for his edification . . . Lily's history, then, illustrates the terrors not of the word made flesh but of the flesh made word" (81).

The terrors of Lily in *The House of Mirth* and of the women in "The Lady's Maid's Bell" were Wharton's own. As her unpublished autobiographical fragment "Life and I" reveals, Wharton saw her childhood as a Gothic text and young Edith Jones as its heroine, trapped in suffocating Victorian interiors, isolated by her passion for words, tortured by her acute sensibilities: "My little corner of the world seemed like a dark trackless region 'where ignorant armies clash by night,' and I was oppressed by the sense that I was too small and ignorant and alone ever to find my way about in it" ("Life" 28).

The contrast between her spontaneous verbal reactions to the world around her and the demands of social decorum caused "the most excrutiating moral tortures" (2). How acutely Wharton remembers "the darkness of horror that weighed on [her] childhood in respect to this vexed problem of truth-telling, & the impossibility of reconciling 'God's' standard of truthfulness with the conventional obligation to be 'polite' & not hurt anyone's feelings" (7).

Words, for Wharton, became imbued with the taboo—erotic pleasure enjoyed in secret. Time spent in her library was "a secret ecstasy of communion" with books, "enraptured sessions" that she shared with no one (*Backward* 69–70). The sight and sound of words produced "sensuous rapture," she reveals in "Life and I" (10). Words, she writes there, were "visible, almost tangible presences" that "almost lured me from the wholesome noonday air of childhood into some strange supernatural region" (10). Storytelling became a "devastating passion" (11), "my perilous obsession" (12). Indeed, as Judith Fryer points out in *Felicitous Space*, writing, for Wharton, was an act both spectral and sexual (159–60). Wharton herself suggests this when she explains her family's "awe-struck dread" of the literary and their "tacit disapproval" of her writing, as if she were a "bad" woman (*Backward* 122).[12]

Sexuality itself was kept a shameful secret during Wharton's youth. The adult Wharton remembers that any time she asked about "the shadow of a reality," she was given "a penetrating sense of 'not-niceness,'" a "vague sense of contamination" (33–34). The mystery of sex only intensified as her marriage approached. When the young woman, "seized with a dread of the whole dark mystery" (34), approached her mother for information, she was rebuffed with "icy disapproval" (34).

Writing Gothic stories was a way for Wharton to enact the psychic drama of repressed female language and eroticism that was part of her own experience. Encouraged to "hold her tongue" in her childhood and youth, the adult Wharton undertakes, in her Gothic fiction, the "perilous" task of recording the terrors of powerlessness, isolation, silence, and suppressed sexuality that haunt and may even destroy women. In doing so, Wharton not only tells the "unutterable" story of women's lives, but also asserts her right to speak and be heard.

Notes

1. Wharton's ghost stories have been discussed but not as Gothic fiction. The three best articles on Wharton's ghost stories are Margaret McDowell's "Edith Wharton's Ghost Stories," Allan Gardner Smith's "Edith Wharton and the Ghost Story," and R. W. B. Lewis's "Powers of Darkness." McDowell argues that Wharton's ghost stories are crafted fiction, revealing her psychological and moral insight; however, she does not see any unifying theme among them. Smith argues that Wharton uses the ghost story to address topics that her society preferred not to discuss, primarily the topic of sexuality, and that, in these stories, the horror of the "suppressed 'natural'" is greater than that of the conventional supernatural. Smith suggests but does not discuss male oppression of women in Wharton's ghost stories. Lewis posits that Wharton, like other Victorian and Edwardian ghost story writers, "deployed the supernatural as a way of getting at certain aspects of human nature and experience— the aberrant, the perverse, the lawless, the violently sexual—which

could not be dealt with in realistic fiction" ("Powers" 644). Lewis also briefly discusses the ghost stories in *Edith Wharton, A Biography* and in his introduction to *The Collected Short Stories*. Judith Fryer, in *Felicitous Space*, emphasizes that the process of creativity itself is a ghostly one for Wharton and that, as Lewis explains, the stories express her "hidden and suppressed side," an alternative to order and control. Gilbert and Gubar present an argument about the ghost stories, which I broaden in my discussion of them as Gothic, that these stories are a means of "saying the unsayable" about female desire, rage, and pain (*No Man's Land* 2:159). Critics like Lindberg, Nevius, Ammons, and Wolff, who believe Wharton is a realist above all, mention the ghost stories only briefly in their books.

2. Like G. R. Thompson, but for different reasons, I am assuming that the ghost story is a Gothic form. Wharton does not see the real world as apparitional, the way Thompson contends early nineteenth-century American Gothic writers do, but rather she sees the apparitional in the real world as one clue to reality's hidden Gothic story. My sense of Wharton's Gothic is close to Alfred Bendixen's definition of supernatural fiction by women as "the unspeakable . . . given form" (1). But Bendixen dismisses the Gothic as less subtle and complex than nineteenth- and twentieth-century supernatural tales, while I believe Wharton revises the Gothic to tell the hidden story that may or may not involve the supernatural.

3. Wharton's perspective of the supernatural suggests Freud's definition of the uncanny as "that class of the frightening that leads back to what is known of old and long familiar," which is "in reality nothing new or alien, but something which is familiar and old-established in the mind and which has become alienated from it through the process of repression" (221). It is something that "ought to have remained hidden but has come to light" (241). Wharton emphasizes, however, that the frightening ought *not* to remain hidden.

4. Both Lewis and Wolff discuss this period of illness in Wharton's life. In "Powers of Darkness," Lewis makes the important point that "The Lady's Maid's Bell" was written within six months of Wharton's mother's death, and notes: "With the source of her childhood terrors removed, the mature writer could now deploy her memory of them to expert literary purposes" (646).

5. Poe's description reads: "During the whole of a dull, dark, and soundless day in the autumn of the year, when the clouds hung oppressively low in the heavens, I had been passing alone, on horseback, through a singularly dreary tract of country; and at length found myself, as the shades of the evening drew on, within view of the melancholy House of Usher. I know not how it was—but, with the first glimpse of the building, a sense of unsufferable gloom pervaded my spirit" (95).

6. Elizabeth Ammons points this out (36) as does Lewis in his introduction to *The House of Mirth*.

7. As Gilbert and Gubar have noticed, Bertha Dorset suggests a revised version of Bertha Mason in *Jane Eyre*, who also represents the displaced, monstrous sexuality of the heroine (*No Man's Land* 2: 145). The parallel is emphasized in Carry Fisher's comment to Lily that " 'Bertha has been behaving more than ever like a madwoman' " (384).

8. Mary Jacobus discusses how, just as Lucy Snow writes a secret, passionate letter, so *Villette* contains a "buried letter of Romanticism" which "becomes the discourse of the Other, as the novel's unconscious—not just Lucy's—struggles for articulation within the confines of mid-nineteenth century realism" (42). Supernatural haunting disrupts the text because it cannot formally recognize the Gothic mode. I think Wharton deliberately uses Gothic elements, in this case Lily's horrified enthrallment with Bertha's letters, to articulate what realism cannot.

9. Key to the Gothic is the internal battle between "immediate ego-preservation" and "the apprehension of larger, less personal values that first makes itself known as dread," Judith Wilt explains in her discussion of the Gothic in Eliot's *Daniel Deronda* (177).

10. Lily's suggestion of promiscuity among the working class is perhaps one reason why Margaret McDowell, otherwise an astute reader of Wharton, mistakenly assumes that Nettie is a former prostitute (*Edith Wharton* 45).

11. Relevant here is Susan Gubar's observation that George Eliot "criticizes the idea that beauty is an index of moral integrity by demonstrating how narcissism infantilizes the female, turning her from

an autonomous person into a character in search of an author or a page in search of a pen" (79).

12. Gilbert and Gubar have brilliantly described the "anxiety of authorship" a woman suffers because of "her culturally conditioned timidity about self-dramatization, her dread of the patriarchal authority of art, her anxiety about the impropriety of female invention" (*Madwoman* 50).

Works Cited

Ammons, Elizabeth. *Edith Wharton's Argument with America.* Athens: U of Georgia P, 1980.

Bendixen, Alfred. Introduction. *Haunted Women: The Best Supernatural Tales by American Women Writers.* New York: Ungar, 1985. 1–12.

Day, William Patrick. *In the Circles of Fear and Desire: A Study of Gothic Fantasy.* Chicago: U of Chicago P, 1985.

Freud, Sigmund. "The 'Uncanny.'" *The Standard Edition of the Complete Works of Sigmund Freud.* 24 vols. Trans. and ed. James Strachey. London: Hogarth, 1968, Vol. 17.

Fryer, Judith. *Felicitous Space: The Imaginative Structures of Edith Wharton and Willa Cather.* Chapel Hill: U of North Carolina P, 1986.

Gilbert, Sandra M. and Susan Gubar. *The Madwoman in the Attic: The Woman Writer and the Nineteenth-Century Literary Imagination.* New Haven: Yale UP, 1979.

———. *No Man's Land: The Place of the Woman Writer in the Twentieth Century.* 3 vols. *Sexchanges.* New Haven: Yale UP, 1989, Vol. 2.

Gubar, Susan. "The 'Blank Page' and the Issues of Female Creativity." *Writing and Sexual Difference.* Ed. Elizabeth Abel. Chicago: U of Chicago P, 1982. 73–93.

Jacobus, Mary. "The Buried Letter: Feminism and Romanticism in *Villette.*" *Women Writing and Writing About Women.* Ed. Mary Jacobus. New York: Barnes, 1979. 42–60.

Kahane, Claire. "The Gothic Mirror." *The (M)other Tongue: Essays in Feminist Psycoanalytic Interpretation*. Eds. Shirley Nelson Garner, Claire Kahane, and Madelon Sprengnether. Ithaca: Cornell UP, 1985.

Lewis, R. W. B. *Edith Wharton: A Biography*. New York: Harper, 1975.

————, ed. *The House of Mirth*. New York: Houghton, 1963.

————. "Powers of Darkness." *Times Literary Supplement* 13 June 1975: 644–46.

Lindberg, Gary H. *Edith Wharton and the Novel of Manners*. Charlottesville: UP of Virginia, 1975.

McDowell, Margaret B. "Edith Wharton's Ghost Stories." *Criticism* 12 (1970): 133–51.

————. *Edith Wharton*. Indianapolis: Bobbs-Merrill, 1976.

Moers, Ellen. *Literary Women*. Garden City: Anchor, 1977.

Nevius, Blake. *Edith Wharton: A Study of Her Fiction*. Berkeley: U of California P, 1961.

Poe, Edgar Allan. "The Fall of the House of Usher." *The Selected Writings of Edgar Allan Poe*. Ed. Edward Davidson. Cambridge: Riverside, 1956. 95–112.

Punter, David. *The Literature of Terror: A History of Gothic Fictions from 1765 to the Present Day*. New York: Longman, 1980.

Rabuzzi, Kathryn Allen. *Motherself: A Mythic Analysis of Motherhood*. Bloomington: Indiana UP, 1988.

Showalter, Elaine. "The Death of the Lady (Novelist): Wharton's *House of Mirth*." *Representations* 9 (1985): 133–49.

Smith, Allan Gardner. "Edith Wharton and the Ghost Story." *Women and Literature* 1 (1981): 149–59.

Stein, Karen F. "Monsters and Madwomen: Changing Female Gothic." *The Female Gothic*. Ed. Juliann E. Fleenor. Montreal: Eden, 1983. 123–37.

Thompson, G. R. "The Apparition of This World: Transcendentalism and the American 'Ghost' Story." *Bridges to Fantasy*. Eds. George E. Slusser, Eric S. Rabkin, and Robert Scholes. Carbondale: Southern Illinois UP, 1982.

Wershoven, Carol. *The Female Intruder in the Novels of Edith Wharton*. Rutherford: Fairleigh Dickinson UP, 1982.

Wharton, Edith. *A Backward Glance*. New York: Appleton-Century, 1934.

———. *The Descent of Man and Other Stories*. New York: Scribner, 1904.

———. *The House of Mirth*. New York: Scribner, 1905.

———. "Life and I." Wharton Archives. Yale University, New Haven, CT.

———. *A Motor-Flight Through France*. New York: Scribner, 1908.

———. Preface. *Ghosts*. New York: Appleton-Century, 1937.

———. *Sanctuary*. New York: Scribner, 1903.

Wilt, Judith. *Ghosts of the Gothic: Austen, Eliot, and Lawrence*. Princeton: Princeton UP, 1980.

Wolff, Cynthia Griffin. *A Feast of Words: The Triumph of Edith Wharton*. New York: Oxford UP, 1978.

Jennice G. Thomas

Spook or Spinster?
Edith Wharton's "Miss Mary Pask"

Faced with being spooked, Spinsters are learning to
Spook/Speak back. . . . Tactically, Spooking means learning to refuse the seductive summons by the Passive Voices
that call us into the state of Animated Death.
　　　　　　　　　　　　—Mary Daly, *Gyn/Ecology*

LONG BEFORE MARY DALY began her explorations of the
power potential in feminist spaces, women writers concerned
with female powerlessness in a patriarchal world were exploiting
the supernatural for weapons of retaliation against the patriarchy
that limits the images and options available to women. The free-
doms offered by the ghost story genre allowed Edith Wharton
to create possibilities of vengeance for a supposedly powerless
spinster in her story "Miss Mary Pask." The title character must,
however, pay the price exacted of women who push their way out
of patriarchal definitions. She is given the power to frighten the
arrogant male narrator literally out of his senses. But her reward
is loneliness because she is denied the benefits of sisterhood.

In the "Third Passage" of *Gyn/Ecology*, Mary Daly traces

the journey of Spinsters through the realm of Spooking into the energy arousal of Sparking. Daly acknowledges that in patriarchal parlance "spinster" is a deprecating term, but she traces its deep meaning from the dictionary's "a woman whose occupation is to spin" and redefines it: "A woman whose occupation is to spin participates in the whirling movement of creation. She who has chosen her Self, who defines her Self, by choice, neither in relation to children nor to men, who is Self-identified is a Spinster" (3). Once the Spinster has reclaimed her powers of self-definition, she begins the passage into her potential for Spooking. Spooking entails not only responding to "the call of the wild" (Daly 343) from within and without but also learning means of "dispossessing" the patriarchy of what rightfully belongs to women, their selfhood and their history (Daly 337–47). Spinsters who have learned to Spook link with their sisters to rekindle the fires of an innate energy that patriarchy has sought to extinguish or steal. Miss Mary Pask, in learning to spook the narrator, exorcises an enfeebling image, escapes into her own space, and finds the process indeed inspiriting, but she never arrives at that stage of completion and reward that Daly associates with the Sparking of female friendship.

In Wharton's story, a nameless male narrator, a bachelor who suffers from a recurring nervous disorder, recounts his meeting one foggy night with the ghost of a lonely spinster, Mary Pask. He has undertaken a journey to her isolated cottage near the *Baie des Trepasse* (Bay of the Dead) on the Brittany coast to pay her a social visit, Mary being the elder sister of Grace Bridgeworth, a friend's wife. As he waits in the hall for Mary Pask to acknowledge the servant's summons, he suddenly remembers that Mary has been dead for over a year. The memory of Grace Bridgeworth's mourning for her sister surfaces in his confused consciousness just as a spectral figure in white descends the stairs to greet him. He recognizes his hostess as the ghost of Mary Pask and remains mesmerized while she expresses an urgent desire to

The dramatic lighting suggests that Wharton's narrator feels his masculinity threatened by the specter of Miss Mary Pask. Photo by Ken Van Dyne from Harold Brett's illustration for *The Pictorial Review*, 1925.

hear details of her sister's response to the news of her death, explains the sources of strength and freedom that she has recently found, and jokes about her own loneliness. As soon as the narrator can regain enough self-possession to move, he attempts to escape. Mary Pask urges him to spend the night and share her company since he has made the effort to pay a visit, but a gust of wind blows out the candles and, under the cover of darkness, he pushes past her and flees into the night. This event continues to haunt him through a nervous collapse and a return to America, where he pays a visit to Grace and Horace Bridgeworth and discovers that the report of Mary Pask's death was a mistake. This news so humiliates him that he repudiates both the pity and the terror that he has experienced and retreats into indifference.

Wharton's narrator is indeed spooked by his experience. He begins in a position of power as he patronizingly contrasts his own sense of social and artistic achievements to Mary Pask's pitiful loneliness and "the extremely elementary nature of her interest in art" (Wharton 224). Once in her presence, however, he quickly succumbs to her power to terrorize him into a state of utter passivity. Reversing the stereotype that gives hysteria its female name, Wharton portrays the narrator as a hysterical bachelor, whose intermittent artistic pursuits are punctuated by frequent visits to various European sanatoriums for rest cures. Thus the reader is invited to judge the cruelty and absurdity of patriarchal pretensions in the form of his easy assumption of superiority over a woman who can command a social situation, maintain a sense of humor, analyze her own experience with perceptiveness, and assert her independence and individuality.

Mary Pask can profoundly spook the narrator because his male ego distorts his vision not only of her but of himself as well. Wharton reverses the stereotypes of the active bachelor and the passive spinster to expose the narrator's false sense of security. She comments ironically on the male artist's sources of self-confidence, and she draws from a long tradition that associates women with nature to demonstrate how the dread of darkness and death is linked in the masculine imagination with a fear of women.

As the narrator stumbles through pitch darkness toward the deserted seacoast cottage where Mary Pask lives, the fog, the sound of the sea, and the darkness disorient and confuse him. At this point, nature, like woman, is vaguely threatening to him, and it does not help that the place is called the Bay of the Dead. Indeed the narrator associates something female with the sea's insistent noise: "the sea whose hungry voice I heard asking and asking . . . the sea whined down there as if it were feeding time, and the Furies, its keepers, had forgotten it" (228). With an image of the Furies, those ancient Greek goddesses of vengeance whom many scholars now acknowledge as the voices of a betrayed and defeated matriarchy, Wharton suggests the buried power of female anger. The narrator's dread of being fed to the hungry waves is soon translated into his fear of becoming consumed in Mary Pask's schemes to seduce him. For, although she should be in her grave, she seems to be beckoning him into a ghastly embrace. Indeed, as gusts of wind whip the night fog into a storm, so her power to enthrall him increases.

In contrast to the narrator, with his dread of nature, Mary finds the sounds of wind and sea companionable in her isolation from other people. She prefers darkness to light, sleeps during the daylight hours in a shady corner of her garden, and spends the night awake and alone in the house. She tells the narrator, "I like the darkness. . . . The dead naturally get used to it" (234). Mary's very real power to spook the narrator with her reversals of night and day, indoors and outdoors, allows Wharton to suggest, perhaps playfully, perhaps seriously, that the image of the witch that has so terrified the patriarchal imagination can be used by women to turn the tables of patriarchal terror tactics. For Mary Pask is hardly the pitiful and powerless creature the narrator expects to find as he stumbles through the fog on his mission of mercy.

On the other hand, the role of spook that Mary has chosen

bears a superficial resemblance to the role of spinster that she
has rejected, and this irony intensifies the narrator's horror. Both
the spook and the spinster dress habitually in white and move
about silently. Wharton further empowers Mary by permitting
her to use the rituals of courtship ironically; the spook, like the
derided spinster of patriarchal myth, practices the "wiles of a
clumsy capering coquetry" (233), according to the narrator, but
these become weapons of terror that enable Mary to "captivate"
him. The narrator can do nothing but stare and tremble as Mary
Pask draws him "in her wake like a steel cable" (233) and jokes
slyly about her isolation: "It's such an age since I've seen a living
being" (233). Mary Pask's manipulation of the narrator's expectations to increase his horror makes her the active and controlling
agent and him her passive victim.

To maintain some semblance of self-control, the narrator attempts to reassure himself that, in spite of her supernatural appearance, Mary Pask is still a weak and timid soul, using another
double-edged image of seductive spinsters: "Dead or alive, Mary
Pask would never harm a fly" (234). Mary's pleas that he remain
for the night to relieve her loneliness with news about her sister strike him as both threatening and pathetic. Although Mary's
loneliness is clearly caused by the desertion of her sister, the
narrator feels himself to be the object of Mary's desires. Mary
complains:

> "I used to think I knew what loneliness was . . . after Grace
> married, you know. Grace thought she was always thinking
> of me, but she wasn't. She called me 'darling,' but she was
> thinking of her husband and children. I said to myself then:
> 'You couldn't be lonelier if you were dead.' But I know better
> now . . . There's been no loneliness like this last year's . . .
> none!" (236–37)

But Mary's appeal for companionship is interpreted by the narrator as an appeal for masculine protection and a ploy for sexual

entrapment. Ghost or not, in his mind Mary is a spinster still eager to catch an eligible bachelor in the bonds of matrimony. He cannot quite tell whether she wants to drag him into her bed or into her grave, and he is not amused to reflect that there may no longer be any real difference between the two. In fact, his experience with Mary raises questions for him about the validity of other supernatural figures of power: "Old tales and legends floated through my mind: the Bride of Corinth, the mediaeval vampire—but what names to attach to the plaintive image of Mary Pask!" (238). The mediaeval vampire sucked the life's blood from her betrothed. The Bride of Corinth arose from the dead to defy her parents and lie with the man she loved, who, like the narrator, was not comforted to discover that his lover was a corpse, three days buried.

Such legends, of course, serve to reinforce the links between death, evil, and female sexuality within the male imagination. Indeed, the narrator's assumption that a woman can attain validity only through her connections with a man make it impossible for him to understand that Mary is lonely because she has lost a sister, not because she has failed to find a husband. Mary clearly despises Horace Bridgeworth because he has taken Grace from her, but the narrator, who knows Horace to be a "ladies' man" and who is incapable of seeing any relationship between women that does not revolve around a man, finds it easier to believe that Mary's dislike of Horace is simply a mask for her own illicit attraction to her sister's husband. So clearly does the narrator see spinsterhood as the source of Mary's loneliness that he speculates, "I wonder if she isn't better off than when she was alive" (235). Indeed, spinsterhood so clearly strips identity from a woman that the narrator admits, "The dead Mary Pask . . . was so much more real to me than ever the living one had been" (239). Mary's presentation of herself as a spook rather than a spinster implies Wharton's protest against a world in which women must be perceived as dead in order to escape masculine scorn and claim an empowering autonomy.

Mary Pask is a spinster by choice not default, as the narrator assumes. Her sister's marriage has left her alone and she uses that aloneness to explore opportunities for autonomy, to gain a sense of freedom, and to cultivate her sensibilities. Grace, Mary's sister, credits Mary's interest in art with providing the motive for her solitude. Wharton is clearly aware that women were often forced to choose between marriage and an artistic career, and that loneliness and contempt were the price patriarchy expected women to pay for their devotion to art or literature. (Wharton may have modeled Mary on the Queen Recluse herself, Emily Dickinson, who dressed in white, devoted her life to her art, and suffered the misunderstanding of male critics.) The narrator's jealousy dismisses Mary's artistic sensibility as trivial and pretentious while insisting on his own artistic seriousness and importance. He contrasts his own ability to choose a single life with Mary's failure to be chosen by a mate. But, clearly, Wharton expects us to see through his pretensions. Even the fact that Wharton leaves him nameless while giving Mary a name with so many powerful associations helps us to see through his empty vanity to a reality that either escapes him or threatens him. Mary's choice of spinsterhood so spooks the patriarchy that it can see her only as a ghost of a woman.

The tragedy of Mary Pask's loneliness is not that she has lost a companion through her own failure to marry but that she has lost a companion to marriage. Before Grace married, the sisters were inseparable. Again, Wharton's choice of names underscores the potential for spiritual power in the bonding of these two sisters. That Grace deserts Mary for a heterosexual relationship that allows her neither time nor energy for the sister she has abandoned is a situation that Wharton and many other women of her time felt was inevitable. But sisterhood need not fail.

The concept of sisterhood that Mary Daly links with spook and spinster in *Gyn/Ecology* offers women the possibility of achieving autonomy without loneliness. Indeed the sparking of female friendship inherent in the concept of sisterhood gives women access to a creative power that not only challenges patriarchy's scorn of women but also exposes the feeble imagination beneath the veneer of vain pretension that has often characterized masculine attitudes toward feminine independence. Mary Pask, however, cannot benefit from such an empowering process, for although she has found her own identity in spinsterhood and learned to spook her detractors, loneliness mars her achievements; her sister fails her.

Loneliness, almost a living death, is indeed a hard price to pay for autonomy and that Wharton saw such loneliness as the inevitable result of a woman's attempts to live outside the boundaries of marriage explains, perhaps, the necessity she felt to grant this spinster a supernatural power. Wharton's exposure of sisterhood's failure to alleviate the sufferings of single women contributes another dimension to this tale. One can only speculate about the sparks that a satisfying sisterhood might have ignited in this spinster who all alone learns how to "Spook/Speak" back at the specter of patriarchal power.

Works Cited

Daly, Mary. *Gyn/Ecology: The Metaethics of Radical Feminism.* Boston: Beacon, 1978.

Wharton, Edith. "Miss Mary Pask." In *Ghosts.* New York: Appleton-Century, 1937. 221–43.

Lynette Carpenter

Visions of Female Community
in Ellen Glasgow's Ghost Stories

Shade after shade, they passed before me in that first
year of my homecoming. Shade after shade, they approached, looked at me without stopping, and vanished
into complete darkness. . . . The house belonged to the
dead. I was living with ghosts.
　　　　　　　　　—Ellen Glasgow, *The Woman Within*

The old gray stucco house at One West Main Street in
Richmond, Virginia, is said to be haunted. It is the house
where Ellen Glasgow lived, wrote, and died. Believers in
ghosts claim to have seen a vision of Miss Ellen in white,
standing on the landing or in the garden doorway. . . .
Nonbelievers might feel close to Miss Ellen only through
the reading of her novels; but if ever a house should be
haunted with the ghosts of the past and intimations of the
future, hers should be.
　　　　　　　　　　　　　　　—William Godbold,
　　　　　　　　　Ellen Glasgow and the Woman Within

IN 1916, WITH HER FATHER and closest sister recently dead, Ellen Glasgow returned to the family home in Richmond, Virginia, and entered into one of the most difficult periods of her life. She felt keenly the loss of her family, and the war played upon her imagination. Her physical and mental health worsened; she became even more painfully self-conscious about her deafness. She felt herself haunted by the ghosts of dead loved ones, as she described it later in *The Woman Within*: "Ghosts were my only companions. I was shut in, alone, with the past." She added, "This is not rhetoric. This is what I thought or felt or imagined, while I stood there alone, in that empty house" (237).[1]

Yet the house was not always empty. Anne Virginia Bennett, who had nursed Glasgow's father and sister, stayed on in the house as Glasgow's private secretary. A frequent visitor was Henry Anderson, Glasgow's close friend and probable fiance. Anderson's influence on the Glasgow novels from this period, *The Builders* (1919) and *One Man in His Time* (1922), has been noted by critics and biographers, and chronicled by Anderson himself in his correspondence with the author. Rarely discussed are the contemporaneous ghost stories, written, according to Miss Bennett, at her own instigation.[2] The differences between Glasgow's novels and her ghost stories suggest something of the dynamics of her household at the time. More importantly, however, they portray Glasgow's exploration of the alternatives of conventional heterosexual romance and female community. At a time when she was contemplating marriage, Glasgow wrote some of her most radical critiques of marriage in both the novels and the ghost stories, but only the ghost stories envision the possible substitution of relationships between women for the conventional resolution of happy marriage.

Marriage was clearly a subject of preoccupation for Glasgow in these years, for despite her well-documented cynicism about it, by her own admission she was attracted to the prospect of marriage with Anderson, confessing: "It is true that conscience and reason are not inflexible motives" (*Woman Within* 228). A chronology of events in the development of their relationship is difficult to establish (Anderson destroyed all of Glasgow's letters to him following her death), but they were probably engaged when Anderson left for Rumania in 1917 for an administrative post with the Red Cross.[3] Glasgow's own account blames their estrangement on Anderson's infatuation with Queen Marie of Rumania. In any case, the war seems to have effectively ended their engagement, although they may have continued to discuss marriage for years. Glasgow commented: "For seventeen months out of twenty years we were happy together" (*Woman Within* 227). That happiness, however, cannot have seemed secure to one who confessed to "a deep conviction that [she] was unfitted for marriage" (153). Indeed, Anderson's letters to her between 1916 and 1920, dated only by day and not by year, record a troubled relationship punctuated by hurt and humiliation on her part, and misunderstanding on his. Plagued by physical illness and mental depression, she may have felt especially betrayed at a time when she was especially vulnerable. Yet in retrospect, she relates the episode to "the illusion of [her] disillusionment" (215), acknowledging that her disappointment with romance and marriage antedated her experience with Anderson.

More enduring was her relationship with Anne Virginia Bennett, of whom she wrote: "More than anyone else since I lost [my sister] Cary, Anne Virginia has had my interests at heart; and she has shared my compassion for all inarticulate creation, and even turns that compassion upon me" (216). William Godbold writes of other attitudes in common: "They shared a love of dogs and a dislike of men. Ellen liked to think of men as intellectual and social inferiors and unsatisfactory lovers, but she enjoyed teasing them and often sought their company. Anne Virginia hated men almost violently" (196). Godbold observes that Miss Bennett especially disliked Henry Anderson, and Marcelle Thiébaux records that she did not welcome his presence at Glasgow's funeral (22). Like Anderson, Miss Bennett left Glasgow to go abroad with the Red Cross during the war, but unlike Anderson, in Glasgow's view, she returned with her loyalty intact. She did not share Anderson's interest in Glasgow's work; her editorial influence cannot be documented in the way that Anderson's can. Yet she was the most likely prototype for the sympathetic heroines of the ghost stories, who offer an appealing alternative to masculine cruelty and insensitivity.

The ghost stories value sympathy, compassion, and sensitivity, and portray these qualities as a primary source of bonds between women. These are qualities that men neither possess, nor understand, nor value, the stories imply. Glasgow's familiarity with a female tradition in the ghost story is suggested by her personal library holdings at the time of her death: in addition to Bronte's *Wuthering Heights* and Radcliffe's *The Mysteries of Udolpho*, she owned two of Cynthia Asquith's ghost story collections, Edith Wharton's *Tales of Men and Ghosts* (1918) and *Ghosts* (1937), Katherine Fullerton Gerould's *Vain Oblations* (1914), Isak Dinesen's *Seven Gothic Tales* (1934), Virginia Woolf's *A Haunted House and Other Stories* (1944), and miscellaneous collections by Mary Wilkins Freeman, Elizabeth Bowen, Marjorie Bowen, and Vernon Lee. Perhaps most significant among these literary influences was Edith Wharton, whose 1904 story, "The Lady's Maid's Bell," featured a compassionate lady's maid who struggled first to understand and then to help her victimized mistress (see Fedorko, this volume); if Anne Virginia Bennett was the actual prototype for Glasgow's heroines, Wharton's Hartley was a likely literary model.

In the earliest of the stories, "The Shadowy Third," their counterpart is the narrator, Miss Randolph, a nurse who finds herself siding with her female patient against two powerful professional men. Miss Randolph is flattered when the great surgeon Dr. Maradick chooses her as personal nurse to his wife, vaguely described as a "mental case" (4). Yet she feels an immediate empa-

Nurse Randolph witnesses the tearful farewell between mother and ghostly daughter in Ellen Glasgow's "The Shadowy Third." Photo by Jay Yocis from Elenore Plaisted Abbott's illustration for *Scribner's Magazine*, 1916.

thy with her new patient, an empathy manifested by their shared vision of Mrs. Maradick's little girl by her first marriage, dead two months previous from pneumonia. Mrs. Maradick accuses her husband of murder, telling Miss Randolph that he had married her for her fortune and killed the child who stood in the way of his inheritance. Questioned by the surgeon, Miss Randolph refuses to confirm his opinion that his wife is insane. Finally, however, she cannot prevent Mrs. Maradick's commitment to an asylum, and she witnesses the tearful farewell between mother and ghostly daughter. She stays on as office nurse to Dr. Maradick, learning of Mrs. Maradick's death and then of his engagement to a wealthy young woman he had known before his marriage. She also learns that Mrs. Maradick's beloved house, the house in which her ghostly daughter lives on, will be torn down upon Dr. Maradick's marriage. On the eve of his second wedding, he is called to the hospital late, but as he starts downstairs, the nurse looks up to see a child's jump rope coiled on a stair in the darkness. He has fallen to his death before she can reach the light.

The story emphasizes sympathetic bonding between women. Nurse Randolph's initial sympathies are with the husband, who is "charming . . . , kind and handsome" (5)—a man, she says, "born to be a hero to women" (6). Even before she is singled out for the attention of the great surgeon, Miss Randolph succumbs to the force of his personality, observing, "But I am not the first nurse to grow love-sick about a doctor who never gave her a thought" (7). The hospital superintendent suspects that she is too sympathetic and imaginative for her own good, and asks, " 'Wouldn't you have made a better novelist than a nurse?' " (5). Miss Randolph's first personal encounter with Dr. Maradick leads her to confess: "I felt I would have died for him" (13). By the time Miss Randolph does in fact write her story, however, Dr. Maradick is not its hero but its villain.

When Miss Randolph meets Mrs. Maradick, her sympathies are again besieged, and her loyalties divided. Mrs. Maradick's "sweetest and saddest smile" (16) and her "gentle voice" (17) win over Miss Randolph at once: "There was something about her— I don't know what it was—that made you love her as soon as she looked at you" (18). Despite Mrs. Maradick's accusations of murder against her husband, Miss Randolph concludes, "She was not mad" (20). Understandably, the young nurse has found her first night in the house emotionally draining: "By seven o'clock I was worn out—not from work but from the strain on my sympathy" (21). When next Miss Randolph sees the surgeon and is questioned about his wife's condition, she lies to protect Mrs. Maradick: "How the warning reached me—what invisible waves of sense-perception transmitted the message—I have never known; but while I stood there, facing the splendour of the doctor's presence, every intuition cautioned me that the time had come when I must take sides in the household. While I stayed there I must stand either with Mrs. Maradick or against her" (26). She may be willing to die for Dr. Maradick, but she is not willing to sacrifice his wife to his convenience. Standing with Mrs. Maradick also means risking her career to contradict the opinion of the nerve specialist, Dr. Brandon.

In actuality, the decision has already been made for Miss Randolph by her cultural background and her gender: she is a Southern woman. She shares with Mrs. Maradick a Southern heritage, since she is from Richmond and her patient's mother was from South Carolina. When she chooses loyalty to the wife over loyalty to the husband, Miss Randolph acts on "intuition," on a message transmitted by "invisible waves of sense perception." The "power of sympathy" (35) that Miss Randolph herself recognizes extends to Mrs. Maradick's attachment to the house in which she was born, the house in which her ghostly daughter lives on.[4] Miss Randolph's own sensitivity to place—an attribute Glasgow frequently portrays as both female and Southern—allows her to see the ghostly child even before she has met Mrs. Maradick, a vision shared only by the black servant. After Mrs. Maradick's death, Miss Randolph does not see the ghost again until she hears that Mrs. Maradick's beloved house is to be torn down (38).

The men in the story are associated with materialism, lack of imagination, and absence of sympathy. Dr. Brandon is the less sinister of the two. Miss Randolph recalls him bitterly: "It wasn't his fault that he lacked red blood in his brain . . . and I hadn't talked to him ten minutes before I knew that he had been educated

in Germany, and that he had learned over there to treat every
emotion as a pathological manifestation" (24). It is Dr. Brandon
who comes to take Mrs. Maradick away at what Miss Randolph
describes as the height of her recovery: "Things couldn't have
been better with her than they were" (29). Dr. Maradick, despite
Miss Randolph's periodic disclaimers, emerges from her narrative as the supreme egotist, determined to gratify his own desires
at all costs. Of their first meeting, Miss Randolph says, "I have
suspected since that he was not entirely unaware of my worship"
(14). Later, she is more blunt: "His vanity was incredible in so
great a man. I have seen him flush with pleasure when people
turned to look at him in the streets" (36). He dines out every evening while his wife is ill. Finally, whatever the narrator claims to
believe, the narrative suggests that he allowed his stepdaughter's
death and caused her mother's death to acquire the fortune he
needed to attract the woman who had once jilted him.

But who causes Maradick's death? Critic Marcelle Thiébaux
observes that the ending is ambiguous, implicating Miss Randolph for her failure to light the stairs. Up until the revelation
of Dr. Maradick's engagement, Miss Randolph has succeeded,
she says, "in . . . acquitting him altogether" (37) and in convincing herself that she had never really seen the ghost. In short,
when Mrs. Maradick leaves, she again falls victim to the force
of his personality. With his engagement comes confirmation of
his guilt, although Miss Randolph continues to resist the inevitable conclusion. Sensitive to the atmosphere of the house, however, she anticipates—and ultimately aids—its ghostly vengeance.
Dr. Maradick's death avenges his mistreatment of mother, child,
and Miss Randolph herself, whose adoration of him is rewarded
by his engagement to another.

Glasgow had numerous opportunities during this period of her
life to compare the intelligence, insight, and skill of doctors and
nurses; "The Shadowy Third" intimates the extent of her confi-
dence in male doctors to diagnose and treat female illness. From

the perspective of "The Shadowy Third," it is difficult to understand why Glasgow critics have been so willing to accept the
reliability of the two male narrators of Glasgow's second ghost
story, "Dare's Gift"—one of them a doctor, the other a law-
yer (Anderson's profession).[5] In Part 1, the lawyer-husband of
Mildred Beckwith recounts the story of their removal to a lonely
colonial mansion in Virginia, Dare's Gift, after his wife's first
nervous breakdown. Preoccupied with his defense of a railroad
against charges of corruption, and mindful of the significance of
the case to his career, Beckwith leaves Mildred alone a great deal
while he commutes to the city, although he notices that she looks
increasingly tired. When he contemplates suppressing incriminat-
ing evidence that he has uncovered, Mildred betrays him to the
press, saying, " 'I had to do it. I would do it again' " (73). Beckwith concludes, "Then it was I knew that Mildred's mind was
unhinged" (73). But the elderly local doctor has a different interpretation. He claims that the house is "haunted by treachery"
(77), telling the story of Lucy Dare, a staunch Confederate who
had once betrayed her former lover, a Yankee, to Confederate
soldiers at Dare's Gift. When the young man had been shot and
killed, she had said to the doctor, "I had to do it. I would do it
again" (100).

The contradictions in both narratives call into question the
validity of masculine perception. Beckwith expresses his sincere
concern for his wife's condition, but does not explain its cause.
Nor does his concern induce him to remain at Dare's Gift and
care for her. Mildred's own response to Dare's Gift contradicts
his idyllic portrayal. What Beckwith describes as "just the place"
for Mildred (69) is in actuality a prison for her, complete with
an isolated setting, "walls of box" and "iron gates" (97) reminiscent of the asylum-house in Charlotte Perkins Gilman's "The
Yellow Wallpaper." Similarly, the real Mildred emerges only from
between the lines of her husband's narrative insensitivity. Once
Beckwith has implied a history of mental illness from his refer-

ence to Mildred's "first nervous breakdown" (48), the reader must question his description of "the perfect matrimonial harmony in which we lived" (97). The real Mildred seems to be paying a heavy price for maintaining the harmony of which Beckwith is so proud.

Dr. Lakeby's portrayal of Lucy Dare is even more confusing.[6] He calls her "cold," and reflects, "I knew half a dozen men who would have died for her—and yet she gave them nothing, nothing, barely a smile" (92). He describes a recent visit to her in a home for the elderly, but her reported words and actions belie his characterization of her as senile, and she is likely, in any case, to be younger than he is.

Lucy Dare's place in the "haunting" of Dare's Gift is questionable, since at least one of the local betrayal stories involves an ancestor of Lucy's. Yet the men are correct in presuming a relationship between Mildred Beckwith and Lucy Dare, two women victimized by male assumptions about feminine nature. Of Lucy Dare's betrayal, the doctor says, "She has forgotten, but the house has remembered" (104). If the house has remembered anything, however, it has remembered the courage of a woman who placed public commitment above personal commitment, loyalty to a cause above loyalty to a lover. Just as Lucy Dare had believed that her betrayal would save the Confederacy, Mildred Beckwith believed that her betrayal could salvage the public trust. Both women recognize a moral imperative: "'I had to do it. I would do it again.'" Although Beckwith records no ghostly appearance and Lucy Dare is still alive, Mildred may have felt her presence in the same way Miss Randolph feels the tensions present in the Maradick house.

While "Dare's Gift" does not portray the deliberate masculine cruelty of "The Shadowy Third," it suggests that masculine insensitivity can be harmful to women. "The Past" suggests that insensitivity can be deadly. In a narrative that recalls both "The Shadowy Third" and Wharton's "The Lady's Maid's Bell," a secretary, Miss Wrenn, tells her story. Miss Wrenn responds with immediate sympathy to the tragic air of her new employer, the beautiful Mrs. Vanderbridge, and suspects cruelty on the part of her employer's husband. Upon dining with the couple that evening, however, Miss Wrenn is surprised to discover that her host is kindly if preoccupied, and she is astonished when they are joined by another, a graceful, frail young woman to whom no one speaks. The housekeeper afterwards confides that this woman is the "Other One," the first Mrs. Vanderbridge, dead fifteen years. Mrs. Vanderbridge herself first explains that this "Other One" materializes only when Mr. Vanderbridge is thinking of her, that his own feelings of guilt about her death during pregnancy make him imagine her, and make her appear to him, as "hurt and tragic and revengeful" (134). Yet Mrs. Vanderbridge also believes that the apparition appears of her own will, and she has often contemplated an appeal to this ghostly predecessor. Miss Wrenn unwittingly provides the opportunity for such a confrontation when she discovers in a desk old love letters written not by Mr. Vanderbridge but by his adulterous first wife's lover. Miss Wrenn urges Mrs. Vanderbridge to use the letters to break her rival's power over her husband, but instead Mrs. Vanderbridge burns the letters, addressing her nemesis directly for the first time: " 'I can't fight you that way. . . . Nothing is mine that I cannot win and keep fairly' " (145). To Miss Wrenn's amazement, the apparition responds to the "great pity, . . . sorrow and sweetness" (145) in that voice with a transformation from "evil" to "blessedness," "just as if a curse had turned into a blessing" (146), and vanishes—presumably for good.

As in "The Shadowy Third," the narrator sees the ghost, first because of her sensitivity to atmosphere, and then because of her sympathy for another woman; she begins her narration, "I had no sooner entered the house than I knew something was wrong" (108). Engaged by Mrs. Vanderbridge, she says, because of "the remarkable similarity of our handwriting" (108), she also

An affinity between women: Lucy Dare (left) and Mildred Beckwith (right) turn their backs on the male narrators of their stories in "Dare's Gift." Photos by Jay Yocis from C. E. Chambers's illustration for *Harper's New Monthly Magazine*, 1917.

shares with her employer a common cultural and educational heritage as a Southern woman educated "at the little academy for young ladies in Fredericksburg" (108). Before she ever sees Mrs. Vanderbridge, then, she observes, "This was a bond of sympathy in my thoughts at least" (108). Overwhelmed by her new employer's beauty, kindness, and air of tragedy, she expresses her devotion at the end of their first meeting: " 'I am ready to help you in any way—in any way that I can,' . . . and I was so deeply moved by her appeal that my voice broke in spite of my effort to control it" (111).

Miss Wrenn's sympathy for Mrs. Vanderbridge is encouraged by another woman, the elderly maid, Hopkins. Tearful at their first encounter, Hopkins immediately confides in Miss Wrenn, telling her, " 'You look as if you could be trusted' " (115). Her plea is for Mrs. Vanderbridge: " 'She needs a real friend—somebody who will stand by her no matter what happens' " (115). Hopkins provides Miss Wrenn with her first information about the ghost's identity; although she has never seen the ghost, she feels its presence and accepts it as only white and black women, black men, and children do in Glasgow's stories: " 'I know it is there. I feel it even when I can't see it' " (116). She is the one who tells Miss Wrenn that Mr. Vanderbridge sees neither the ghost nor its effect on his wife.

The ghost herself is an interesting figure, because she too must ultimately become an object of sympathy. When Miss Wrenn first sees the ghost, she compares the young woman to a child: "I was aware, from the moment of her entrance, that she was bristling with animosity, though animosity is too strong a word for the resentful spite, like the jealous rage of a spoiled child, which gleamed now and then in her eyes" (121). As if to further dilute the ghost's malevolence, Glasgow added several lines at this point when editing the original *Scribner's* text for the *Shadowy Third* collection: "I couldn't think of her as wicked any more than I could think of a bad child as wicked. She was merely wilful

[sic] and undisciplined and—I hardly know how to convey what I mean—elfish" (121). According to Mrs. Vanderbridge's somewhat illogical theory, Mr. Vanderbridge is at least partly responsible for the ghost's demeanor since she supposedly appears the way *he* thinks of her: " 'His thought of her is like that, hurt and tragic and revengeful' " (134). Yet Mrs. Vanderbridge also considers a direct appeal to the ghost, despairing of her husband's capacity to change, or presumably, to understand: " 'I've wondered and wondered how I might move her to pity' " (135). Miss Wrenn's depiction of the ghost in the final scene contradicts to some extent her own earlier description; the phantom is now malignant and sinister. Yet as she watches husband, wife, and ghost together, the violence Miss Wrenn advocates is directed not at the ghost but at Mr. Vanderbridge. Concerning the treacherous love letters, she says, "If I had my will, I should have flung them at him with a violence which would have startled him out of his lethargy. Violence, I felt, was what he needed" (144). In Miss Wrenn's view, Mr. Vanderbridge is killing his wife through his neglect, weakness, and insensitivity; he is far more dangerous to her than the ghost.

Instead of violence, Mrs. Vanderbridge chooses feminine weapons: the moral superiority and boundless sympathy of the angel in the house. Turning her sympathy on the ghost, she says, " 'The only way, my dear, is the right way' " (145), though whether she is addressing her husband or the ghost here is unclear. Only then can Miss Wrenn see the ghost differently, perhaps because the specter has become a reflection of Mrs. Vanderbridge's thoughts rather than her husband's: "I saw her clearly for a moment—saw her as I had never seen her before—young and gentle and—yes, this is the only word for it—loving" (146). Of Mrs. Vanderbridge, Miss Wrenn concludes: "She had won, not by resisting, but by accepting; not by violence, but by gentleness; not by grasping, but by renouncing" (146). In short, Mrs. Vanderbridge's victory apotheosizes the cardinal feminine virtues of

Glasgow's time, an appropriate ending to a drama played out primarily among women, yet indicative of Glasgow's ambivalence as a feminist to a feminine ideal she often criticized.[7]

The vision of female community offered briefly in the final scene of "The Past" is at the heart of the last Glasgow ghost story, "Whispering Leaves." Appropriately, Glasgow borrowed the ghost of "Whispering Leaves" from her own maternal legacy, modeling Mammy Rhody on the Mammy Rhoda who was nursemaid to her mother and sisters. Like three of the four stories, "Whispering Leaves" is narrated by a woman; here, it is Effie, who has gone for a visit to her ancestral home, a plantation now owned by an unknown cousin named Blanton. Also in residence, she learns, are Blanton's second wife, her children, the new baby, and a little boy from Blanton's first marriage, Pell. When Effie first encounters Pell, he is courting disaster in a mulberry tree, but when he falls he is caught by "an old negro woman" (73), who disappears as quickly as she has appeared. Effie soon learns that Pell's first nurse, Mammy Rhody, had died several years before, after faithfully fulfilling a promise to his dying mother "that she would never let the child out of her sight" (162). Effie worries about Pell—his pallor, gravity, and shyness seem to her signs of loneliness and parental neglect. As she grows more attached to him, she has several mysterious encounters with the old black woman she had seen the first day. She feels that this silent figure wants something of her, but she does not know what it is. One night, the house catches fire, and Effie is frantic to learn that Pell is trapped inside. When she sees the dark figure emerge carrying Pell, however, she understands at last and steps forward with outstretched arms to claim the child from his ghostly guardian.

The story emphasizes throughout the significance of female history and the strength of female bonding. Effie describes Whispering Leaves as "the house in which my mother and so many of my grandmothers were born" (152). Female history seems to be the only significant history here, and Effie's sensitivity to the house's female past allows her to see the ghost that no one else can see but Pell. After her first glimpse of the apparition, Effie muses about the woman's place in her own past:

> Though I had had only the briefest glimpse of her, I had found her serene leaf-brown face strangely attractive, almost, I thought oddly enough, as if her mysterious black eyes, under the heavy brows, had penetrated to some secret chamber of my memory. I had never seen her before, and yet I felt as if I had known her all my life, particularly in some half-forgotten childhood which haunted me like a dream. Could it be that she had nursed my mother and my grandmother, and that she saw a resemblance to the children she had trained in her youth? (166)

Before she even learns Mammy Rhody's identity, Effie acknowledges a female bond based on caring, and associates Mammy with her own foremothers.

In fact, she discovers that Mammy Rhody is linked to the female history of Whispering Leaves because Rhody had nursed the first Mrs. Blanton, Clarissa. Effie sees herself as tied to these two other women—her predecessors at Whispering Leaves—by their shared love of nature. Nature is one expression of the house's history which is visible and audible—beautiful, fragrant, and melodious. Effie is warned about the profusion of birds around Whispering Leaves; the black driver tells her, "'Hit seems dat ar place wuz jes made ter drive folks bird crazy'" (155), and the white driver calls them "'the ghosts of Mammy Rhody's pets'" (163), the birds Mammy was said to have tamed for Pell. In one scene, a vision of the red turbaned Mammy Rhody resolves itself into a scarlet tanager (184). But Effie insists, "I liked birds!" (156), and later has a vision of "the bright ghosts of all the birds that had ever sung in this place" (184). The neglected garden that Effie admires is Clarissa's: "Never until that moment had I known what the rapture of smell could be" (184). An observation about the garden elicits from her cousin Pelham, Pell's father, the response,

" 'That sounds like Clarissa' " (178). Except for Pell, Effie alone seems capable of appreciating the female legacy of Whispering Leaves. Mrs. Maradick's love for her house in "The Shadowy Third" is here replaced by the women's love for the garden surrounding the house, and it is the garden that remains when the house burns down.

But the force that most strongly draws the three women together is their love for Pell, who falls out of a tree, behaves like a bird at dinner, and spends his days in his mother's garden. Effie, alive to the feminine past of Whispering Leaves, sees the woman who haunts the garden in order to keep her promise to another woman, and out of love for the two generations of children she nursed. Effie's sympathy for the anguished apparition and her growing love for Pell eventually allow her to translate the "inaudible language" (172) of the ghostly appeal. Pell informs her: " 'Mammy says you must take me away with you when you go away' " (191). Yet Effie resists the responsibility; to herself, she says she felt the resistance "as if [she] were disputing with some invisible presence at [her] side" (193). Her love must undergo a literal trial by fire before she fully understands the necessity for her action: "I knew, in that moment of vision, what the message was that she had for me" (197). Effie will continue the female maternal tradition of Whispering Leaves, and will do so unhampered by masculine intervention.

Both parents are insensitive to Pell's suffering, but Glasgow reserves particular contempt for Pell's father, a man of limited interests whom Effie dismisses as "one Pelham Blanton, a man of middle age, who was, as far as we were aware, without a history" (151). To be without a history at Whispering Leaves, where history is so important, is to be utterly insignificant. Effie describes Blanton as "vain, spoiled, selfish, amiable as long as he was given everything he wanted, and still good-looking in an obvious and somewhat flashing style" (176). Her empathy with Clarissa leads her to speculate on the happiness of their marriage: "I wondered

A ghostly guardian passes her charge on to the female narrator of "Whispering Leaves." Photo by Jay Yocis from Elizabeth Shippen Green's illustration for *Harper's New Monthly Magazine*, 1923.

how that first wife, Clarissa of the romantic name and the flaming hair, had endured existence in this lonely neighborhood with the companionship of a man who thought of nothing but food or drink. Perhaps he was different then; and yet was it possible for such abnormal egoism to develop in the years since her death?" (176). Her own antipathy for the man is Effie's only basis for presuming an unhappy marriage, yet Mammy Rhody is also clearly unwilling to leave Pell in his hands. Effie accepts the responsibility of motherhood without the burdens of wifehood, and the story suggests that she is better suited for motherhood as a single woman than as a victim of marital misery.

Of all the ghost stories, "Whispering Leaves" offers the most radical alternative to conventional romance; building upon the bonds of female sympathy portrayed in "The Shadowy Third," "The Past," and "Dare's Gift," it envisions a sense of female community that exists outside of marriage and transcends heterosexual love. As a whole, the stories constitute a forceful and unflinching critique of heterosexual love and marriage. The contemporaneous novels, however, demonstrate Henry Anderson's influence in their sexual politics as well as in their national and regional politics. Despite their bleak portrayal of marriage, both *The Builders* (1919) and *One Man in His Time* (1922) end with a promise of happy marriage for their heroines.[8]

The conflicts Glasgow experienced during these years—between marriage and singleness, between Henry Anderson and Anne Virginia Bennett, between convention and anomaly—are best illustrated by a comparison of the novels with the ghost stories. The stories, for example, contain no exemplary male characters: at their best, men are unperceptive and insensitive; at their worst, they are malicious and deadly. Nurse Randolph must learn, in "The Shadowy Third," not to confuse a distinguished man's good reputation with the reality. In both *The Builders* and *One Man in His Time*, on the other hand, the heroine must be won over to a man judged harshly by people in general. In the case of David Blackburn, hero of *The Builders*, that judgment is particularly harsh and unjust where women are concerned. *The Builders* allows Blackburn to play a role Anderson often played in his letters—that of long-suffering victim to female irrationality.

The inaccuracy of the heroines' initial perceptions in the novels disputes the value of female intuition and sympathy. These qualities are under particular attack in *The Builders*, the novel on which Anderson probably collaborated most heavily.[9] When Miss Randolph chooses sides in the Maradick household in "The Shadowy Third," she feels compelled to conceal both her own sympathy and Mrs. Maradick's sensitivity; in a passage quoted earlier, she responds to Dr. Maradick's question concerning his wife's sanity: "Every intuition cautioned me that the time had come when I must take sides in the household. While I stayed there I must stand either with Mrs. Maradick or against her. . . . 'She talked quite rationally,' I replied after a moment" (26).

The Builders, in its portrayal of David Blackburn, values rational intelligence, commitment to a generalized public good, and a strong sense of justice. When nurse-protagonist Caroline Meade praises her female employer's sympathy, she demonstrates her own naivete: " 'Her sympathy is wonderful!' Almost in spite of her will, against the severe code of her professional training, she began by taking Mrs. Blackburn's side in the household" (*Builders* 93). In the course of the novel, Miss Meade must come to mistrust her own sympathy, and to recognize that Mrs. Blackburn's is shallow, calculated, false. Presumably, once Miss Meade has learned her lesson, she will return to the "severe code of her professional training"—a phrase recalling Miss Randolph's scornful description of Dr. Brandon's German medical training. Perhaps Anderson hoped that the sympathetic Miss Bennett would follow suit.

In the ghost stories, adherence to rationality prevents white men, and especially professional men, from seeing ghosts. The same quality promotes a generalized insensitivity to atmosphere and environment, and to the feelings of the women around them. It may make them distinguished politicians, but it hardly suits them for matrimony; "Dare's Gift" and "The Shadowy Third" suggest that it may make them renowned doctors, but it cannot make them good ones. Thus while contemplating marriage and accepting a male collaborator for her work, Glasgow continued her more radically feminist tradition in her ghost stories, choosing a genre she knew to be appropriate to her concerns. Living unhappily in a house she perceived to be haunted, she wrote of other unhappy women and their hauntings. Sensitive to the presence of the past at One West Main Street, she portrayed other houses as texts in a female history available to anyone sensitive enough to read them properly. Dependent upon a female companion for the understanding and sympathy her male lover seemed unable to offer, she celebrated the bond of female friendship as a more fulfilling tie than that of heterosexual romance and marriage.

Notes

1. A typescript draft of *The Woman Within* in the University of Virginia's Alderman Library records a previous version of this line: "It is an exact description of my sensations while I stood there in that empty house" (Accession no. 5060, box 5, TS 190).

2. "Ellen and Anne Virginia were sitting before the fire one night when Anne Virginia said: 'Ellen, we need money. Why don't you write a story?' Ellen agreed, and wrote 'The Shadowy Third'" (recounted in Godbold 115). Glasgow's own distaste for short stories has contributed to the critical neglect of the ghost stories. In 1918, she told an interviewer, "I cannot write short stories" (Overton 26). She had published three short stories early in her career but had otherwise devoted herself to novels. That she specifically wrote the ghost stories to earn money is corroborated by Richard Meeker: "While hardly poor by ordinary standards, Miss Glasgow had large medical

bills, traveled extensively, and had to maintain One West Main Street in Richmond after her father's death in 1916" (5).

3. Marjorie Kinnan Rawlings's attempts to document Glasgow's engagement for a projected biography are recorded in E. MacDonald. A primary source of information on this complex relationship, however, is Anderson's correspondence with Glasgow from this period, which is held by the Alderman Library. In addition, Anderson's mother, Laura E. Anderson, wrote Glasgow on 19 November 1918: "Henry . . . told me of the congeniality of feeling existing between you and himself" (Accession no. 5060, box 11). Godbold suggests that "the engagement was abandoned rather than canceled" in the fall of 1919 (124).

4. Glasgow critic Julius Raper believes that all of the Glasgow ghosts are suspect, merely reflections of their viewers' state of mind. With respect to "The Past," he writes: "We spend the story trying to outwit the narrator (and the author) concerning the motive and conditions for her seeing the ghost of Dr. Maradick's daughter Dorothea. . . . Margaret's [Miss Randolph's] doubts about the ghost (after Mrs. Maradick dies in an asylum) tend to reestablish her credibility just before she reports the fourth appearance of the girl" (68). This is so far from my own experience in reading the story that I question the wisdom of that gender-neutral, generalized "we." Nor would I consider calling Dorothea "Dr. Maradick's daughter," which appears to me to support the doctor's diagnosis of his wife's insanity and paranoia by granting him credibility as a father. Odder to me still is Raper's introduction of the ghost stories with physiological justifications for the supernatural experience: "Today we know enough about the effects chemical alterations have on consciousness to acknowledge that sane people may sometimes *see things that are not there,* and see them as substantially as though they were there—even when these phenomena exist *only* as chemical changes in the brain. We also know that strong emotions . . . involve significant chemical changes throughout the body" (67). These explanations recall Miss Randolph's description of the great nerve specialist, Dr. Brandon, through whom, I argue, Glasgow is satirizing the psychological profession.

5. I include "Dare's Gift" among Glasgow's ghost stories because of the unresolved possibility that it describes some kind of haunting, even though an actual ghost is not likely. For a fuller discussion of the story, see my own essay in *Studies in Short Fiction*.

6. Again, Raper and I disagree. Whereas Raper argues that Mildred's repression led to her nervous breakdown, and thus that Beckwith is an unreliable narrator, he finds Dr. Lakeby a credible narrator, faulting Beckwith for lacking the "objectivity the old doctor brought to the case of Lucy Dare" (70). I am arguing that objectivity is not a stance valued in the ghost stories.

7. For a scathing analysis of Glasgow's feminism, see Frazee.

8. In the case of *The Builders*, although Caroline Meade and David Blackburn cannot marry until his wife dies, the novel ends with an understanding between them, and it is obvious that his wife does not have long to live.

9. Anderson's letters to Glasgow in the Alderman Library sometimes refer to chapters he has received from her and recommended revisions. Accession no. 5060, box 9.

Works Cited

Anderson, Henry. Letters. Accession no. 5060, box 9. Ellen Glasgow Papers. U of Virginia, Charlottesville.

Anderson, Laura. Letter. Accession no. 5060, box 11. Ellen Glasgow Papers. U of Virginia, Charlottesville.

Carpenter, Lynette. "Lucy's Daring Gift in Ellen Glasgow's 'Dare's Gift.'" *Studies in Short Fiction* 21 (1984): 91–105.

Colvert, James B. "Agent and Author: Ellen Glasgow's Letters to Paul Revere Reynolds." *Studies in Bibliography* 14 (1961), 177–96.

Frazee, Monique Parent. "Ellen Glasgow as a Feminist." *Ellen Glasgow: Centennial Essays*. Ed. M. Thomas Inge. Charlottesville: U of Virginia P, 1976. 167–89.

Glasgow, Ellen. *The Builders*. Garden City, NY: Doubleday, Page, 1919.

————. *One Man in His Time.* Garden City, NY: Doubleday, Page, 1922.

————. *The Shadowy Third and Other Stories.* Garden City, NY: Doubleday, Page, 1923.

————. *The Woman Within.* New York: Harcourt, Brace, 1954.

Godbold, E. Stanly, Jr. *Ellen Glasgow and the Woman Within.* Baton Rouge: Louisiana State UP, 1954.

MacDonald, E. "A Retrospective Henry Anderson and Marjorie Kinnan Rawlings." *Ellen Glasgow Newsletter* 12 (March 1980): 4–16.

Meeker, Richard. Introduction. *The Collected Stories of Ellen Glasgow.* Baton Rouge: Louisiana State UP, 1963. 3–23.

Overton, Grant M. *The Women Who Make Our Novels.* New York: Dodd, Mead, 1918.

Raper, Julius Rowan. *From the Sunken Garden: The Fiction of Ellen Glasgow, 1916–1945.* Baton Rouge: Louisiana State UP, 1980.

Thiébaux, Marcelle. *Ellen Glasgow.* New York: Frederick Ungar, 1982.

Tutwiler, Carrington C., Jr. *A Catalogue of the Library of Ellen Glasgow.* Charlottesville: Bibliographical Society of the U of Virginia, 1969.

Geraldine Smith-Wright

In Spite of the Klan

Ghosts in the Fiction of Black Women Writers

WHILE THE GHOST TALE in recent African-American literature has its deepest roots in West African culture, the genre's more immediate development is traceable to the era of slavery in the American South. Ghost stories, along with staged ghostly encounters, were an important part of the stock-in-trade that slave owners used to discourage Blacks from moving around at night unsupervised. Yet Black folklorists subsequently commandeered and altered these ghost stories in ways that reconciled African beliefs about the supernatural with their experience as slaves. Folktales involving the supernatural, which the slaves told in the new world, extended the rich African oral tradition and became fixed in the African-American literary canon. Ghosts in the selected fiction of four Black women writers from 1925 to 1983 represent interesting and varied uses of the supernatural in the twentieth century. Like their slave forebears, Zora Neale Hurston, Ann Petry, Toni Morrison, and Paule Marshall employ the supernatural to reflect in their own time the status of African Americans in the African diaspora.

The effort to control slaves' mobility occurred in the aftermath of a number of well-planned slave insurrections, which, though not decisive, were particularly traumatic for the Southern white slave-holding classes. Although slave owners instituted physical measures, namely, beatings, torture, and the patteroller system, to monitor the movement of slaves, these strategies were largely ineffective in preventing slaves from convening secret night meetings. Gladys-Marie Fry, in a careful study of the use of ghost stories as a special method of limiting slave movement, shows how this strategy was meant to exert psychological control over the slaves with less physical brutality and better results (see Fry 45–80).

Supernatural tales created by slave owners were specifically designed to capitalize on slaves' worst fears. These stories described haunted places to which ghosts and witches were attracted, detailed unprovoked attacks on slaves by supernatural animals, and predicted that the dead would return for slaves at night. To press their advantage, whites often disguised themselves as ghosts, donning white sheets, walking on stilts, and using tin cans as noisemakers to create mayhem near the slave quarters—tactics that would later become the mainstays of the official Ku Klux Klan. While ghost narratives, coupled with ghost improvisations, produced the desired results, whites reinforced the intended effect by deliberately circulating rumors about ghosts among the slaves. As these tales became fixed in the Black oral tradition, they were exaggerated with each retelling, so that it was virtually impossible to trace them to their sources. Nor, as the evolution of the ghost story makes clear, did Black raconteurs worry especially about documenting their narratives.

However, while the fear motif remained essential in ghost tales, Black storytellers shifted their emphasis, often with a great deal of humor, to the prowess and quick thinking of the slave victim. Even in stories where encounters with ghosts were especially threatening, their comic tone was derived from the storytellers' accounts of the way extreme fear motivated them to escape the clutches of the supernatural. Humor was inherent in the slaves' fright—wide-eyed, panting, and sweating profusely, victims won the chase, often by a hair. The main objective of Black folklorists was to embroider the ghost tale to such a degree that listeners would marvel at the ingenuity of nimble slaves in the face of deadly odds.

Slaves' supposedly innate fear of ghosts, coupled with their enthusiasm for regaling eager audiences with tales of how intended victims survived, shows how thoroughly African perceptions of the supernatural and the African oral tradition influenced slaves' responses to severe racial challenges. According to Fry, even when slaves were aware of the whites' deception—for example, "ghosts" were often familiar slave owners in costume— they still believed that supernatural beings did exist (7). Although slave owners correctly assessed Blacks' extreme fear of the supernatural, they failed to understand that slaves often intensified the Step-'n'-Fetchit facade to trick their oppressors into believing that their shoddy tactics were successful. Slaves consciously perfected the art of dissembling to free them to stoke the fires of their own deeply rooted African traditions in an alien land. Sterling Stuckey has observed, "The final gift of African 'tribalism' in the nineteenth century was its life as a lingering memory in the minds of American slaves" (3). That whites were able to control slaves through fear of the supernatural despite slaves' familiarity with ghosts can only be explained by the cultural traditions about the spirit world that slaves brought with them.

In the transplanted African community, among the most important traditions was slaves' strong conviction that the spirit world was an integral part of the life force. In African traditions regarding the supernatural, the living and the dead are intimately connected, this relationship often taking the form of ancestor worship. For Africans, it is essential to be on good terms with ancestral spirits (Stuckey 43). In fact, deceased family members are considered part of the present family unit. As John Pobee notes, "To start with the family, it consists of the living, the dead, and the still unborn. It is not only the living. Consequently, these ancestors, though dead, are still believed to be concerned with and involved in the affairs of the living. . . . In short on the ancestors depends the well-being of the living" (8). The reverence for ancestral spirits is one facet of a pervasive sense of a host of spirit beings, both good and evil, that monitor the activities of the living (Pobee 11). It is the inclusive definition of being that ultimately confounded whites' efforts to use bastardized forms of African traditions to control the slaves but which bound together enslaved African peoples in a common heritage.

The survival of African beliefs about the spirit world in the African-American oral and literary traditions is paradigmatic of Blacks' survival in the diaspora. Although the slaves' supernatural tales were modified in accord with their historical experience in America, one significant feature of these folk tales is the emphasis on the heroic exploits of suppressed people (Fry 9–10). The ghost tale as it evolved during and after slavery described, often metaphorically, creative ways that Blacks coped with white oppression and also suggested codes of conduct to strengthen the Black community. Lawrence Levine has specifically noted the teaching aspect of slave folk tales: "If slave tales only infrequently dealt with the sacred world, they nevertheless were often infused with a direct moral message. In Africa, tales which taught a moral, either implicitly or explicitly, were widely used for didactic purposes" (90).

Both the interracial and intraracial concerns in the ghost tale are central focuses in the works by Hurston, Petry, Morrison, and Marshall that will be discussed here. Ghosts in a tale included in Hurston's *Mules and Men* (1935) and in Petry's "The Bones of Louella Brown" (1947) highlight the historical division between Blacks and whites in America, while ghosts in Hurston's "Spunk" (1925) and Petry's "Has Anybody Seen Miss Dora Dean?" (1958) affect interpersonal relationships in the Black community. Through ghosts or references to ghosts, characters in all four of these stories are sufficiently empowered, even if only temporarily, to set things right in their racially divided environment or in a Black setting where individual members' priorities conflict with values deemed necessary for racial prosperity and wholeness.

While ghosts in the works of Hurston and Petry shape Black characters' participation in both Black and racially mixed environments, principal Black characters in Morrison's *Tar Baby* (1981) and Marshall's *Praisesong for the Widow* (1983), Jadine and Avey, respectively, encounter ghosts mainly because they stand outside the collective experience of Black culture. Specifically, these characters are unable to see the value of the Black historical past for the present generation. Jadine permanently rejects her Black past, while Avey eventually embraces her heritage after a wrenching conversion experience. In light of Jadine's and Avey's difficulties in reconciling their lives with their racial pasts, Morrison and Marshall use ghosts in these novels to develop mythic explorations of ways for culturally disenfranchised Black characters both to acknowledge their heritage and to forge a more satisfying connection with their communities.

THE GHOST STORY THAT CALVIN tells in *Mules and Men*, Hurston's important collection of folklore from Eatonville and New Orleans, evokes the supernatural to change the traditional balance of power between Blacks and whites. In this tale a master sends his slave, John, to bring him a pitcher of water from a spring. Although John is reluctant to venture out at night, he obeys because he has always tried to behave respectfully toward his master. Frightened by the noise John makes dipping up the water, a bullfrog sitting on the edge of the spring jumps into it. John drops the pitcher and runs toward the big house, convinced that the bogeyman is after him. When the master orders John to return for the water, the slave refuses, telling him, " 'No, indeed, Massa, you and nobody else can't send me back there so dat booger kin git me' " (12). In view of the fact that John has never disobeyed him, the master relents and asks for a description of the bogeyman. John, whose belief in the power of the spirit world is, no doubt, firmly grounded in his ancestral memory, remembers that " 'he had two great big eyes lak balls of fire, and when he was standin' up he was sittin' down and when he moved, he moved by jerks, and he had most no tail' " (12).

Although Calvin's story ostensibly focuses on the victim's fear and survival instinct, it is actually the account of a power struggle, which the slave wins. Because John is more afraid of the ghost than he is of retribution from a *human* being, slave and master temporarily change places. By refusing to return for the water, John runs the risk of being severely punished for disobeying his master. However, when the master, whether from shock or compassion, does not force John to repeat the dangerous errand, he forfeits some of his power. No matter what repercussions may follow for the slave, the immediate truth is that the master will have to get his own water or draft another slave to perform this service. Hurston has not missed the central irony in Calvin's story. If slaves had not been so thoroughly conditioned to fear everything that goes bump in the night, the master could have had his water. Clearly, the narrative of John's ordeal serves specific psychological needs of Black audiences: namely, it describes the victory of a slave over his oppressor, even though the shift in power is inadvertent and short-lived. John's story has reaffirmed for members of the Eatonville community one foolproof way to use fear to their own advantage.

With a great deal of humor, Ann Petry also uses the supernatural to empower the Black community and to set the record on racial equality straight for future generations. In "The Bones of Louella Brown," the title character's ghost visits her former employer's son to reveal the hypocrisy of burying Blacks and whites in segregated cemeteries. As the story opens, Old Peabody and Young Whiffle, funeral directors of the prestigious undertaking firm of Whiffle and Peabody, Incorporated, receive a contract from Governor Bedford of Massachusetts to remove all the deceased Bedfords from Yew Tree Cemetery and place them in a crypt in the newly constructed Bedford Abbey. Old Peabody, whose father buried Louella in Yew Tree Cemetery to please his wife, intends to use this opportunity to move Louella to a Black cemetery near the edge of Boston.

After all the bodies have been exhumed, Peabody and Whiffle hire a Harvard medical student, Stuart Reynolds, to identify the remains according to records completed at the time of burial. However, he cannot distinguish between the remains of Elizabeth Bedford, the Countess of Castro, and those of Louella. Since the governor is planning to open Bedford Abbey officially with the most elaborate funeral service ever held in Boston, Peabody and Whiffle know that disaster is waiting for them if Reynolds cannot tell the difference between the countess and Louella. Each woman had thick glossy hair, a small bone structure, and all of her own teeth. Also, they died two weeks apart in 1902 when they were in their seventies. Reynolds, unable to keep this startling turn of events to himself, notifies the nighttime city editor at the *Boston Record* of his findings. When the story is released to local and national newspapers, the governor is outraged, and Peabody and Whiffle worry that their establishment will be forced out of business.

During the furor, Louella's ghost begins to appear to Peabody in the daytime. He is annoyed that he sees her more clearly with each passing day. Soon, she even appears in his dreams and laughs at his cowardice and fickle loyalty: "In the dream, she came quite close to him, a small, brown woman with merry eyes. And after one quick look at him, she put her hands on her hips, and threw her head back and laughed and laughed" (Petry 177). Peabody tries to avoid Louella's visitations by sitting up all night or by going to bed early, but the ghost continues to visit each night. When Peabody realizes that he cannot win, he tells Whiffle that

Louella was a fine woman and that " 'her bones will do no injury to the Governor's damned funeral chapel' " (Petry 178). But because Whiffle is unwilling to challenge the racial status quo, the partnership is dissolved. Then Peabody goes to the governor and suggests that the names of both women be placed on a marble slab in Bedford Abbey. He even informs the governor about Louella's nightly visits and warns that unless he follows this suggestion, Louella will visit him too. When the governor imagines that he can already hear Louella laughing, he agrees to take Peabody's advice. Both men write the following epitaph on one slab:

HERE LIES

ELIZABETH, COUNTESS OF CASTRO

OR

LOUELLA BROWN, GENTLEWOMAN

1830–1902

REBURIED IN BEDFORD ABBEY JUNE 21, 1947

"They both wore the breastplate of faith and love;

And for a helmet the hope of salvation"

(Petry 180)

While Petry offers a humorous solution to one example of racial inequality, her intent is deeper than the comic surface of the story. Louella's ghost teaches Peabody that racist attitudes are empty habits masquerading as considered thought. When Peabody meditates on the value of Louella's life and loyal service, he realizes that he has been the victim of his own stale thinking rather than of the fallout from Louella's burial in the wrong cemetery. Petry shows that the monster of racial hatred will be subdued not by reassigning graves but by reordering one's thinking about the issue of race. This is the only legacy that can be of any value to future generations, who will evaluate the attitudes of earlier generations as they confront racial conflict in their own place and time.

Petry's decision to set "The Bones of Louella Brown" in a

white community may be the measure of her belief that the burden of improving Black-white race relations in America rests with the majority culture. Differing from Hurston, whose narrative ghosts exclusively empower members of the Black community, Petry unfolds her story at the source of racial conflict to empower both Blacks and whites. Even after her death, Louella receives the legacy of equality, while Peabody receives the gift of understanding, which he can now pass on to the next generation. Ultimately, "The Bones of Louella Brown" differs from the kind of ghost story in which many early Black folklorists portrayed an autonomous but insular Black community. Here Petry replaces one-upmanship with hard-won cooperation between the races.

In "Spunk" and "Has Anybody Seen Miss Dora Dean?" Hurston and Petry leave the overt conflict between Blacks and whites to concentrate on intraracial issues in the Black community. Here, the use of the supernatural particularly illustrates how divisiveness in Black communities and Black families undermines the values that sustained enslaved Blacks in the new world. Ghosts in these narratives serve two functions: to expose faulty relationships in the Black community or in the family unit; and to show that the truly empowered Black community and family derive from individual members' morally responsible behavior and racial pride.

The title character in "Spunk," who has been parading around Eatonville with Joe Kanty's wife, Lena, is completely insensitive to her husband's public humiliation. Tiring of the constant teasing and ridicule the community heaps on him, Joe follows Spunk to the woods and attacks him from behind with a razor that is no match for Spunk's gun. Shortly after Joe's death, Lena and Spunk move into a new house he is buying as a wedding gift. One night, as they prepare for bed, a black bobcat wanders menacingly around the outside of the house, and when Spunk stares into the cat's eyes, he gets so nervous that he cannot shoot it. Spunk is convinced that Joe has returned from hell in the form of a cat to seek revenge. A few days later, at his job in a saw mill, Spunk is pushed, he believes, by Joe's spirit and falls in the path of a moving saw. Spunk dies cursing Joe for his cowardice, telling his friends at the mill that " 'it was Joe . . . the dirty sneak shoved me . . . he didn't dare come to mah face' " (Hurston, "Spunk" 173).

This story differs in two important ways from the ghost stories that early Black folklorists created to comment on race. First, "Spunk" depicts ghosts in an autonomous Black setting, thus illustrating that ghosts can be the exclusive property of Blacks in an American as well as an African setting. Moreover, Joe returns from the grave not to scare Blacks into submission but to ensure that justice is served. Robert E. Hemenway, Hurston's biographer, observes that the supernatural force in this story corrects the wrongs of the natural world and that the community does not question Spunk's deathbed interpretation of the events leading to his demise (Hemenway 67). In the narrative world of Eatonville, characters accept that supernatural occurrences do provide solutions to human predicaments that appear to have little to do with interracial conflict.

A second change relating to race in "Spunk" involves an intriguing narrative point of view. Members of the store-porch community relate the series of events surrounding Spunk's death; neither Joe nor Spunk is allowed more than a few lines to advance the story from his perspective. Hurston suggests here that the collective voice of the Black community is a bona fide medium through which reality can be defined and transmitted. "Spunk," therefore, explores the issue of race in a more complex way than the face of the story suggests. Although the townspeople do not arrive at any overt conclusions about the sociological importance of their porch conversation, they are aware of the need to assign meaning to the significant events in their racially separate environment.

Another of Petry's stories involving ghosts and the subject of race, "Has Anybody Seen Miss Dora Dean?", is an unusual example of intraracial cooperation. Sarah Forbes, a Black woman in her seventies who is dying, informs her son, Peter, and grandsons, Boodie and Lud, that she wants to leave valuable pieces of china to a friend's forty-two-year-old daughter, the speaker in the story. Sarah's husband, John, had been butler, social secretary, and general caretaker for the Wingates, an affluent white couple, before he committed suicide for reasons not entirely clear to his family. Having indicated in a suicide note that he was tired of living, he then lay down across some railroad tracks in the red-light district of Bridgeport, Connecticut. Before its abrupt conclusion, the Forbes marriage had gradually deteriorated, owing in part to John's excessive loyalty to his employers. Sarah tells the speaker that she cried for three days after her husband committed suicide, not because she felt sorry for him but because he had ruined her life. Her son and grandsons did not provide much comfort, since they were apparently trying to follow John's example by taking up with local prostitutes.

The only valuable possessions that Sarah has managed to save from the wreck of her life are six perfect white cups, which belonged to her grandmother, and several chocolate cups, which were a wedding gift from Mrs. Wingate and reportedly once belonged to a French king. She gives them to the speaker, explaining, " 'Those cups are yours. I'm giving them to you so that I'll know where they are. I'll know who owns them. If they should stay here . . .' " (Petry 110). When the speaker protests that the china should be left to Sarah's grandsons, Lud replies, " 'Oh no . . . I don't want them. What would I do with them? Besides, Nana's ghost would come back and bug me. . . . And if Nana's ghost bugged anybody, they'd flip for sure' " (111). Shortly after the speaker arrives home with her gift, Peter calls to tell her that his mother has just died.

Although this story does not describe an actual encounter with a ghost, the threat is sufficient to clarify Petry's main concern. Sarah's ghost will appear if her important cultural legacy, symbolized by the china, finds its way into the wrong hands. The gift represents something of value from both races. Sarah knows intuitively that Mrs. Wingate's cups are a symbolic gift from her husband's modern-day slave mistress. Thus, an appreciation for the high cost of servitude, during slavery in its past and present forms, is the first legacy she bequeaths to the next generation. Her grandmother's cups symbolize her slave ancestor's determination, much like Sarah's own, to save something precious in spite of a degraded and unhappy life. This ability to survive with dignity and to recognize the value of life's small treasures is the second bequest.

Petry suggests that it is at once the privilege of current Black generations to receive something of value from their foreparents and their responsibility to correct the failures that are part of the legacy. Sarah believes that contributing to the welfare of her racial family is a higher good than rewarding moral ineptitude in her immediate family for the sake of appearances. In "Has Anybody Seen Miss Dora Dean?" Petry suggests that developing racial and personal pride is the surest route to the Black community's empowerment.

TWO RECENT NOVELS elaborate on the connection between racial pride and personal well-being from the perspective of characters who have difficulty achieving either. Toni Morrison's *Tar Baby* (1981) and Paule Marshall's *Praisesong for the Widow* (1983) focus on the ways in which their principal characters' confusion about the value of a firmly defined racial identity prevents the development of a coherent self. Ghost visitations in these novels provide the substance of liberating myths for these troubled characters, who will be freed from the prison of self-devaluation disguised as autonomy. In both novels, American Blacks are displaced in the Caribbean, where they are separated from their homeland and from their adopted communities. What both writers suggest through this double separation is the analogous psychological diaspora that is created when individuals cannot or choose not to acknowledge any manifestation of Black culture in their lives.

In the Caribbean, Jadine and Son, the central characters in *Tar Baby*, are removed from Black-American culture and, by extension, from their African pasts as well. The first is too stylistically different from their present lives, and the second too remote to provide them with a validating ancestral memory. However, the characters take opposing positions regarding their ethnic backgrounds.

The beautiful and worldly wise Jadine resides with her aunt and uncle, Ondine and Sydney, who are servants in the luxurious household of an eccentric white couple, Valerian and Margaret Street. Valerian, given to excessive displays of generosity, has paid for Jadine's education in the finest schools in Europe. Allowed to live free from financial pressure and familial restriction, Jadine is spoiled and takes for granted the easy life and secure place provided by her extended family. The unfortunate trade-off is her failure to take pride in her Blackness. She lives without a racial past, behaving as if her birthright has decreed her uncommitted lifestyle. Dorothy Lee succinctly describes Jadine as being "adrift somewhere between kitchen and drawing room" (357).

Unlike Jadine, Son yearns to validate his life by returning to the security of his (largely imagined) past. He is a merchant sailor who, tiring of his rootlessness, jumps ship and literally swims his way into Jadine's life. After landing on the beach at Isle des Chevaliers, he finds his way to the Streets' home and is eventually taken in by them. Attracted to each other, Jadine and Son become lovers. Although differences in class and attitudes toward race threaten to separate them, the couple set out to achieve some kind of permanence in their relationship. Son takes Jadine to visit his family and friends in Eloe, Florida, where he hopes to settle down. Jadine, however, feels stifled by small-town life and runs off to New York, where a quarrel about their future precipitates her departure. Son follows her to the island, but arrives only to learn that she has left for Paris.

While the plot outline details a tragic love story, Morrison indicates broader intentions in the novel through an organic supernatural component that invests narrative events with mythic significance. The local story of Son and Jadine essentially represents the more general fate of personal and intraracial divisiveness for Blacks in the diaspora. To show that the history and politics of American race relations translate finally into the personal, Morrison creates ghosts that assume identities familiar to displaced characters. Ghosts are not strange beings from the netherworld, a fact recalling African views of the supernatural. They hover just outside of documentable experience, much like the ghostly one hundred horsemen whose nightly journeys through the hills of the Isle des Chevaliers are never far from the periphery of daytime reality. In this novel, it is the virtually claustrophobic space between the natural and supernatural worlds that locks into focus the tragic void informing the main characters' incomplete lives.

In light of Jadine's inappropriate but impervious self-image, Morrison shows the pointlessness of Son's attempt to change Jadine's values when he believes she is most vulnerable. As she sleeps, he tries to replace her dreams with purified visions of women from his childhood home. Determined to align her values with his own, he wants her to dream of "yellow houses with white doors which women opened and shouted Come on in, you honey you! and the fat black ladies in white dresses minding the pie table in the basement of the church and the white wet sheets flapping on a line, and the sound of a six-string guitar plucked after supper while children scooped walnuts up off the ground and handed them to her" (Morrison 102). Son knows that his dreams are only air castles; in fact, he fears that she might "press her dreams of gold and cloisonné and honey-colored silk into him and then who would mind the pie table in the basement of the church?" (103). Susan Willis has perceptively observed that Son's dream for Jadine is rooted in private nostalgia rather than in fact. His recollection of yellow houses and church women tending pie tables "bears no resemblance to his real past as we later come to understand it out of what the book shows us of Eloe, Florida, where tough black women with little time for pie tables have built their own rough-hewn, unpainted houses" (Willis 269). Son's inability to create a viable replacement fantasy allows Jadine to emerge the clear winner in this contest of wills.

While Son makes a poignant effort to reshape Jadine's goals, it is the women in this novel, functioning on the levels of reality and symbol, who censure Jadine most dramatically for denying her Black womanhood. Once, in a Paris supermarket, Jadine, proud of her light skin and Caucasian features, confronts a beautiful black-skinned African woman dressed in yellow who has captured the attention of everyone in the store; as the woman leaves the market, she stares into Jadine's eyes and spits on the ground in contempt for her "sister's" defection. Although Jadine feels her beauty is superior to the African woman's, she admits to herself that she wants the woman to like her.

Another incident revealing Jadine's aversion to her blackness involves her confrontation with the symbolic tree-woman. Once, seeking shelter under some trees from the hot sun, Jadine becomes mired in black, slimy mud. To save herself, she grabs hold of a tree in a group of swaying trees that seem to be women delighted that a child wants to play with them. When they see that Jadine is trying to get away from them and the black forest, their mood changes: "They wondered at the girl's desperate struggle down below to be free, to be something other than they were" (Morrison 157). When Jadine finally frees herself, she tries to remove the tarlike substance from her clothes and skin, using leaves from the tree. This symbolic effort to wash off her blackness is also paradoxical; by using *black* female leaves to rid herself of blackness, she is also washing away the "sacred property" of her Black womanhood.

These two examples illustrating Jadine's renunciation of her

Black womanhood prepare for a crucial scene involving ghost women that occurs during Son and Jadine's visit in Eloe. As the couple make love, women suddenly take shape in the bedroom, women seeming to crowd Jadine's imagination but who, she is certain, exist separately from her. Ondine and Thérèse from the Isle des Chevaliers, the African woman, and even Son's dead mother, as well as Jadine's own, come to reprove her for neglecting the privileges and responsibilities of Black womanhood. She is taken aback by their response when she asks these ghost figures what they want: "They looked as though they had just been waiting for that question and they each pulled out a breast and showed it to her. Jadine started to tremble. They stood around in the room, jostling each other gently, gently—there wasn't much room—revealing one breast and then two and Jadine was shocked" (222). When the African woman in yellow shows her three big eggs she bought in the Paris supermarket, Jadine begins to cry. The eggs and the bared breasts symbolize female reproductive power and the genesis of Black womanhood. Though shaken by her experience with the ghost women, Jadine does not alter her values. Instead, she escapes to New York. It is clear that the night women's intentions have failed; even ghosts have not changed Jadine so much as annoyed her. Thérèse, the visionary who sees through to the core of Jadine's deficiency, warns Son at the end of the novel that " 'she has forgotten her ancient properties' " (263).

Morrison uses ghosts in a rather unusual way to communicate the failure of Son's life. Unlike Jadine, who perceives the ghost women as intrusive and materially different from her, Son himself is described in ghostlike terms to show his intense displacement in a world outside his value system. Son's ghost existence is a paradigm for an essentially false life that only allows him to intuit the deeper displacement he merely courts as a drifter. The space between his free-lance perceptions and the actual shape of his life marks the division between freedom and rootlessness, and therefore between power and defeat.

Several passages in the novel suggest that Son's life is compatible with both the real and spirit worlds. When Gideon, the Streets' gardener, informs his Aunt Thérèse that he has seen Son standing in Jadine's bedroom window, she is convinced that Son is " 'a horseman come down here to get her' " (91). Earlier Thérèse, in a dream, has seen him riding away wet and naked on a stallion and Gideon's story is final proof to her that she is right about Son's identity.

Thérèse's theory could easily be dismissed as colorful fabrication by an island native trying to explain unusual events according to her folkloric traditions, except that Morrison extends to other contexts the possibility that Son is a ghost. For example, Son perceives himself as different—that is, different in essence— from other people. After jumping ship and wandering around the island before falling asleep near the Streets', "he woke up, *in a manner of speaking*" (118, my emphasis) and entered the house. Much later when he and Jadine are at a picnic, Son chides her for tucking in her legs as if she were afraid of him, explaining, " 'I don't have a real life like most people, I've missed a lot. Don't take your feet away from me too' " (152). Finally, when Son takes refuge in New York following a bitter argument between Ondine and the Streets at Christmas dinner, he checks into a hotel where the clerk gives him a hard time because he prefers to pay cash instead of using a credit card or writing a check. After threatening the clerk with bodily harm, Son concludes, "It was less an error in judgment than it was being confronted with a whole new race of people he was once familiar with" (187).

Morrison increases the odds that Son may be a ghost, in an enormously powerful scene at the end of the novel. Thérèse delivers Son in a boat to the outlying shore of the Isle des Chevaliers and instructs him to forget Jadine and join the one hundred ghost horsemen. Morrison suggests here that Thérèse offers Son the only chance for salvation symbolically possible for him. By choosing to wander in search of Jadine, perhaps forever, Son continues his life as a ghost-drifter who will never return to a documentable past or know an emotionally secure future. The only recourse for him is to cast his lot with the community of ghosts who, according to Thérèse, " 'gallop [and] race those horses like angels all over the hills where the rain forest is, where the champion daisy trees grow' " (263). By joining them, he will gather their power to himself and thus validate his life. If he accepts this option, he can avoid floating endlessly among the disparate islands of incoherent or partial selves.

While Morrison shows how supernatural encounters, and even a kind of supernatural transfusion in Son's case, fail to change Jadine's and Son's self-destructive values, Marshall uses ghosts in *Praisesong for the Widow* to encourage the central character, Avey Johnson, to celebrate her ethnic heritage. As she will learn in the course of the novel, the elegant house in White Plains, New York, the expensive clothing, and her yearly cruises have telescoped the empty places in her life rather than diffused them. A disturbing dream-vision recalling her childhood vacations on Tatem Island near Beaufort, South Carolina, marks the beginning of Avey's suspicion that her inner life is woefully deficient.

As the novel opens, Avey (Avatara) and two friends are on a cruise in the Caribbean. While Thomasina and Clarice have been enjoying their long-awaited vacation, Avey, having a miserable time, plans to leave the *Bianca Pride* as soon as it docks in Grenada, and fly home on the first plane to New York. As readers will discover, the ironic name of the ship, which translates to "white pride," emphasizes the inappropriateness of Avey's dependence on white values. During the cruise, Avey cannot make sense of her intense discomfort but is certain that a dream about her great-aunt Cuney and the fact that she could not eat her parfait at dinner that night are implicated. These two events, related to Avey's mind, function equally in forcing her to abandon the cruise.

The dream is based on the child Avey's and great-aunt Cuney's ritual walks to Ibo Landing on Tatem Island, but with an important difference. In the real-life counterpart of the dream, each August during Avey's vacation on Tatem Island, the old woman and young girl made the journey to their ancestral past, symbolized by a group of Ibos who, arriving on American shores from Africa, reportedly saw into the troubled future and walked on water all the way back to Africa. They sang joyfully as they renounced the promise of a brutal slave existence in America. This story had been handed down to Cuney's grandmother, also Avatara, who had not only witnessed the event but claimed that her mind returned with the Ibos while her body remained in Tatem. But in Avey's dream when Cuney beckons the adult Avey to accompany her once again, Avey protests that she is on her way to a social function sponsored by her husband's Masonic lodge, and the two women have a fist fight. In the dream Avey is particularly upset because she knows that her aunt should be dead; Cuney has returned from the grave to humiliate her. Avey "[swings] away her face, telling herself, hoping, that when she looked back, she would find that the old woman had given up and gone on a walk alone; or better yet had returned to her grave in Tatem's colored cemetery" (Marshall 41). Still dreaming, Avey wonders "how could her flesh still be so warm and her smell the same homey mix of brown washing soap and the asafetida she wore in a sac pinned to her undershirt to ward off sickness? How could she still be so strong?" (43).

As Avey wrestles with the import of the dream resurrection of her dead aunt, Marshall describes Avey herself as a kind of ghost figure to reinforce the hollowness of her life. In an important narrative moment, she becomes the thing she most fears in order to give physical form to her moral and psychological deficiencies. In her cabin, the deck lights render Avey ghostlike as she hurriedly packs in preparation for her departure: "For illumination she had opened the drapes at the picture window of a porthole and was making do with the reflection of the deck lights outside, along with the faint glow of the nightlight filtering through the divider. . . . The pale satin sheen of the nightgown she had on added to the small pool of light, as did the subtle aura, unbeknown to her, which her dark skin had given off since birth" (11). Later she zips a garment bag "as if sealing a tomb . . . and still working feverishly, like someone pursued, folded the bag over on itself, [and] latched the two halves together" (16). This small detail presages the ghosts that will not be sealed but instead will haunt the halves of her divided self that she cannot latch together. It is further significant that Avey plans to escape in the middle of the night—the time for ghosts to appear.

When Cuney, in the dream, and later Avey's husband, Jerome, return as ghosts, each parallels an aspect of her divided self. The lesson Cuney teaches aims to relate the Ibos' victory to Avey's own life. Avey has broken the chain of remembrance that would have linked her to her African forebears, and by implication to all American Blacks of the past and future, in a bond of power and pride. Unlike the Ibos, who renounced physical slavery, she has not resisted her emotional slavery to white middle-class values. It is apparent that Avey is not Avatara, as Cuney had insisted she be called out of respect for Cuney's grandmother, who named the child to be born several generations later. The shortened form of her name is appropriate since she is a lesser incarnation of her namesake. Sent to prophesy, Avey, instead, is lost in the wilderness of her own racial confusion.

While Cuney's ghost accuses Avey of ignoring her great African heritage, Jerome returns from the grave to reprimand her for jeopardizing the middle-class lifestyle he has killed himself to attain. He confronts her on the balcony of her hotel room shortly after she arrives in Grenada. Avey is certain this is not the Jerome she knew when he was alive because he is wearing the white apron and white gloves he was buried in as a Master Mason. He specifically criticizes her for wasting hard-earned money by leaving the cruise early and accuses her of wishing to return to the poverty of their early years together. Even from his grave, he cannot forgive

Avey for trivializing the ultimate sacrifice he has made on her behalf.

Since ghosts in *Praisesong* act to emphasize Avey's moral dichotomy rather than to resolve it, it is to be expected that both ghosts would be unwilling to relinquish their places at the extreme ends of the spectrum of values. Avey is caught in the middle position of hybrid values that honor neither the Ibo legend nor the goal of social achievement that characterized her marriage. If she adopts Cuney's values, she will incorporate the stunning example of the Ibos in her own life and thereby establish her familial connection with African ancestors and American Blacks. If she reaffirms the importance of Jerome's middle-class values, she will destroy the familial bond. Because Avey is incapable of sorting out the conflicting values in her life, the solutions to her dilemma must occur outside the usual frames of experience.

Avey's salvation begins when she meets the old man Lebert Joseph, the proprietor of a grog shop on a beach in Grenada, and is completed on the nearby island of Carriacou during an annual ceremony in praise of ancestors and strong cultural identity. On the boat ride to Carriacou, Avey, after becoming desperately ill, is cleansed of her guilt and false pride. Still feeling drained upon her arrival in Carriacou, she is gently restored to health by Joseph's daughter, Rosalie, who administers a ritual bath that completes Avey's purification. After her baptism, she is ready to be introduced to the islanders' observances. The ceremonies marking the occasion—the Beg Pardon, nation dances, Creole dances—are significant for Avey by virtue of their contrast with her unproductive memories and by their relation to African traditions of ancestor worship. In the Beg Pardon, the islanders pay homage to their ancestors by asking forgiveness for offenses committed against the Old Parents throughout the year. Avey has paid no such respect to her individual or cultural ancestors, especially to Cuney and Cuney's grandmother, for safely transmitting the priceless legacy of the Ibos to future Black generations. Participants in the nation dances, restricted to old people, express pride in their individual nations through spirited song and dance. Avey is emotionally drawn into the rituals, unable to deny any longer that she is moved by the old Carriacouans' tenacious hold on their living pasts. She realizes that "it was the essence of something rather than the thing itself she was witnessing. Those present— the old ones—understood this. All that was left were a few names of what they called nations which they could no longer even pronounce properly, the fragments of a dozen or so songs, the shadowy forms of long-ago dances and rum kegs for drums. The bare bones. The burnt-out ends. And they clung to them with a tenacity she suddenly loved in them and longed for in herself. Thoughts—new thoughts—vague and half-formed slowly beginning to fill the emptiness" (240).

She eventually joins the circle during the Creole dances, and now feels the kinship of peoples descended from Mother Africa. Her transformation is so complete that the islanders, following Joseph and Rosalie's example, bow before her to show their respect. Avey need never again fear ghosts from her past. She assumes her role as prophet to define for present generations the true nature of wealth for Black Americans—the strength of Blacks in America depends on an intimate connection with and reverence for the ancestral past. In addition, the continuity of the extended Black family must never be sacrificed to personal greed or benign neglect through the failure of memory. By the end of the novel, Marshall shows that Avey will perform the same function as Cuney's ghost. Avey, as a living ghost, will haunt middle-class Blacks in the hectic passages of their lives and bring them into the circle of memory:

> Her territory would be the street corners and front lawns in their small section of North White Plains. And the shopping mall and train station. As well the canyon streets and office buildings of Manhattan. She would haunt the entranceways of skyscrapers. And whenever she spotted one of them amid

the crowd, those young, bright, fiercely articulate token few for whom her generation had worked two and three jobs, she would stop them. (233)

The novel closes as Avey plans to fix up the house Cuney has left her in Tatem. She will retire there and insist that her grandchildren walk with her to Ibo Landing when they visit each summer.

WHILE THESE INDIVIDUAL ghost tales necessarily share a contrapuntal relation, together they are linked through their implicit assertion that one area of kinship between African and American Blacks is the belief that the living and the dead are intimately connected. Encounters between human and ghost characters show that *all* phases of the life cycle exist in an unbroken circle of being; rather than abdicate, the dead participate actively in temporal experience—a participation dramatized even more forcefully in Morrison's recent novel, *Beloved* (1987). In the American setting for these narratives, ghosts offer the proposition that African Americans can achieve justice, autonomy, and racial pride in an environment that from the era of slavery exacted their submission and fear. That Hurston, Petry, Morrison, and Marshall define an overall similitude between African and African-American views of the supernatural suggests that empowerment for African Americans depends on the sense of connection with their rich African past. The ghost tale is both narrative strategy and theme. The final result, then, of slaveholders' efforts to infiltrate the African canon of supernatural traditions with their own versions of ghost stories is that early African-American storytellers and their literary descendants continued to warm their traditions in the sunlight of Mother Africa, reasserting the clan in the face of the Klan.

Works Cited

Fry, Gladys-Marie. *Night Riders in Black Folk History*. Knoxville: U of Tennessee P, 1975.

Hemenway, Robert. *Zora Neale Hurston: A Literary Biography*. Chicago: U of Illinois P, 1977.

Hurston, Zora Neale. *Mules and Men*. Bloomington, IN: Indiana UP, 1935.

———. "Spunk." *Opportunity* 3 (June 1925): 171–73.

Lee, Dorothy H. "The Quest for Self: Triumph and Failure in the Works of Toni Morrison." *Black Women Writers: A Critical Evaluation*. Ed. Mari Evans. Garden City, NY: Doubleday, 1984.

Levine, Lawrence. *Black Culture and Black Consciousness*. New York: Oxford UP, 1977.

Marshall, Paule. *Praisesong for the Widow*. New York: Dutton, 1983.

Morrison, Toni. *Tar Baby*. New York: New American Library, 1981.

Petry, Ann. "The Bones of Louella Brown." *Miss Muriel and Other Stories*. Boston: Houghton, 1971.

———. "Has Anybody Seen Miss Dora Dean?" *Miss Muriel and Other Stories*. Boston: Houghton, 1971.

Pobee, John. "Aspects of African Traditional Religion." *Sociological Analysis* 37 (1976): 1–18.

Stuckey, Sterling. *Slave Culture: Nationalist Theory and the Foundations of Black America*. New York: Oxford UP, 1987.

Willis, Susan. "Eruptions of Funk: Historicizing Toni Morrison." *Black Literature and Literary Theory*. Ed. Henry Louis Gates, Jr. New York: Methuen, 1984.

Tricia Lootens

"Whose Hand Was I Holding?"

Familial and Sexual Politics in
Shirley Jackson's *The Haunting of Hill House*

SOME TIME DURING THE late 1950s, Shirley Jackson set out to write "the kind of novel you really can't read alone in a dark house at night" (1D).[1] *The Haunting of Hill House*, the novel she ultimately produced, is the story of four people who agree to participate in a ghost-hunting expedition reminiscent of those that took place early in this century: Dr. Montague, an academic who has organized the expedition; Luke, the charming if disreputable heir of Hill House; Theodora, a sophisticated beauty; and Eleanor, a lonely, vulnerable woman who has been chosen, like Theodora, for her history of susceptibility to psychic manifestations. They are a congenial group, and, from the beginning, they play at being a family. The premise of the novel is standard ghost story fare, but by the end of the book, it is clear that this is no ordinary haunting. For what devastates Hill House's victims is not a losing struggle with the forces of the next world, but a brutal, intimate exposure of the ineffectuality of their own dreams. Hill House's ghosts come not with the face of the unknown, but with that of each character's most intimate fears.

Surely one of the most terrifying aspects of Hill House's haunting is its intimacy, which is simultaneously familial and erotic. What happens in Hill House is a process, not merely a "sighting"; a haunting, not merely a ghost. At its source is the house's growing knowledge of its inhabitants' illusions and of their deadly needs. Hill House's ghosts are what Jackson called the "statement and resolution" of its inhabitants' apparently insoluble problems (1D); the haunting is personally designed for the haunted. What Hill House reveals to its guests is a brutal, inexorable vision of the "absolute reality" (*Hill House* 3) of nuclear families that kill where they are supposed to nurture. In this perception, Jackson touches on the terror of her entire culture.

Hill House sets out to separate its guests, and it locates Eleanor as the weak link. Although each of the others has reasons to cherish the illusion of belonging together, Eleanor cannot even pretend to herself that she belongs anywhere else. She is ready to give her life for love, and she fixes her romantic fantasies both on Luke and on Theodora. As it becomes clear that neither is willing or able to reciprocate, the haunting increasingly singles her out. It (and the desperation it reveals in her) separates her from the others even as it seduces her into believing that Hill House, and Hill House alone, wants and needs her. As the original "family" of guests begins to disintegrate, the house is invaded by representatives of spiritualist sentimentality and criminally unimaginative common sense, in the persons of Dr. Montague's overbearing wife and her martinet companion. By the time the others discover that Eleanor is vulnerable to murderous manifestations that she alone perceives, it is too late. She reveals what the reader—and the house—have known all along: she has nowhere else to go. In a ruthless ending, she kills herself rather than leave the only home she knows. She dies in vain, for after her death as before it, "whatever walk[s] in Hill House, walk[s] alone" (1).

By the time she began *Hill House*, Jackson had already explored the establishment (and destruction) of women's coherent sense of self in such works as *Hangsaman* and *The Bird's Nest*.

As Lynette Carpenter has noted, inquiry into "causes and consequences of female victimization" runs throughout Jackson's work (32). She had written about human sacrifice, not only in its most brutal, literal sense as in "The Lottery" or perhaps in "The Summer People," but also in connection with seduction and demon lovers, as in "The Visit" and "The Rock." In *Life Among the Savages*, she had written in a far different vein about the vicissitudes of family life. Given all this, what could be more natural than to turn to domesticity, self-sacrifice, and the disintegration of a woman's personality as sources of terror?

It is for this reason that the drafts of *Hill House* in the Library of Congress come as such a surprise. Jackson's early versions of the novel are unmistakable proof that the character of Hill House's haunting was not clear from the beginning. She seems to have set out to write a fairly standard ghost story, not a horror story about the ways in which people, especially women, are destroyed by the nuclear family, sexual repression, and romantic notions of feminine self-sacrifice.[2]

At the very earliest stage of her work on *Hill House*, Jackson seems to have created a series of sketches that briefly explore a possible past for her haunted house, a cast of characters, and above all a vision of the character she first calls Vancey, and later, Theodora Vane. "The book is told in the first person by a woman named Vancey," Jackson writes in a typed paragraph that seems to introduce her first description of the manifestations at Hill House: "She is one of four people hired to spend three months in a house which has acquired a bad reputation because no one will live there. The owners and the renting agents are most anxious to prove that there is nothing wrong with the house, without at the same time involving themselves in any of the wild joy with which newspapers handle any stories about haunted houses" (TS).

Jackson devotes the majority of her sketches on the "woman named Vancey" to character development. We see Vancey on her way to a weekly dinner at her sister's house (1D, TS), being recruited for Hill House (TS), possibly facing the house for the first time (as an unnamed narrator; TS), engaging in fantasies about herself for the entertainment of her fellow guests at the house (1D), facing her first manifestation (1D), and most importantly of all, facing herself and her fantasies in order to tell the reader her story (1D, TS). "Well," she says in one passage of self-introduction,

> "My name, as I've said, is Mary Bothwell Stuart Vance, and most people—*most* people? I have perhaps ten friends—call me Vance, or Vancey; if you could see me you'd know why no one ever thinks twice to call me Mary . . . What I am trying to say is that I am one of those curious creatures who is (well!) not lovely. I've spent a number of years facing it and I don't know why it's so hard each time I say it, but there it is—I am conten[t], I think, and I've managed to carve myself a good life, and I don't go around bawling on other people's shoulders, unless I get into that particular drunken state where feeling sorry for yourself is a lovely thing, and even then I usually try to feel sorry for myself for something else—even then, you will say, refusing to face it. Say what you please; I defy you to match my life." (TS)

The tone is characteristic. Vancey is the feminine equivalent of the bluff, hearty bachelor narrator of so many classic Victorian ghost stories—with a difference, of course. Invited to Hill House because she appears to be a "sensible young woman" (TS), Vancey is not entirely what she seems. Jackson clearly intends to play not only with outsiders' assumptions of what it means to be a sensible young woman, but with those of Vancey herself.

Vancey may present a front of common sense, but she is also a romantic, lonely woman who feels entrapped by the peaceful, ordered existence symbolized by her weekly visits to her married sister's house. In a half-ironic, half-rueful tone, she informs the reader that she was "made to die for love," and that love "hasn't asked" (TS). Her position is nevertheless far stronger than that of any of the women who will succeed her as Jackson's protagonists. She is her own woman, both intellectually and economically.

In different sketches, Vancey lives on her inheritance (TS) or her salary (1D), but she always survives by her wits. In her dry humor and intellectual independence she is also not unlike Jackson herself. She even dreams of being an author: "I'm going to be a great writer," the young Vancey tells a little suitor, "and I'm never going to get *married*. . . . If I ever *do* get married it will be Humphrey Bogart, or somebody like that" (1D).

Such a story is typical of her. At another point, she wryly evokes Shakespearean comedy, tragic love, and her sister's matchmaking, all on the basis of a hardware store sign:

> "I turned the corner and thought, 'O stay and hear, your true love's coming, that can sing both high and low. . . .' That was because R. Sweeting Hardware store stood on the corner; 'Trip no further, pretty sweeting: journey's [sic] end in lovers [sic] meeting. . . .' Poor Pretty Sweeting Hardware; were *his* lovers all untrue?
>
> They did frequently end in lovers [sic] meetings, my visits to my sister. . . . Carrie wanted me to get married, for some inscrutable reason. Perhaps she found the married state so excruciatingly disagreeable herself that it was the only thing bad enough she could think of to do to me." (1D)

Vancey's choice of song is significant: her private jest evokes the comic world of *Twelfth Night*, in which an exiled, sexually ambiguous heroine finds a new home, a lost brother, and true love. Like a "blind motif" in a fairy tale, retained long after it has lost its original context and meaning, Vancey's "R. Sweeting" song will be passed down to the central figure of each draft. By the time it reaches Eleanor in the final draft of *Hill House*, the phrase "journeys end in lovers' meeting" has become a ritual invocation of faith by a woman who does not know its origin; who does not even believe in the value of knowledge; and who is afraid that if she remembers the whole song, she will discover it is "improper."

This expression of Vancey's saving grace—her wit and her rich inner life—will become the expression of Eleanor's bankruptcy and the voice of her downfall.

Two more main sketches in the *Hill House* papers seem to have been narrated by Vancey: her account of the first view of Hill House and that of the first manifestations within the house (1D). Both are retained essentially untouched in later versions; but as Jackson's protagonist changes, their significance, like the significance of the R. Sweeting song, is vastly altered. Vancey's successors echo her loneliness, her motherlessness, her hunger for change, and certain aspects of her situation, but none has her independence or her humor—and none has the first-person narrator status, which guarantees that somehow she will survive.

In order to distinguish her from the character later named "Theodora," I will call the protagonist of what seems to be the next series of sketches, "Trapped Theodora Vane." She is a weakened version of Vancey, both in descriptive vividness and in personality. Where, for example, Vancey responded to her sister's announcement of a male dinner guest with "Do you think *he'll* want to marry me?" (TS), Trapped Theodora goes out to buy new shoes (TS). In her, emotional vulnerability is matched by economic vulnerability: Trapped Theodora has lost not only Vancey's brashness, but her home and independent means. She may have an apartment, but metaphorically speaking, she has no room of her own (TS).

What Trapped Theodora loses in self-sufficiency, she gains in family ties. Vancey's affection for her sister was limited at best; she may have longed for romantic adventures, but she was openly critical of nuclear families (TS). Theodora's reaction to her baby sister's matchmaking seems to temper exasperation with genuine affection, perhaps even gratitude (TS). She combines longing for a family of her own with lack of a strong sense of self. Where Vancey went to Hill House because she was bored with her ordered life, Trapped Theodora goes because she is bored with herself. Where Vancey was clearly sane, Trapped Theodora may not be. One brief letter in the *Hill House* files, signed "Theodora," is clearly that of a madwoman (TS).

As the novel's protagonist becomes more vulnerable, Hill House's evil becomes more specific. What confronted Vancey at Hill House was arrogance and, above all, humorlessness—the ultimate evil in the eyes of a woman who measures her self-respect and sanity by her ability to laugh. What confronts Trapped Theodora in the house is another negation: "It has never been anyone's *home,* if you know what I mean," she is told. "There seem to be houses like that—one meets them sometimes—which have never known families growing up . . ." (TS). Nothing could make the depth of Hill House's coming transformation clearer. From a house that has "never known families," it is destined to become one that knows entirely too much on the subject.

The haunting itself, which began by threatening Vancey with physical violence, now moves to exploit Trapped Theodora's vulnerability by underscoring her emotional isolation. The Trapped Theodora sketches mark the first appearance of the "cousins" scene in which two women, newly arrived at Hill House, establish a fantasy family connection and lazily plan a picnic—until Jackson shatters the intimate moment with a rush of icy air and the view of spectral footsteps (1D).

As with Vancey's manifestations, this scene remains essentially untouched as the novel develops, but its resonance is radically transformed. Jackson has already created a house for which the innocent pleasure of picnics is anathema; what she has yet to create is a house that entraps its inhabitants with fantasies of domestic bliss even as it forces them to recognize such fantasies as delusions. The "cousins' " playful assertion of kinship will come to reveal more and more desperation; their dream of sharing everyday celebrations of domesticity will become increasingly poignant and sinister. By the final draft, Theodora will still be holding out the futile promise of a picnic at Hill House moments before Eleanor smashes into a tree.

With the next draft, which I call the "Erica draft" (TS/C4), Jackson seems to have undertaken her first full sketch of *Hill House*'s plot.[3] There are pages missing from this draft, but it is nevertheless clear that with Erica, Jackson moved the haunting beyond her initial plans and beyond most of the "real" hauntings she had studied.[4] "Experience and Fiction" offers an oblique explanation for her decision to take the haunting's outcome beyond exile into death: "The ghosts were after me" (203). One morning, she says, she came downstairs and found "a sheet of copy paper moved to the center of my desk, set neatly away from the general clutter. On the sheet of paper was written DEAD DEAD in my own handwriting. I am accustomed to making notes for my books, but not in my sleep; I decided that I had better write the book awake, which I got to work and did" (203).

In this draft, Erica Vance, an angry, defensive, and lonely woman with none of Vancey's or Trapped Theodora's wit, is driven to Hill House by "self-disgust and dullness" (1D). She meets a stock romantic hero, Luke; a glamorous rival, Theodora; and a happily married scholar, Dr. Montague. *Hill House*'s basic plot is set: "The story is primarily about Erica, who is going to have to be a good deal more complex than she seems now," Jackson explained in a note to her publisher, adding: "the emphasis upon (yippee) togetherness; the house wants to separate them and drive them away, the people want to stay together in the house; where the others want to stay together because they are afraid to be alone in the house Erica wants to stay with them because she is afraid to be alone anywhere, anytime; her life will be indicated as a pattern of loneliness which she is trying to break" (1D).

Though Jackson seems to implicate Erica as a potential human agent behind the manifestations of haunting in this draft, she has nevertheless begun to transform Hill House into its final form. This draft begins with the sentence that will open the published novel: "No live organism can continue for long to exist sanely under conditions of absolute reality" (TS/C4 1). With the house's transformation in this draft, the transformation of characters seems to be accelerating. Erica goes to Hill House to find herself (TS/C4 26); and we are told that she has had a secret desire for death "for no very clear reason, since she was seventeen years old" (TS/C4 37). Although the draft does not contain a final scene, it seems clear that her secret wish will be fulfilled.

Even after writing the "Erica draft," however, Jackson still seems to have been making "comfortable" assumptions about being able to haul in a standard moaning specter at the crucial moment. "There are going to be some dandy ghosts," she vaguely assured her publisher. "I set up the story of the house so that any of its previous inhabitants might enjoy coming back to haunt it, and—although my own preference is for a veiled lady, moaning— I think it may turn out that different people see different things; see, in fact, just exactly what they are expecting to see" (1D). As it turns out, of course, the final draft has no woman with a veil, and no ghost that is exactly what any character expects to see, unless one counts the absurd monks and nuns obligingly dished up by Mrs. Montague's planchette. There is a reason: between the Erica Vance draft and the one that followed, Jackson seems to have found her "real" ghosts.

When Vancey arrives at Hill House, she knocks on a heavy wooden door (1D); when Erica arrives, she finds a knocker with a lion's head (TS/C4 7); but by the time Jackson walks her final protagonist, Eleanor Vance, up the steps to Hill House, the knocker has become a child's face (TS1 16). Jackson had found the source of Hill House's peculiarly intimate brand of horror: what her final heroine, Eleanor Vance, enters is above all a family home.

Two words are scrawled on the bottom of a page of notes for *Hill House*: "FAMILY, FAMILY" (1D). Given Jackson's story of having written "DEAD DEAD" in her sleep, it is easy to imagine that her notes express a parallel though presumably waking revelation. In any case, there is no question that some time between the Erica Vance draft and that which followed, the first

Eleanor draft (TS1), Jackson reached a decision. The final or "second Eleanor draft" (TS1/C) that follows only expands the transformation the first Eleanor draft has begun. By the time Jackson's haunting of Hill House reaches its culmination, "FAMILY, FAMILY" and "DEAD DEAD" are close to synonymous.

From a sinister shell to be filled up with ghosts and observers (as though a literary moving van had been drawn up to the door), the Hill House of Jackson's final version has become a vicious travesty of a family home, the leering equivalent of James Thurber's personified housefront. In this version, the characters are trapped within a nightmare embodiment of the nuclear family, an insidious Home Sweet Home that will not allow its victims to belong or to be happy, but will not let them go.

On the basis of her readings of both Freud and the psychic researchers, Jackson had come to believe that ghosts provided the "statement and resolution" of their percipients' problems—problems that could not "be solved realistically" because "impossible problems require impossible solutions, after all" (1D). Perhaps in part as a result, she transformed the haunting of Hill House into the "statement and resolution" of the irreconcilable conflict between Jackson's characters' dreams of belonging in "one big happy family" and the reality of the family's failure in their lives. "Hill House is the haunting," Jackson wrote in pencil somewhere among her notes for the novel (1D). With each succeeding draft, the house becomes a more brutal parody of a family home, and its guests more vulnerable to delusions of togetherness.

Designed to satisfy the arrogance of the family's founding father, Hugh Crain, and to "suit his mind" by mirroring its distortion (*Hill House* 105), the house of the final draft has surpassed any human being in its capacity for evil. In the first Eleanor draft, we hear that Hill House's founder must have "disliked the sensible square houses he saw other people building" (TS1 64); by the final version, we are told that he "must have detested other people and their sensible, squared away houses, because he made his house to suit his mind" (107). For all its upright walls and firm floors, Hill House has become a "masterpiece of architectural misdirection," a structure whose proportions deliberately undermine one's "senses of balance and reason" (107). Once begun, the house has eluded human control: "This house, which seemed somehow to have formed itself, flying together into its own powerful pattern under the hands of its builders, fitting itself into its own construction of lines and angles, reared its great head back to the sky without concession to humanity" (35).

In its form, Hill House is now a parental house. Warped to fit the mind of the vicious patriarch, it is furnished with symbols of the destructive power of motherhood. "It's all so motherly," says Luke, who has no mother. "Everything so soft. Everything so padded. Great embracing chairs and sofas which turn out to be hard and unwelcome when you sit down, and reject you at once—" (209). For him, it is "a mother house . . . a housemother, a headmistress, a housemistress" (211). The "heart of the house" (119) is like the "doorway of a tomb" (118): it is the nursery, decorated by two "grinning heads" whose "separate stares, captured forever in distorted laughter, met and locked at the point of the hall where the vicious cold centered" (120). Gathered comfortably into the heavy, pressing surrounding hills, Hill House is the original womb/tomb, with all the comforts of home. There are good beds, excellent cooking, companionship; and nothing to do but die in a house that does not want you—that "almost" shudders around you and the mess you make by opening doors (92, 97, 115)—but that does not want to let you go. Like the worst kind of family, Hill House "takes care" of its inhabitants in both senses of the phrase.

For Eleanor, the house is associated with both mother and father. On the same page on which Jackson wrote, "FAMILY, FAMILY," she wrote, "*Leaving house = betrayal of mother.* Eleanor does not belong anywhere. Betray mother by being born —taking away part of mother" (1D). If Eleanor has betrayed her mother by being born, there is only one way to assuage her guilt: to be "unborn." The house exudes the smell of the grave, a reminder of her mother, from the library door, the entrance to the tower in which one woman is said to have died already. The library, with its tomblike smell and maternal associations, is only the entryway to its male counterpart, a tower of "gray stone, grotesquely solid, jammed hard against the wooden side of the house, with the insistent veranda holding it there" (112). Built to fit the mind of its founder, who "guarded" his daughter's "virtue" by a combination of threats, obscene pictures, and promises of a heavenly end in "her father's arms" (171), Hill House has become more phallic with each rewriting. In the final draft, as Eleanor joins the haunting on the last night, she asks Hugh Crain's grotesque statue to dance with her—and the house takes her hands. She goes out for a last look at the tower, "held, so tightly in the embrace of the house, in the straining grip of the house" (231) and then walks up the library steps toward seduction and death: "And here I am, she thought. Here I am inside. It was not cold at all, but deliciously, fondly warm, . . . Under her feet the stone floor moved caressingly, rubbing itself against the soles of her feet, and all around the soft air touched her, stirring her hair, drifting across her fingers, coming in a light breath across her mouth, and she danced in circles . . . she thought, . . . I have broken the spell of Hill House and somehow come inside. I am home, I am home, she thought . . ." (232). Eleanor is about to reverse the birth process through which she "betrayed" her mother.

In the last two drafts, as the house becomes an increasingly more powerful parent, the haunting it creates for its guests most frequently takes the form of a child: a child who calls for mercy in the night (162); a child whose "little caressing touch," moving "intimately and softly" on the doorknob, and whose "wheedling to be let in" accompany the house's onslaught against its guests' doors (201); a child who scrawls names and pleas or demands on walls (145–46, 55); and a child whose "voice, singing sweetly and

thinly, . . . 'Go in and out the windows' " (226), evokes childhood
games of connection and entrapment for Eleanor alone. When
Eleanor runs down the halls of Hill House, nearly following a
ghostly "mother" to her death, she seems to be dreaming that she
is already one of Hill House's children, taunting the grown-ups
in residence: "What fools they are," she thinks, "we trick them
so easily" (230).

The ghostly manifestations of some of the earlier drafts had
already pointed to the longing for family: the "cousins" scene,
for example, or the night walk into the ghostly picnic. Others are
rewritten in this draft to emphasize family. The writing on Hill
House's walls, originally "Help, Eleanor Come Help" (TS3 93)
becomes "Help Eleanor Come Home" (146). The manifestation
on the second night, which told Vancey to go away (1D), now
leads Eleanor to believe her mother is knocking against the wall
for help (127). More awake, she consoles herself that the noise
"sounds like something children do," and hears "little pattings,"
"small seeking sounds," the sound of something "fondling" the
doorknob, and "little sticky sounds" (131). Mad ghostly children
outside the door, human counterparts within: when the manifestation's "thin little giggle" ends, Eleanor and Theodora are
clutching each other "like a couple of lost children" (131).

All of these manifestations and descriptions combine to make
the Hill House of Jackson's final version a house of delusions of
family. Hill House will be glad to give you a hand to hold in
the night, someone to be there, a sense of belonging. When it
is too late, you will realize that all along you were really alone,
clinging to your enemy—or to nothing at all. The house's furnishings have "hands everywhere," Luke says: "Little soft glass
hands, curving out to you, beckoning—" (209). So do its ghosts.
In a scene which Jackson marks as containing the "key" to the
book (1D), Eleanor clutches Theodora's hand as she works up
the courage to cry out against the torture of a ghostly child. She
suddenly looks up to see Theodora on the other side of the room.
She screams: "*Whose hand was I holding?*" (162–63). The hor-

ror behind Eleanor's scream is not that she was alone in the dark, but that she believed herself to have someone there.

In these last drafts, Jackson restructures her characters' personal histories to reveal their vulnerability to fantasies of belonging in a family. On a single sheet of paper Jackson wrote, among other things, "Theo divorced? excitement / Luke—too wise—indolent / doctor foolish / Eleanor IS house /" and then, in large capital letters, "ALL DISTORTED LIKE HOUSE" (1D). Although Theodora's background changes, the plan seems clear: each character will be rewritten to emphasize a weakness Hill House can exploit, a literal kinship with the house. Luke, Theodora, and Eleanor, for example, the three "children" (69, 142) are all in some sense orphaned. Theodora has symbolically rejected all ties by eliminating her patronym (8); she had "thousands of uncles," she says (53), and her family "sent her away to boarding school" (45, 53). Luke's only family is his aunt, who doesn't trust him with the family silver (10); and though his confession of suffering from motherlessness may be as banal and self-pitying as it seems to Eleanor, that need not make it any less true (166–67). Eleanor herself has had no home, even nominally, since her mother died (8). Vancey had her house; Trapped Theodora, her "apartment 3B"; Erica, her dim apartment in the city (TS 4/C 50, 59–60). Eleanor has an apartment in one early sketch (1D), but by the time Jackson includes her in a full draft, she is defined by her lack of a home. "ELEANOR IS HOMELESS," Jackson scrawled on a page of notes (1D).

Jackson's introductions of her three "orphans," written as she was creating Hill House's family haunting, are worth watching. Luke is a liar and a thief (9); Theodora is "not at all like Eleanor" (8); Eleanor "hates" only her sister now that her mother is dead (7). All these statements seem to be true; but so are their opposites. In fact, Luke plays into Hill House's hands through his honesty; Theodora, through her ties to Eleanor; and Eleanor, through her desperate need for a family to love.

In their isolation as perhaps in the disintegration of the initial easy affection between them, Theodora, Luke, and Eleanor are heirs to Hill House's first children. Jackson had experimented with several versions of Hill House's past, but only in the final draft does she envision the house's history as one of death, betrayal, and homelessness, especially for women. Founder Hugh Crain's first wife is killed on the grounds before she ever reaches the house (75); his second dies of a mysterious fall (76). The third, a consumptive, leaves the country—and leaves her stepdaughters to Hill House until she too dies (76). One sister takes "a girl from the village to live with her" at Hill House as "a kind of companion" (77); when she wills Hill House to the "little companion," the other sister (perhaps aided by the house itself) engages in wild attacks on Hill House's new owner until she hangs herself—reportedly in the library tower (77–81). Only one man is said to have died at Hill House—a guest who made the mistake of attempting to leave after dark and was crushed against a tree (75). As Dr. Montague points out, the family history and the house's nature are intimately connected: "Essentially, the evil is in the house itself, I think. It has enchained and destroyed its people and their lives, it is a place of contained ill will" (82).

In the final version, there are other parallels between the house's past and the histories of its guests. Eleanor may say that she and her sister are nothing like the sisters of Hill House, for example; but her denial only points up the way in which the Hill House sisters' struggles over the house echo the conflict that forced her to reach Hill House by "stealing" a car that was half her own (10–12). When Luke's aunt fears that he will abscond with the family silver, she is continuing a Hill House tradition that began with accusations about stealing the house's china (78). Even the story of the little companion has its bitter echoes, not only because Eleanor had been forced to live as a kind of companion to her invalid mother, but because the younger woman's vulnerability is a mocking reminder that Theodora can never extend the security of family status to her own roommate/companion/lover.

Like the house, the guests come to be defined by the failures of their family ties. Hill House makes deadly use of both Dr. Montague's willingness to play "father" (69, 142) and the fatuous pride he takes in "his" haunted house. Initially an impersonal elderly scholar whose work has been devoted to the "suppression and elimination of superstitious beliefs" (TS), he is described in the final draft as a man who belongs "before a fire in a pleasant little sitting room, with a cat on his knee and a rosy little wife to bring him jellied scones" (60). His wife is no such figure. In the first Eleanor draft, she is a foolish, absurdly girlish woman, but a loving mother to her children (TS); Dr. Montague is portrayed as patient with her foibles. By the final draft, the happy children and the fondness have disappeared: Mrs. Montague makes no pretense of having the slightest respect for her husband, thus exposing his ability to imagine himself happily married as absurd and painful. What is more, she brings another "housemaster" to take over her husband's pretense at being a protector (211).

Mrs. Montague not only assists in effecting her husband's transformation, she plays a crucial, independent role in the creation of the house's familial haunting. If Theodora, Luke, Eleanor, and the doctor represent outsiders in a world of family homes, Mrs. Montague is an insider. Certainly her sentimentality about the needs of "spirits" and her imperviousness to both the needs of the living and to actual manifestations provide needed comic relief. Yet there is a more disturbing side to the counterpoint she provides. When she and the housekeeper, Mrs. Dudley, settle for a cozy chat in the kitchen of Hill House, they do not render the house any less vile. Rather, the house creates a new and sinister context for their prosaic occupation. The dishes "belong on the shelves" (101) in Hill House; and by extension, the same drive for domestic order that moves Mrs. Montague and Mrs. Dudley to handle their dishtowels moves the house to close doors after its guests when they leave the room. Hill House, which almost "shudders" at the noise and confusion of living inhabitants, is the original self-cleaning house, ready to exterminate or expel anyone or anything that makes a mess. In an early draft, when Mrs. Dudley says, "The dishes belong on the shelves," Theodora asks "wickedly, 'And the guests?'" (TS1 60).

Like the characters, the novel's plot essentially remains stable, even as the shift in the nature of the haunting profoundly alters its significance. From the beginning, Jackson seems to have assumed that sexual tension between the two women at Hill House would play a central role. She seems to have left the nature of such tension open as long as possible: as late as one draft of scenes including Eleanor, she was still experimenting with one scene in which the two women openly argue over Luke and another in which Theodora's lesbianism is openly discussed and the attraction between the two women clearly acknowledged (1D). By the final draft, of course, Eleanor is drawn both to Luke and to Theodora, neither of whom can offer her the familial love she so desperately needs.

In the final version, the main sexual tension is clearly not competition over Luke. Luke has been transformed from the stock romantic hero of earlier versions to a more ambiguous figure. Eleanor does experiment with romantic fantasies about him, but these do not take real form until the breach with Theodora is virtually inevitable, and they are short-lived. "The only man I have ever sat and talked to alone," Eleanor thinks, "and I am impatient; he is simply not very interesting" (167). The focus of Eleanor's romantic and sexual longings throughout virtually the whole novel is now Theodora. In the final haunting, the sexual tension between Eleanor and Theodora becomes an inexorable and tortuous battle over the nature of identity and morality. Eleanor's reactions to Theodora crystallize not only her longing for a sister who loves her, and for a lover, but her hopeless attempt to assert a new sexuality and sense of self without questioning the family structure and morality that have governed her life before Hill House.

It is no accident that Jackson's final version presents Theodora in opposition not only to family but to Eleanor herself. Theodora has cast off her surname, we learn from Jackson's introduction—and she is "not at all like Eleanor" (8). As usual, the characterization must be approached with skepticism. In many ways, the Theodora of the final draft is Eleanor's mirror image, an image of the kind of woman Eleanor is afraid even to dream of becoming. Eleanor has tried to forget the terrifying poltergeists who threw stones at her house when she was an adolescent (and who, according to most theories of poltergeist manifestations, may have arisen in response to her own psychological turmoil at the death of her father); Theodora tells the others that after having thrown a brick through a greenhouse window she "thought about it for a long time, remembering the whipping but remembering also the lovely crash, and after thinking about it very seriously I went out and did it again" (73). When the groundskeeper at Hill House is rude to Eleanor, she is shocked by her fleeting impulse to run him down (30). Theodora actually aims the car at him (46). Eleanor is nearly overwhelmed by her daring in having bought slacks, a red sweater, and red sandals. "Mother would be *furious*," she thinks, and hides them in the bottom of her suitcase (41). Theodora wears slacks and bright colors without apparently caring "at all what other people [think] of her" (96).

Theodora's mirroring of Eleanor is fortunate, dangerous, erotic; she is her other self, her potential sister, lover, murderer. The following passage in the *Hill House* papers is crossed out and replaced by the note, "Precede by Nell—Theo talk—I'm going where you do—semi-comic / Theo against Nell, of course: to each of us—if we are fortunate—is given one other person, the true doppelganger, the other half of the self, and the union here is sometimes star-crossed, sometimes illicit, always deadly; it is the moment of perception when the victim sees his murderer, the brother discovers his sister, beauty destroys [embraces] the beast" (TS3 n.p.).

Jackson's handwritten notes include another more cryptic indication of the complex ways in which Theodora both personifies
and negates Eleanor and her family: "Theo *is* Eleanor / "NO
ONE TO LOVE ME" = NO HOUSE Therefor [sic] Eleanor invisible / THEO = SISTER" (1D). The deep connections between
the women are too complex to be set out in rational terms; but
Jackson's final haunting clearly evokes their power.

When Theodora paints Eleanor's toenails red in a scene added
to the final draft, the gesture is both seductive and aggressive. She
mockingly validates Eleanor's earlier fantasy of being a "famous
courtesan," but she also says, "By the time I'm through with you,
you will be a different person; I dislike being with women of no
color" (116).

This scene and Hill House's response to it are roughly framed
by two others. In the first, in a rare moment of pleasure in her
own separate identity, Eleanor finds herself "unexpectedly admir-
ing her own [unpainted] feet" (83). That same evening, Theodora
tells Eleanor she is attractive and touches her hand (86). Eleanor,
who tells herself she hates to be touched, is suddenly afraid she
herself is not "clean": "Her fingernails *were* dirty, and her hand
was badly shaped," she thinks, "and people made jokes about love
because sometimes it was funny" (86). After the toenail paint-
ing and its sequel, the guests discover a ghastly book of precepts
for one of the original daughters of Hill House, compiled by the
self-proclaimed "author of [her] being and the guardian of [her]
virtue" (171)—complete with obscene illustrations, expressions
of fanatical morality, and a signature in blood. The juxtaposi-
tion of Eleanor's sexual self-hatred and Hugh Crain's teachings
has everything to do with what happens between Theodora and
Eleanor.

"Your feet are dirty," Theodora says casually, as she paints
Eleanor's toenails—and Eleanor panics: "It's *horrible*," she said
to Theodora, "it's *wicked*," wanting to cry. Then, helplessly, she
began to laugh at the look on Theodora's face . . . I hate having

things done to me. . . . I don't like to feel helpless . . . My mother—
. . . It's wicked. I mean—on *my* feet. It makes me feel like I look
like a fool" (117).

"You've got wickedness and foolishness somehow mixed up,"
a startled Theodora tells her (117). In part, of course, she is right.
In part, however, she misses the point. Eleanor has been raised in
the ideological world of Hugh Crain's precepts; she may surrep-
titiously buy red clothing, but to glory in her own sexuality, to
be a "woman of some color," she would have to be a "different
person" indeed. If it is fine for her to do so, what does that say
about her entire past? Either such self-indulgence is wicked, or
she has been played for a fool.

The message is clear: Eleanor cannot cope with her own sexuality. Henceforth, she will pursue Theodora as an intimate companion, but she will shrink in disgust from her touch. Theodora
seems to sense how serious matters are. "You're about as crazy as
anyone I ever saw," she says cheerfully at first; and then "gravely,"
"I have a hunch that you ought to go home" (117). What she cannot know is that Eleanor has no home; and that she, Theodora,
has exposed herself as Eleanor's true double, able simultaneously
to seduce and annihilate.

The haunting's strategy of separating the guests seems to aim
particularly at separating Eleanor and Theodora. By the next
day, Eleanor's name has been scrawled on the walls, and the
two women have begun to fight. What follows is probably Hill
House's most vicious manifestation: a stinking, bloody attack
on Theodora's room, with "HELP ELEANOR COME HOME
ELEANOR" scrawled on the walls (152–58). Earlier drafts
showed blood on Theodora's walls and dressing table alone (TS),
and one even shows Mrs. Montague later soaking it out with
cold water (TS/C4 211–12). Now the attack is spectral, and it is
extremely intimate. The menstrual imagery seems unmistakable
here: Hill House echoes and amplifies Eleanor's hatred of "dirty"
female bodies, including her own. Theodora's bright clothes are

trampled and soaked in blood (155). Even more significantly, she herself is bloodied—literally rendered a scarlet woman—and Eleanor's name, like Hugh Crain's in the obscene book of "moral" instruction, is written on the walls in blood (155, 157–58). Beside herself, Theodora blames Eleanor, whose wild, secret hilarity reveals the extent to which Hill House has indeed fulfilled her hidden desires. "Journeys end in lovers meeting," she says silently to steady herself (154).

In the end, however, Hill House is a treacherous ally even in retaliation. The morality of Eleanor's upbringing is only momentarily vindicated. True, she may now call Theo "filthy" (158) and tell herself she has "never felt such uncontrollable loathing" for anyone (157), but she must watch as Theodora, newly scrubbed and cheerily admitting to being a fool, casually appropriates her own cherished and daring red sweater, asserting with equal casualness that she and Eleanor are "practically twins" (158). The haunting has thus moved to cut Eleanor off not only from Theodora but also from her own timid dreams of becoming more colorful. Even Theodora's assertion of kinship seems a form of aggression to Eleanor now, and it is true that she can no longer rely on Theodora's good will. It is no accident that the manifestation that follows is what Jackson called the key scene of the novel: the scene in which Eleanor holds Theodora's hand, only to discover there was no one there.

Is Theodora a kind of demon lover, a human parallel to the ghostly hand that offered Eleanor transitory, delusive comfort? Is she too a victim of Hill House? Or is she both? It is never quite clear whether Jackson implies an intrinsic relationship between the selfishness she seems to attribute to Theodora, Theodora's dangerous function as a double, and Theodora's lesbianism. (The connection between the latter two was much stronger in *Hangsaman*.[5]) What does seem clear is that Theodora betrays Eleanor in part because she betrays her own desires. The evening before Eleanor reaches for Theodora's hand and finds that of Hill

House, the four guests talk about fear. "I am always afraid of being alone," Eleanor confesses, but for Theodora, fear comes from " 'knowing what we really want' . . . She pressed her cheek to Eleanor's hand, and Eleanor, hating the touch of her, took her hand away quickly" (159–60). Just as she fought with her lover rather than admitting to her need to go to Hill House (9), Theodora is drawn into fighting with Eleanor rather than admit to the sexual awareness that makes her realize that she is unable to cope with Eleanor's confused longings for intimacy.

Later, when the two women walk into negative light, fighting over Theodora's anger at Eleanor's willingness to listen to Luke's confidences, one of the first manifestations Jackson wrote takes on new irony and poignancy. Originally written as a vicious parody of the famous "adventure" at Versailles, which Jackson believed had united two real British schoolmistresses, Miss Moberly and Miss Jourdain, in bonds of labor and probably of love, the manifestation now reverses its model in function as well as form.[6] In earlier drafts, the haunting shatters the women's intimacy before either can ask a question about Luke (1D). This time, the question Hill House does not allow them to ask is "Do you love me?" (174).

In her own way, Theodora, too, seems to have been seduced by Hill House's delusive promises. Just before Eleanor is sent away, she says, "Oh Nellie, my Nell—be happy; please be happy. Don't *really* forget me . . . Oh, Nellie! I thought you weren't going to say good-by to me" (244).

We have seen the destruction of Eleanor's romantic fantasies. "Journeys end in lovers meeting," she thinks, meaning first Luke and then Theodora; but as they themselves admit, she cannot trust them (213). In the "absolute reality" of Hill House, Eleanor begins to face a second truth she has tried to flee: her self-sacrifice has been inadequate and ultimately pointless. On the one hand, she could never give her family enough: "It was going to happen sooner or later in any case," she says of her mother's death. "But

of course no matter when it happened it was going to be my fault"
(212). On the other hand, what she did give, she seems to have
given for nothing. She hated her mother and hates her sister; and
she has no home. "Do you *always* go where you're not wanted?"
an exasperated Theodora asks her at one point. "I've never been
wanted *anywhere*," Eleanor "placidly" replies (209).

Hill House comes to embody what Claire Kahane calls a "primary Gothic fear" of "nonseparation from the castle as mother":
in the secret center of Hill House, "the secret center of the Gothic
structure . . . boundaries break down, . . . life and death become
confused, . . . images of birth and death proliferate in complex dis-
placements" (Garner 337–38). Eleanor herself increasingly swings
between what Kahane calls "the polar oppositions of experience
within the symbiotic bond: the illusion of being all or nothing"
(338). By the last night, Eleanor *is* the haunting for the other
guests who hear her pounding at their doors (228–29).

Hill House's spectral "family," initially a mirror of all the
guests' deepest conflicts, now belongs to Eleanor alone, and with
secrecy a new dynamic emerges. As the violence of Hill House's
most dramatic manifestation reaches its peak, Eleanor can no
longer differentiate herself from the haunting. She thinks the noise
is in her own head, and she feels as if she is "disappearing inch
by inch" into the house. The house begins to rock as it is literally tearing itself into pieces. "We are lost," she thinks, "lost; the
house is destroying itself. She heard the laughter over all, coming
thin and lunatic, rising in its little crazy tune, and thought, No;
it is over for me. It is too much. . . . I will relinquish my possession of this self of mine, abdicate, give over willingly what I never
wanted at all; whatever it wants of me it can have" (204). "I'll
come," she says; and the manifestation stops (204). Once more, a
woman has sacrificed her own identity to hold her "family" home
together. Eleanor's surrender leaves one with an uneasy question:
can a woman sacrifice herself if she has never really had, or perhaps even wanted, a self? Does Eleanor know she has a choice?
Is her death suicide—or murder?

To sacrifice oneself, after all, Jackson implies, one must have been allowed to develop a "self," and one must have a choice; it is not clear that Eleanor has either. Her death is only the dramatic accomplishment of a domestic murder that began long ago. Even her suicide is not her own: "In the unending, crashing second before the car hurled into the tree she thought clearly, *Why* am I doing this?" (246). What is left at the end of *Hill House* is a vision of failed human bonds, and of the forced sacrifice of a victim too weak, and too drugged by fantasy, to resist.

Perhaps the greatest horror of Jackson's haunting is not that the house seduces Eleanor into literally sacrificing herself for the sake of belonging, but that having done so, it still does not let her belong. Eleanor may imagine herself to be joining the ghostly children who try to enter her room, sing to her, hold her, and ask her for help, but this promised intimacy is as delusive as any other in Hill House. In Kahane's terms, Eleanor has given her life to become "everything" and has become nothing. The house does not want her any more than anyone else does; it wants her dead. After all, whatever walks in Hill House walks alone.

Notes

1. I believe I can distinguish four main versions in the drafts of *Hill House* at the Library of Congress. For the sake of convenience, I have named them after their protagonists (Vancey, Trapped Theodora, Erica, and Eleanor), assuming that those sketches that are furthest from the final draft were probably written first.

The "Vancey" and "Trapped Theodora" versions are drawn from folders labeled "First Draft" (1D) and "Typescript" (TS). These same folders contain a series of jumbled and, for the most part, unpaginated sketches for what I believe are later drafts, the "Erica" and "Eleanor" versions. They also contain Jackson's introduction and publishing house readers' reactions to an early draft (probably the Erica version); unused sketches for Hill House's history; drawings and floor plans for the house; notes and commentary on Jackson's research into psychic manifestations; and a description of *Hill House*'s composition, which appeared in shortened form in her essay, "Experience and Fiction"; as well as one or two sketches which seem to be unrelated to the novel.

The majority of the "Erica" version appears in the folder labeled "Typescript Carbon 4" (TS/C4). This folder contains pages one through sixty-six of a draft of the novel's opening. It also contains two short sketches of scenes about a protagonist named "Eleanor." These pages (136–40 and 211–18) appear to be part of a lost draft; the incidents they describe had not yet been integrated into the "Erica" draft.

The final, or "Eleanor," version may be found in two sets of files. One set is marked "Typescript 1," "Typescript 2" and "Typescript 3" (TS1, TS2, TS3); the other, "Typescript Carbon 1," "Typescript Carbon 2," and "Typescript Carbon 3" (TS/C1, TS/C2, TS/C3). "Typescript Carbon 3" also contains unnumbered pages. The set marked "Carbon" is not a copy of the first set, but it does incorporate corrections penciled on that set. Both are numbered, and both drafts are very close to the final form of *Hill House*. Uncorrected page proofs are also in the collection.

2. The personal context from which Jackson wrote about the destructiveness of the nuclear family is suggested by the recent Oppenheimer biography.

3. Erica appears as the protagonist of sketches scattered through the "Typescript" and "First Draft" folders as well. In the most disturbing of these, she suddenly walks into a hospital emergency room "because she genuinely wanted to be in touch, somehow, with another human being to whom some ultimate thing was happening, because she was lonely" (TS). On the same page, Jackson wrote, "Reality is an interminable sentence, but as long as it allows for the slight irregularity of hope it is bearable."

4. In writing *Hill House*, Jackson embarked on "a lot of splendid research reading all the books about ghosts I could get hold of" ("Experience" 202). She seems to have read and drawn on accounts of some of the most famous hauntings in the English-speaking world, particularly the hauntings at Borley Rectory and Ballechin Castle, which are mentioned by Dr. Montague in the novel (*Hill House* 141). Accounts of these hauntings include: Eric J. Dingwell,

Kathleen Goldney and Trevor H. Hall, *The Haunting of Borley Rectory* (London: Gerald Duckworth, 1956); Harry Price, *'The Most Haunted House in England': Ten Years Investigation of Borley Rectory* (London: Longmans, 1940); *The End of Borley Rectory, The Most Haunted House in England* (London: Longmans, 1940); and A. Goodrich-Freer, Colonel Lemesurier Taylor and John, Marquess of Bute, eds., *The Alleged Haunting of B— House* [Ballechin Castle] (London: George Redway, 1899).

While Jackson certainly borrowed manifestations and descriptions for *Hill House* from these and other hauntings, she seems to have come away from her research intrigued by the human relationships and self-revelations that come from the groups of psychic researchers pursuing these ghosts. She writes in some undated notes that in every documented case she has investigated, there is "a reason for the perception of the supernatural; that is, the ghost may or may not have a reason for appearing, but the percipient most certainly has a reason for *seeing* it" (1D).

5. When Jackson first discovered that Jeannette Foster had included *Hangsaman* in her *Sex Variant Women in Literature*, she wrote a letter that vilified the lesbian poet and scholar as "some dirty old lady," asserting her own reading as definitive: "damnit, it [*Hangsaman*] is about what I say it is about" (Oppenheimer 232–33). Although Oppenheimer echoes Jackson's horror at what the biographer terms a misreading, apparently accepting the author's statement as conclusive, she quotes enough of the remainder of Jackson's impressive letter to reveal the writer moving beyond her initial response and engaging in a self-critical exploration of the fear and denial suggested by her own overwhelming response to the association of her characters with a "named sin" (233–34).

6. Jackson made frequent references to the "adventure" of Charlotte Moberly and Eleanor Jourdain, in which apparitions at Versailles helped to create a lifetime union between these two British schoolmistresses. A version of this adventure appears as one of Hill House's most frightening manifestations. An account of the women's experiences is given in Charlotte Moberly, *An Adventure* (London: Macmillan, 1911); and in *An Adventure with Appendix and Maps* (London: Macmillan, 1913).

Works Cited

Carpenter, Lynette. "The Establishment and Preservation of Female Power in Shirley Jackson's *We Have Always Lived in the Castle.*" *Frontiers* 8 (1984): 32–38.

Garner, Shirley Nelson, Claire Kahane, and Madelon Sprengnether, eds. *The (M)Other Tongue*. Ithaca: Cornell UP, 1985.

Jackson, Shirley. "Experience and Fiction." *Come Along With Me: Part of a Novel, Sixteen Stories, and Three Lectures.* Ed. Stanley Edgar Hyman. New York: Viking, 1959.

———. *The Haunting of Hill House.* New York: Viking, 1959. (paperback: New York: Popular Library, 1959)

———. Book File 22: "First Draft," "Typescript," "Typescript 1," "Typescript 2," "Typescript 3," "Typescript Carbon 1," "Typescript Carbon 2," "Typescript Carbon 3," and "Typescript Carbon 4." Shirley Jackson Papers, Library of Congress, Washington, D.C.

Oppenheimer, Judy. *Private Demons: The Life of Shirley Jackson.* New York: Fawcett, 1988.

Gayle K. Fujita Sato

Ghosts as Chinese-American Constructs in Maxine Hong Kingston's *The Woman Warrior*

IT IS IRONIC THAT Maxine Hong Kingston's *The Woman Warrior*, one of the most celebrated works by an Asian American, has not been interpreted primarily as Asian-American writing. Critics and reviewers consider Kingston's key metaphors, especially woman warrior and ghost, but do not interpret them as Chinese-American constructs. This essay reads *Woman Warrior* as a distinctly Asian-American text by showing how "ghost" designates a particular as well as a shared Chinese-American existence. In the various forms of her "girlhood among ghosts," Kingston seems to me to represent her life as an undichotomized Chinese-American totality, even as she speaks alternately of what is "Chinese" and what "American" in the process of interpreting her experience. Thus when Kingston says she "had to figure out how the invisible world the emigrants built around our childhoods fit in solid America" (*Woman Warrior* 6), she distinguishes these two places—the "invisible," presumably Chinese, "world" and "solid America"—but also begins an analysis that will ultimately enable their synthesis. Through the writing of *Woman Warrior*, Kingston combines "invisible" and "solid" in the figure of the "ghost" and the word *ghost* to represent the nature of Chinese-American experience.[1]

The substantial body of feminist criticism generated since Kingston's work first appeared helps us to define an ethnic approach that is both responsive to otherness and sophisticated about writing as a strategy for cultural invention and empowerment.[2] The following statement by Suzanne Juhasz, which expresses the stance toward ethnicity informing feminist readings of Kingston's work, provides a point of departure for defining ethnic criticism:

> Taken together, *The Woman Warrior* and *China Men* compose a woman's autobiography, describing a self formed at the source by gender experience.
>
> To say this is neither to ignore nor to minimize the question of national identity everywhere present in Kingston's writing. Born in the United States to Chinese immigrant parents, her search for self necessarily involves a definition of home. Is it America, China, or someplace in between? . . . For Kingston, in fact, who has never been there, China is not so much a physical state as it is a construct used by her parents to define their own identities. America too, especially for her parents, is a psychological state as much as it is a place. My own focus here on sexual identity is therefore not meant to negate the other dimension of the problem, but rather to reveal sexual and national identities as parts of one another. For it is as a Chinese-American woman that Kingston seeks to define herself. (74)

While Juhasz's essay does illuminate the gender issues in *Woman Warrior*, it misconstrues Kingston's construction of ethnic identity. In her opening statement, Juhasz unintentionally repeats the idea *in opposition to which* Asian-American writing is fundamentally defined.[3] For Juhasz accepts dual identity, or the splitting of identity into separate Asian and American components, by asking whether "home" can be located in "America, China, or someplace in between." But Kingston's nationality is not undetermined. She wants to clarify "Asian," but this process begins from the fixed fact of American nationality. An ethnic approach to Kingston would begin with the assumption of a definite culture that is not tentatively situated "someplace in between," but named and located as Chinese America.

THAT THE GHOST OF No Name Woman will play a central role in the writing of *Woman Warrior* and the locating of Chinese America is explicitly stated by Kingston in the first chapter, where she claims the aunt as "my forerunner" (9) and reveals her desire for connections: "Unless I see her life branching into mine, she gives me no ancestral help" (10). The centrality of the aunt's ghost is also richly and powerfully expressed in the way she makes her appearance. When Kingston brings her aunt back to life by telling her story, the aunt surfaces from the drinking well of life and the inkwell of literature in a reenactment of the ancestral crossing from China to America. This association of two kinds of wells, a figure for the splicing of life and literature that constitutes autobiography, is clearly intended by Kingston. To begin with, "No Name Woman" ends with the following passage indicating that the drinking well figures prominently in Kingston's relationship with her aunt:

> My aunt haunts me—her ghost drawn to me because now, after fifty years of neglect, I alone devote pages of paper to her, though not origamied into houses and clothes. I do not think she always means me well. I am telling on her, and she was a spite suicide, drowning herself in the drinking water. The Chinese are always very frightened of the drowned one, whose weeping ghost, wet hair hanging and skin bloated, waits silently by the water to pull down a substitute. (19)

By ending the first chapter of *Woman Warrior* thus, Kingston expresses her kinship with the aunt's ghost through the imagery of the drinking well, a move that underscores her intention to re-store the well as a place of life by restoring her aunt's place in the family history. Kingston's association of the drinking well with an inkwell is also implied in this passage since she says she will purify the well through words, through pages of paper contain-ing her aunt's story. In later chapters, ink figures prominently in Kingston's identification as a woman warrior and a writer. The tale of Fa Mu Lan merges with Kingston's real life through the illusion of entering an ink drawing of White Tigers mountain (24–25). Fa Mu Lan's back was carved and inked with words of revenge, and in her own way Kingston is immersed in ink as a writer. Moon Orchid distinguishes Kingston from her siblings as the "girl smeared in ink" (152), the one with "an American name that sounded like 'Ink' in Chinese" (152). (And in English, too, we might add: *Max-ink*.) The drinking well inhabited by No Name Woman's ghost is thus the autobiographer's inkwell. Being haunted by a nameless ghost will be the means of Kingston's self-naming.

Not just No Name Woman but also the principal subjects of subsequent chapters—Fa Mu Lan, Brave Orchid, Moon Orchid, and Ts'ai Yen—all assist in this process of self-naming. In ref-erence to their collective function, they are called "ghost/role models" by Bacchilega (7) and "tutelary geniuses" by Cheung (171). However, No Name Woman's particular guidance as one of Kingston's ghost writers is fundamental to that of the others. The aunt's narrative illustrates the continuing centrality of filial rela-tions, the foundation of traditional Chinese society, to Chinese Americans.

Caught up in her own battles with parents and parental culture, Kingston understands the absolute negation of identity her aunt's severance from the family line entails. As a Chinese-American daughter seeking and evaluating family ties, Kingston indeed feels kinship with this unacknowledged kin. Kingston's memoirs nar-rate the process of gaining access to a familial, communal memory that is initially ghostlike—elusive and hidden. Her narrative is a deeply filial act, not only because telling about No Name Aunt enacts the writer's own rediscovery of home, but because the aunt's readmission into the family reenacts the larger home-building phenomenon of Chinese emigration. Reclaimed and reborn on paper, No Name Aunt has emigrated in a highly visible way in Kingston's narrative, a fact of greater importance when we consider gender differences in Chinese immigration.

To subvert laws designed to admit a temporary pool of Chinese men while preventing their establishment of permanent communities, many Chinese entered the United States as "paper sons," claiming to be sons of men already admitted or in possession of legal papers. Coupled with the custom of leaving wives at home while they worked abroad, anti-Asian immigration laws restricted the Chinese-American population until World War II to a predominantly male or "bachelor society" as it is called (see Nee, *Longtime Californ'*). By making her aunt a "paper daughter" to permit her emigration to America, Kingston not only grounds self-understanding in Chinese emigration but also expands the terms of that history to acknowledge women as cultural founders. They need not have physically emigrated in order to shape emigrant culture.

When Kingston represents her aunt as a "paper daughter," she acts not only as kinswoman but as writer. As she says, the "pages of paper" devoted to her aunt are "not origamied into houses and clothes" (19). "Origami," the Japanese term for the art of folding paper, is a reference to the Chinese custom of burning "paper suits and dresses, spirit money, paper houses, [and] paper automobiles" (19) as part of the graveside ritual of honoring ancestors. Kingston does make a filial offering on paper, but in a form befitting a writer. In fact, this is the best she can do because there is no gravesite to visit, and because words constitute the best redress for silence. In another sense, too, Kingston's filial offering of words is specifically appropriate to her subject. She says that her aunt "crossed boundaries not delineated in space" (9), and by fleshing out those boundaries, Kingston makes a comparable crossing, a venturing into new territory as a writer. That is, by interpreting No Name Woman as Hester Prynne's sister, Kingston converts her aunt's transgression into an extension of the range of American literature.

Thus Kingston not only reclaims but reimagines her aunt's story. "Adultery is extravagance" (7): with this opening definition, Kingston proceeds to imagine her aunt's motivations. Though she concedes the possibility that her aunt was forced into sex, she prefers to ascribe desire to her aunt, for it is the story of imaginative possibility she seeks to recover. Her aunt, she imagines, was attracted by the curve of a torso or a pigtail tossing in the wind: "For warm eyes or a soft voice or a slow walk—that's all—a few hairs, a line, a brightness, a sound, a pace, she gave up family" (9). Hester Prynne's scarlet letter, "in fine red cloth, surrounded with an elaborate embroidery and fantastic flourishes of gold thread, . . . with so much fertility and gorgeous luxuriance of fancy" (Hawthorne 80), publicizes her own rebellion against a pragmatic economy. Like Hester Prynne, who becomes the town mother, No Name Woman enriches the culture that banishes her, surviving—and thereby transforming the meaning of *ghost*—as an embodiment of the value of extravagance, luxuriance, and passion. Beginning with Kingston, No Name Woman nurtures an American generation of woman warriors.

By showing her aunt's kinship with Hawthorne's creation, and by illuminating her aunt's identity as a "paper daughter," Kingston's ghost tracking is an original act of Asian-American writing in the American grain.[4] It is writing that is grounded simultaneously in American literary history and American immigration history. This double framework, which makes *Woman Warrior* a highly specific ethnic text but not one with a narrow audience, is reflected in the larger organizations of the book. For instance, the narratives of No Name Woman, Fa Mu Lan, Brave Orchid, Moon Orchid, and Ts'ai Yen not only present five versions of female development but also express a concentric movement from imagined or "far away" toward actual or "close" experience. In other words, emigration is embodied structurally in the change of settings from chapter to chapter, the physical relocation from an unnamed Chinese village where No Name Woman lived, to Stockton, California, where the writer grew up. Another important example of Kingston's combining historical and literary structures is the relation between emigration and fiction. The strategy of "paper sons" meant that from the start the Chinese were authoring their American lives, that notions of "real" identity were never uncomplicated. Folklore and fantasy in the creation of self were implicit in the very beginnings of Chinese-American society. Kingston's self-empowerment through the "paper identity" constituted by *Woman Warrior* comes out of this tradition.

Unlike the term *woman warrior*, however, which is clearly understood through its referent Fa Mu Lan, the term *ghost* raises problems in translation, as Kingston explained in a lecture delivered in Kyoto several years ago. She didn't want to follow Pearl Buck's translation of *kuei* as "white devil." She used *demon* for *China Men*, but sought another term to match the situations and language of her women warriors. Generally speaking, male sojourners in America like those portrayed in *China Men* spoke to, traded with, and lived among white Americans more fully than did women. Kingston settled on *ghost*, first of all to reflect immigrant women's indirect interaction with society. She also noted the range of meanings *ghost* embraces—threat and coercion mitigated by indefiniteness, seductive beauty or charm. After this explanation, someone in the audience pointed out that the Japanese translation of *kuei* into *oni* was off the mark even though the same kanji or Chinese character for *kuei* was being used. *Oni* are semihuman Japanese folk creatures. They do not haunt, though they sometimes hurt people. They do not translate easily into English and provide a good example of the degree to which ghost forms can be culture specific.[5]

At least for the original version in English, however, this problematic word proved a wonderful choice. It signifies cross-cultural translation, represents aspects of Chinese-American culture, and generates various metaphors. These functions of *ghost* are sometimes explicit, sometimes not, in a book that is written not for Cantonese-speaking "insiders" or English-speaking "outsiders," but for an in the interests of *creating* an audience like Kingston herself, an audience that shares a kinship like the one between Kingston and her aunt, an audience that is Chinese American in consciousness.

IF THE APPEARANCE of No Name Woman on the American shore, her ghost rising up from the well in a wonderful reversal of the "digging a hole to China" motif, symbolizes the ancestral crossing on both a personal and communal level, it is Fa Mu Lan's warrior skills that enable Kingston to fully possess this ancestral legacy. This is the meaning of the book's title. Before Kingston can recognize and benefit from "a girlhood among ghosts," she must first be able to rescue her aunt's ghost. Through this rescue, she allows herself to be subversive, to criticize her home and culture without denying herself a place in them. This is precisely what Fa Mu Lan, the "woman warrior" of the "White Tigers" chapter, accomplishes by fighting as a man to redeem her village and family on the one hand, and on the other, bearing a son and kneeling happily at the feet of her parents-in-law. The chapter on Fa Mu Lan is a positive counterpoint to the chapter on No Name Woman, a narrative of connectedness and return to family that follows and reinterprets one of severing and abandonment. Fa Mu Lan's avenging of community and acquisition of personal family are for Kingston as writer symbolized and partly constituted by her encounter through narrative with the ghost of the No Name Aunt.

But if rescuing the aunt's ghost is Kingston's primary act as a woman warrior, at the same time she must possess knowledge of ghosts in order to become a capable warrior. This dilemma is one of the many paradoxes that *Woman Warrior* resolves, not by reduction, but through a way of seeing that I call "superimposed vision," which can admit the simultaneous existence of two seemingly opposed ideas or states of being. The paradoxes addressed in *Woman Warrior* are summed up in the paired terms "god" and "ghost," the terms of the book's title and subtitle. Representing two extreme conceptions of existence—omnipotence and oblivion—"god" and "ghost" must become connected in order to have meaning for daily life. Kingston makes such a connection through the cultivation of superimposed vision, in which "god" is viewed and understood through "ghost." This superimposed vision is represented metaphorically in the "White Tigers" chapter, where the writer as Fa Mu Lan says, "I learned to make my mind large, as the universe is large, so that there is room for paradoxes" (35). The tale of Fa Mu Lan's training serves as a paradigm for Kingston's education in illusion, paradox, fantasy, dreams, and heightened senses that enables her to become a woman warrior through writing.

Cultivation of poetic imagination is represented in the landscape of White Tigers mountain, which is fluid and fabulously concrete. The mountain itself is not stable, but merely the top of one dragon's head: "When climbing the slopes, I could understand that I was a bug riding on a dragon's forehead as it roams through space, its speed so different from my speed that I feel the dragon solid and immobile" (34). At the same time, though nothing is solid, everything is concrete: the dragon's tongue is lightning, and "the red that the lightning gives to the world is strong, and lucky—in blood, poppies, roses, rubies, the red feathers of birds, the red carp, the cherry tree, the peony, the line alongside the turtle's eyes and the mallard's" (35). As the second quotation shows, the landscape of White Tigers mountain is also brilliantly colored, a fact that illuminates the nature of the superimposed vision represented in "White Tigers," and how this vision is related to ghosts.

We can see Fa Mu Lan's sensibility for color, for instance the way she interprets nature's red, in Kingston's own attentiveness to color in her writing. One example, a description of the gifts the villagers bring Fa Mu Lan, will suffice to represent the extensive use of color that marks the writing throughout *Woman Warrior*:

> We took the saddlebags of the horse and filled them with salves and herbs, blue grass for washing my hair, extra sweaters, dried peaches. They gave me a choice of ivory or silver chopsticks. I took the silver ones because they were lighter. It was like getting wedding presents. The cousins and the villagers came bearing bright orange jams, silk dresses, silver embroidery scissors. They brought blue and white porcelain bowls filled with water and carp—the bowls painted with carp, fins like orange fire. I accepted all the gifts—the tables, the earthenware jugs—though I could not possibly carry them with me, and culled for travel only a small copper cooking bowl. (42)

To be color*ful* is to be full of physical energy and creative power, to be alive. As in Wallace Stevens's poem "Disillusionment at Ten O'Clock," to be white or without color is to be internally blank. The poem contrasts the emptiness of houses "haunted / by white nightgowns," none of them "purple with green rings / or green with yellow rings," with the potent imagination of "an old sailor, / Drunk and asleep in his boots, / Catch[ing] tigers in red weather" (66). Life's colors register on Kingston's imagination, too: "a yellow, warm world" (25), "oh green joyous rush" (30), "I nodded, orange and warm" (31), "in dark and silver dreams" (47). To speak in colors is to experience diversity and darkness and dreams as sources of creative power.

The mountain of "white" tigers is misleadingly yet aptly named. White could mean the absence of imagination—if Casper is our limited idea of a ghost or if we read Fa Mu Lan's story as fantasy in the superficial sense of "daydream." If, on the other hand, we cultivate illusion, or imaginative depth perception, then we can actually inhabit a "fantasy" like that of Fa Mu Lan and a white world reveals its colors, the full spectrum of colors. We can define the deep, empowering sense of "fantasy" as a ghost existence, or a condition of being available for creative inhabitancy. Kingston's identification with Fa Mu Lan is an example of the empowerment that creative inhabitancy brings. To achieve such a merging requires superimposed vision, or the ability to perceive that reality is layered. Armed with this kind of vision, Kingston can superimpose the glorious life of Fa Mu Lan on that of No Name Woman to reconstruct the context of her own disappointing American life. She presents No Name Woman's obliteration as the inverse of Fa Mu Lan's "perfect filiality" (154) in an effort to reinscribe her own sense of familial identity.

THOUGH THE WAY of seeing represented in "White Tigers" constitutes Kingston's main weapon, her training to become a writer-warrior is incomplete without the living example of her mother, a flesh-and-blood battler of ghosts who thus embodies a link between the folklore heroines and real-life heroism. Through Brave Orchid's talk story about her own exploits as well as Fa Mu Lan's, Kingston is given an indisputable example of the role of ghost knowledge in developing imaginative power and social identity.

Brave Orchid is perhaps the most invisible solidity Kingston must contend with in the process of fitting an invisible emigrant world into solid America. Among the stream of ghosts at the airport, for instance, she seems the only substantial person in an undifferentiated blur, with her bag of food, blanket, and thermos. She hardly seems representative of an invisible world, yet portions of her past life in China and the source of her psychic stamina remain mysteries to Kingston. Ultimately Kingston forges a style out of this doubleness in order to come to terms with it. Her words yoke solid and invisible realities, as in describing her sensations upon opening her mother's medical diploma: "the smell of China flies out, a thousand-year-old bat flying heavy-handed out of the

Chinese caverns where bats are as white as dust, a smell that comes from long ago, far back in the brain" (67). Here as elsewhere, through words that flesh out as magically as bats flapping forth from a hollow tube, Kingston can render the simultaneous mystery and tangible presence of her mother. This literary style of superimposed vision that yokes the invisible and the solid means that Kingston has come to understand her mother's power as consisting of this doubleness. Kingston summarizes Brave Orchid's survival skills thus: "My mother could contend against the hairy beasts whether flesh or ghost because she could eat them, and she could not-eat them on days when good people fast. . . . She was a capable exorcist" (108). Brave Orchid is empowered by her judicious restraint. She is an amazing and mysterious combination of practicality and poetry. She has a fluid sense of invisibility and solidity, of what to accept as reality and what to ignore, and when to do so. This is the superimposed vision that enables her to incarnate Fa Mu Lan, the vision which signals "the presence of great power" (24).

Normally Brave Orchid is practical. Kingston notes: "My mother was not crazy for seeing ghosts" (108). But when the situation demands it, as when she wishes to conquer anxieties about being the only older student in medical school, Brave Orchid will pursue ghosts to make a show of power. She scares her children with stories to test their "strength to establish realities" (5); she does likewise for herself: "Danger was a good time for showing off" (79). What she shows off in the battle with Sitting Ghost is the reality of her existence: "When morning comes, only one of us will control this room, Ghost, and that one will be me" (82). Her steady stream of words is equivalent to asserting the weight of her existence against the immense weight of the sitting ghost, which is symbolic of self-doubts and other obstacles to be overcome in acquiring a medical diploma. The final victory is not just an allaying of fears, but a magnification of self as Brave Orchid embellishes the story to her audience the next morning.

If the private experience of encountering ghosts means entering diversity, darkness, and dreams to test individual power, the
public, narrated experience is one of disengaging from otherness
in order to reconfirm social identity. After schoolmates chant at
her request—"Come home, come home, Brave Orchid, who has
fought the ghosts and won. Return to To Keung School, Kwangtung City, Kwangtung Province" (84)—Brave Orchid's "soul returned fully to her and nestled happily inside her skin, for this
moment not travelling in the past where her children were nor to
America to be with my father" (84). Brave Orchid must reinte-
grate herself into her community: "She was back among many
people. She rested after battle. She let her friends watch out for
her" (84). Entering the world of ghosts is an individual, internal experience of self; separating from ghosts measures the self's
possession of communal identity.

Ghosts, therefore, because they imply both insubstantiality and
solidity, represent both poetry and practicality, isolation and inte-
gration. These are not conflicting definitions of ghost; they simply
represent the two ways of responding to otherness. The "ghost/
role models" in *Woman Warrior* all use or embody the term *ghost*
in both senses. No Name Woman, for instance, gazing at her new-
born, contemplates the simultaneous loss and possession of family
that the baby "ghost" represents: "A child with no descent line
would not soften her life but only trail after her, ghostlike, beg-
ging her to give it purpose. . . . Full of milk, the little ghost slept"
(17). Fa Mu Lan understands her very different separation from
family, one sanctioned by the community, as a kind of ghost existence. Given a glimpse of her future husband, she says: "We will
be so happy when I come back to the valley, healthy and strong
and not a ghost" (37). Brave Orchid's limitations are expressed in
terms of ghosts: "Medical science does not seal the earth, whose
nether creatures seep out, hair by hair, disguised like the smoke
that dispels them. She had apparently won against the one ghost,
but ghost forms are various and many" (98). The ghost that Brave

Orchid cannot control turns out to be her sister, who ends up "a ghost badmouthing her children" (185). Not "very imaginative" (166), according to Brave Orchid's earlier diagnosis, and thus unable to negotiate minimally with otherness, Moon Orchid is subsumed by it to the point of losing home and self: "Her husband looked like one of the ghosts passing the car windows, and she must look like a ghost from China. They had indeed entered the land of ghosts, and they had become ghosts" (178). Ts'ai Yen, Moon Orchid's inverse as Fa Mu Lan is No Name Woman's, thrives in a land of ghosts because she can contain them within herself, shape them into song. The major narratives of *Woman Warrior*, then, are constructed to enact two relationships to the ghost world—entering it to develop imagination and individuality, and leaving it to confirm familial and communal identity.

We can now look at how *Woman Warrior* in its entirety is structured by Kingston's multifaceted relationship to the ghost world —by the autobiographical project defined through the ghost of No Name Woman, by the way of seeing represented in the landscape and events of White Tigers mountain, and by Brave Orchid's example of contending with ghosts. We can say that Kingston's five ghost/role models constitute a structure of superimposed vision. One level of superimposing is the pairing of chapters 1 and 2, and 4 and 5. In each case, the second story enacts a positive reversal of the preceding one. Another superimposition occurs when the middle chapter binds these paired narratives. Because she is a living example of tiger and dragon training—resilient to hardship, productive and empowered, poetic and practical— Brave Orchid stands between Fa Mu Lan, who is totally empowered but not human, and Moon Orchid, who is human but helpless. The overarching superimposition is Kingston's creation of the whole structure as one that unghosts No Name Woman.

Kingston speculates that whatever solace her aunt might have felt holding her child was mitigated by knowledge of the power of

family: "How would this tiny child without family find her grave
when there would be no marker for her anywhere, neither in the
earth nor the family hall? . . . At its birth the two of them had felt
the same raw pain of separation, a wound that only the family
pressing tight could close" (17). No matter how strong, bold, or
talented, no Chinese or Chinese-American woman is defined outside of family. Perhaps the very power of Fa Mu Lan's story to
inspire is its fantasy of perfect filiality. With the contribution of
real-life narratives from her female family—those of her mother,
her aunts, and herself—Kingston bridges anonymity and identity
in an act of confirming her own existence as a Chinese-American
woman and daughter. The superimposition of Fa Mu Lan on No
Name Woman is the paradigmatic unghosting, the reaffirmation
of filial identity. Kingston will name her aunt so that she can join
the ancestral spirits "who act like gods, not ghosts, their descent
lines providing them with paper suits and dresses, spirit money,
paper houses, paper automobiles, chicken, meat, and rice into
eternity" (18–19). By comparing her "pages of paper" to these
origamied paper offerings, Kingston defines her autobiography as
a filial gesture.

Such a gesture marks the narrative as genuinely Chinese American. Even in as careful and willingly inclusive a reading as
Juhasz's, Kingston's definition of home is summarized as a
duality: "In a fierce tirade against her mother she asserts her own
American sense of independence" (Juhasz 183). Juhasz asserts:
"Establishing herself as a talker in opposition to her mother—
as American instead of Chinese, a truth teller instead of a liar—
makes it possible for her to define herself as separate from her
mother. Leaving home at this stage means leaving China, and her
mother's Chinese way of talking" (Juhasz 183). This approach
splits Chinese from American such that the absence of ethnicity
is what defines American selfhood. Yet, as the filial gesture signified by the unghosting of No Name Woman indicates, whatever
alienation Kingston experiences is inherent in the filial dynamic

implicit in Kingston's identification with family. American self-hood is not measured by distance from home, but by how far one can travel within it, or to what extent possession of a home base frees one to be critical and investigative. The confession, the speaking out, the anger, the list of secrets, these are all articulated simultaneously with the exhibition and celebration of a culture. This doubleness—not dual identity—is a form of bilingualness, which is distilled in the transliterated word *Ho Chi Kuei*.

GHOST IS NOT ALWAYS weighted with the metaphoric reso-nance Kingston gives it as a writer and shaper of narrative. In the last chapter, *ghost* is finally heard and explained as part of the language of dailiness. *Ghost* is interchangeable with *person*, as in Ghost Teachers, Sales Ghosts, and Black Ghosts. It is used in anger, as when the Delivery Ghost makes a mistake: "That ghost! That dead ghost! . . . No one's going to sicken my child and get away with it!" (196). And it defines the American-born generations: "They would not tell us children because we had been born among ghosts, were taught by ghosts, and were our-selves ghostlike" (213–14). It is in this last chapter, when Kingston spills her secrets, that we hear *ghost* as the language of mundane complaint and frustration.

Dailiness can be the hardest thing to recognize. Always back-ground, always normal, it is nonetheless complexly constituted. This autobiography, a narrative of Chinese-American dailiness, opens with total awareness of the complexity: "Chinese Ameri-cans, . . . how do you separate what is peculiar to childhood, to poverty, to insanities, one family, your mother who marked your growing with stories, from what is Chinese?" (6). By the end, the question can be restated matter-of-factly: "I continue to sort out what's just my childhood, just my imagination, just my family, just the village, just movies, just living" (239). The event enabling transition from question to assertion is the outburst that provokes the response "Ho Chi Kuei"—Ho Chi Ghost. Like Kingston, we must adjust our understanding of the preceding meanings of *ghost* through this usage.

When Brave Orchid castigates her daughter by calling her "Ho Chi Kuei," Kingston is confronted with the problem of discovering what "Ho Chi" means. She lists thirteen possibilities, and ends up guessing after all. But before recording the results of her dictionary research, she indicates a fairly good sense of the phrase through its typical occurrences: " 'Well, Ho Chi Kuei,' they say, 'what silliness have you been up to now?' 'That's a Ho Chi Kuei for you,' they say, no matter what we've done. . . . The river-pirate great-uncle called even my middle brother Ho Chi Kuei, and he seemed to like him best" (237–38). These occurrences suggest a range of meanings: affection mixed with scorn; impatience; an absent-minded hello. Perhaps the phrase is like *kotonk,* which is what Japanese Americans from Hawaii call Japanese Americans from the mainland. The absence of a clear, agreed-upon definition has not prevented its being widely understood and used to distinguish the mainland from Hawaii, sometimes scornfully, sometimes good humoredly.

These kinds of phrases, *Ho Chi Kuei* and *kotonk,* are not easily translated from any language but they need not be, as Kingston's "explanation" implies. Before presenting results from the dictionary, she writes: "Be careful what you say. It comes true. It comes true. I had to leave home in order to see the world logically, logic the new way of seeing. . . . I enjoy the simplicity. Concrete pours out of my mouth to cover the forests with freeways and sidewalks. Give me plastics, periodical tables, TV dinners with vegetables no more complex than peas mixed with diced carrots. Shine floodlights into dark corners: no ghosts" (237). This irony is possible for her only after leaving home and gaining points of comparison with Chinese food, folklore, ways of seeing. Her language, so fabulously concrete, displays and is its own commentary on the irony of "no ghosts." Hence Kingston's relaxed humor when interpreting the dictionary results, which obviously have not clarified *Ho Chi*: "I like to look up a troublesome, shameful thing and then say, 'Oh, is that all?'" (238). Actually, it is all the experience, reflection, and training as a writer that have intervened between the events and their narration, which have allowed resolution, but not exactness of interpretation.

Sorting out what is just family, just imagination, just living means perceiving different layers of *ghost* ranging from simple idiomatic expression to complex metaphor. Rereading with this in mind, one sees *ghost* comfortably embedded in the text, an ethnic marker, signifying the familiarity and security of home. For instance, right after the passage concerning "nightmare babies" (101) and strategies "to make [her] waking life American-normal" (102), is this introduction of welcomed ghost stories: "When the thermometer in our laundry reached one hundred and eleven degrees on summer afternoons, either my mother or my father would say that it was time to tell another ghost story so that we could get some good chills up our backs" (102). Or, there is this passage describing Kingston's affection for her old home, where her mother will live on when she leaves:

> How can I bear to leave her again? She would close up this room open temporarily for me, and wander about cleaning and cleaning the shrunken house, so tidy since our leaving. . . . The sinks had been built of gray marble for the old Chinese men who boarded here before we came. I used to picture modest little old men washing in the mornings and dressing before they shuffled out of these bedrooms. I would have to leave and go again into the world out there which had no marble ledges for my clothes, no quilts made from our own ducks and turkeys, no ghosts of neat little old men. (118)

Or, there is the endearment "Little Dog," which can unghost Kingston like magic. In the narrative of No Name Woman we first learn that "old-fashioned women gave birth in their pigsties to fool the jealous, pain-dealing gods, who do not snatch piglets" (16). As the aunt held her "little ghost," she "clenched her teeth at its preciousness, lovely as a young calf, a piglet, a little dog" (17). But these names have also been associated with rejection. Kingston remembers when explaining *Ho Chi Kuei*: "It was more complicated (and therefore worse) than 'dogs,' which they say affectionately, mostly to boys. They use 'pig' and 'stink pig' for girls, and only in an angry voice" (238). In the conclusion of "Shaman," and thus midway between these passages, is a usage that combines the positive and the negative. Saying goodnight, Brave Orchid calls Kingston "Little Dog": "A weight lifted from me. The quilts must be filling with air. The world is somehow lighter. She has not called me that endearment for years—a name to fool the gods. . . . 'Good night, Little Dog.' 'Good night, Mother'" (127). Although the chapter actually ends on a dark note, with Kingston still "dreaming the dreams about shrinking babies" (127), the endearment is undiminished. However much Kingston must contend with ghosts, she is not one herself, in the sense that she is never without home, outside of which "the ghosts took shapes nothing like our own" (116).

Ho Chi Kuei is the adjuster that puts the entire cultural fabric signified by *ghost* into perspective.[6] Transliterated but untranslated, it signifies that Kingston's flying language and white-tiger vision are rooted in Chinese America. Her metaphors are attached to a culturally specific history and physical places—Canton, Stockton, the Hong residence. Representative of dailiness, *Ho Chi Kuei* reminds us that not everything needs explanation, that some explanations are a matter of absorbing a whole context, or that what seems alien might be more familiar than we realize. Finally, *Ho Chi Kuei* signifies the writer/warrior's identity. As an act of both criticism and celebration, the writing of *Woman Warrior* required a departure from home in order to discover the ways in which one need not depart. Kingston's simultaneous departure and return is precipitated as well as symbolized in the dinner table confrontation with her mother, who shouts: "Ho

Chi Kuei. Leave then. Get out, you Ho Chi Kuei. Get out" (237).
This scene climaxes the narrative of Kingston's battles to affirm
her identity within the family and Chinese American culture. It is
a turning point like that experienced by Ts'ai Yen. Transformed
by the sound of barbarian flutes that "reached again and again
for a high note, yearning toward a high note, which they found at
last and held" (243–44), Ts'ai Yen is enabled to sing of her own
culture. The song "about China and her family" thus arises out of
separation and is shaped to the music of foreign flutes. This bridging of two cultures into one song frees Ts'ai Yen psychologically
from captivity—"she left her tent to sit by the winter campfires,
ringed by barbarians" (243)—but at the same time such integra-
tion was implicit in the music of the Hsiung-nu, which yokes
opposites: their arrows are "high whirling whistles . . . filling the
air with death sounds" (242), their peace-time music pierces like
"an icicle in the desert" (243). Analogously, Kingston comes to
terms with what she considers to be "barbarian" elements of her
family history and culture, the various ghosts that alienate her
from Chinese America. Pushed to the limit of being denounced
as a Ho Chi Kuei by her mother, Kingston begins to see the
positive meanings of identification with ghosts. Like Hsiung-nu
music, the vitality of Chinese-American culture also consists in
opposed energies, represented in Woman Warrior in the multiple
meanings of ghost. Recognizing and inhabiting the oppositions,
rather than reducing them, leads to song. Ho Chi Kuei, the last
ghost form encountered in Woman Warrior, is the colloquial ana-
log of the writer's high clear note, the distillation of Kingston's
Chinese-American memoirs of a girlhood among ghosts.

Notes

1. I would like to thank Cristina Bacchilega, Stan Yogi, and
Deborah Weiner for their helpful comments on an earlier draft of
this essay.

2. King-Kok Cheung's recent essay comparing *The Woman Warrior* to *The Color Purple* illustrates how feminist theory can inform ethnic criticism without subsuming it.

3. See Frank Chin's Introduction to *Aiiieeeee! An Anthology of Asian-American Writers*.

4. When interviewed on the Dick Cavett Show in 1979, Kingston mentioned William Carlos Williams's *In the American Grain* as a model for the structure of *China Men*. In another interview, Arturo Islas asked Kingston about the implications of Williams's influence: "William Carlos Williams is also cited as a significant influence. His work *The American Dream* was inspirational for her conception of what it means to claim America in a literary way. Does 'claiming America' mean assimilation of American values?" Kingston replied, "No. I mean it as a response to the legislation and racism that says we of Chinese origin do not belong here in America. It's a response to the assumption that I come from Vietnam or another Asian country. When I say I am a native American with all the rights of an American, I am saying, no, we're not outsiders; we Chinese belong here. This is our country, this is our history, we are part of America. If it weren't for us, America would be a different place."

Read as ghost tracking, *Woman Warrior* also brings to mind James's "The Jolly Corner." Essentially, Spencer Brydon, like Kingston, returns to the childhood home to discover the terms of American selfhood.

5. I am grateful to Professor Teruyo Ueki of Kobe Women's University for supplying this information. Kingston's remarks about the term *ghost* are from my translation of a section of Professor Ueki's essay on *Woman Warrior* and *China Men*, which includes a report of Kingston's talk. I also want to thank Leslie Adams, Daniel Lee, and Wing Tek Lum for their various glosses on the Cantonese usage of *kuei*.

6. In this respect, *Ho Chi Kuei* is remarkably similar to the single untranslated phrase in Joy Kogawa's novel *Obasan*. The Japanese expression *ki ga tsuku* likewise represents the whole of the protagonist's cultural legacy, occurs at the end of the book, and enables repossession of cultural identity.

Works Cited

Bacchilega, Cristina. "*The Woman Warrior* di Maxine Hong Kingston: trasgressione e creazione dell'io narrante." *Quaderni di retorica e poetica* 2, 1 (1986): 227–33.

Cheung, King-Kok. " 'Don't Tell': Imposed Silences in *The Color Purple* and *The Woman Warrior*." *PMLA* 103 (1988): 162–74.

Chin, Frank. Introduction. *Aiiieeeee! An Anthology of Asian-American Writers.* Eds. Frank Chin, Jeffery Paul Chan, Lawson Fusao Inada, and Shawn Hsu Wong. Washington, D.C.: Howard UP, 1974. xxi–xlviii.

Hawthorne, Nathaniel. *The Scarlet Letter.* 1850. Ed. Nina Baym. New York: Penguin, 1983.

Islas, Arturo. Interview with Maxine Hong Kingston. *Women Writers of the West Coast Speaking of Their Lives and Careers.* Ed. Marilyn Yalom. Santa Barbara: Capra Press, 1983.

Juhasz, Suzanne. "Narrative Technique and Female Identity." *Contemporary American Women Writers: Narrative Strategies.* Eds. Catherine Rainwater and William J. Scheick. Lexington: UP of Kentucky, 1985.

Kingston, Maxine Hong. *The Woman Warrior: Memoirs of a Girlhood Among Ghosts.* New York: Knopf, 1976.

Nee, Victor G. and Brett de Barry Nee. *Longtime Californ': A Documentary Study of an American Chinatown.* New York: Pantheon, 1972.

Stevens, Wallace. "Disillusionment of Ten O'Clock." *Collected Poems.* New York: Random House, 1982. 66.

Ueki, Teruyo. "Asian American Family of Storytellers: Maxine Hong Kingston's Metaphors." *Eikoku Bugaku Techo [English Literature Journal,* Kyoto] 22 (1984): 55.

Ruth Rosenberg

The Ghost Story as Aggada

Cynthia Ozick's "The Pagan Rabbi" and Sheindel's Scar

ERICH AUERBACH'S ACCLAIMED critical work, *Mimesis*, opens with an interpretation of Odysseus's scar. Its precisely rendered visibility is what makes it typical of Homeric narrative strategy, as Auerbach notes. A consideration of the distinction between Odysseus's scar and the scar of the widow Sheindel in Cynthia Ozick's "The Pagan Rabbi" helps to illuminate the differences between the Hellenic and the Hebraic narrative traditions, and indicates the context within which Ozick has adapted the ghost story genre to Jewish themes and concerns.

According to Auerbach, "The Homeric style knows only a foreground, only a uniformly illuminated, uniformly objective present" (5). In Hellenic epic, he observes, "everything is visible," everything is "clearly outlined" and "totally foregrounded" (2). The Hebraic style is profoundly different. Instead of a clearly delineated and brightly illuminated scene, it presents only heard voices. Auerbach notes that the sacrifice of Isaac opens with God calling Abraham: "We only hear His voice, and that utters nothing but a name . . . and of Abraham too nothing is made perceptible except the words in which he answers" (6). Nothing is described. Nothing is located in time or space. Everything is so indeterminate, so obscure and enigmatic, that it places great demands upon the reader. The biblical epic, like the mark on Sheindel's cheek in the Ozick story, must be interpreted in terms of history. Its narrative style is "fraught with background" (6). Its hidden depths insist upon interpretation. The Greek epic, in its lavish descriptions, sought only to give pleasure. The Hebrew epic, lacking even in adjectives, seeks to impose truth: "The Bible's claim to truth is not only far more urgent than Homer's, it is tyrannical—it excludes all other claims" (12).

The clash of these two cultures has been a persistent theme of Cynthia Ozick's fiction, and nowhere more so than in "The Pagan Rabbi." The narrator of the story has heard of the suicide by hanging of his old friend, Rabbi Isaac Kornfeld, and has gone first to see the tree where Isaac was found and then to visit Isaac's widow, Sheindel, with some hope of marrying her himself. The fathers of both the narrator and Isaac were distinguished rabbis who "vied with one another in demonstrations of charitableness, in the captious glitter of their scholia, in the number of their adherents" (3). The only issue on which they agree is that Greek thought is "an abomination" (3). Vehemently, they both condemn pagan idolatry. Yet both rabbinic dynasties are doomed to be lost. Of the two sons, who had been classmates in the seminary, one, from overmuch reading of philosophy, became an atheist and withdrew from the study of the Law; the other, from too much reading of Romantic poetry, became a pagan and hanged himself from a tree in a public park. What led to Rabbi Isaac Kornfeld's suicide is interpreted by the narrator from two documents removed from the dead man's pockets and given to Sheindel, Isaac's widow. One is a small notebook, containing entries in Greek, Hebrew, and English. The other Sheindel angrily describes as a "love letter" (18); it records Isaac's conversion to animism, his copulation with a dryad, and his confrontation with his newly "liberated" soul, figured as an old man with a pack of books on his back. To the narrator's horror, Sheindel condemns him bitterly: "I think he was never a Jew" (13).

If the unnamed fathers, the anonymous narrator, the unspecified locale, the indeterminate time, and the invisibility of the characters were not enough to mark this narrative as Hebraic, the overheard voices that substitute for description should do so. For example, we know that Sheindel has beautiful hair only because the narrator's "Puritan" ex-wife remarked upon it at Sheindel's wedding (7). For the most part, characters are defined by their moral positions, and this strategy is centrally Jewish. An ethical posture takes the place of a physical appearance. In contrast, as Auerbach notes, Homeric narrative "delights in physical existence" and by making that perceptible, "bewitches, ingratiates, and ensnares us into sharing that reality" (Auerbach 10–11). That reality "conceals nothing, contains no teaching, has no secret second meaning" (11). The Hebraic mode, in contrast, "does not court our favor by pleasing us" (11); rather, it demands that we subordinate our reality to its absolute demand for priority.

Lest we miss this claim, Ozick has pointed to it in her epigraph. Prefacing her story is a lesson from "The Ethics of the Fathers," insisting that scripture takes precedence over nature: "Rabbi Jacob said: 'He who is walking along and studying, but then breaks off to remark, "How lovely is that tree!" or "How beautiful is that fallow field!"—Scripture regards such a one as having hurt his own being'" (3). Ozick's parable contemporizes this description. A Talmudic scholar is deluded into addressing a young oak tree as "Loveliness." The concluding episode dramatizes how deeply this interruption of his study by the beauties of nature has hurt his being. He not only fails to recognize but vehemently repudiates his emanation, his soul, which appears to him as a spectral figure studying Scripture as it walks along a dusty road. At the same instant that he disavows his soul, his body shrivels like a withered leaf. He is already dead, has already separated soul from body.

In rewriting "The Ethics of the Fathers" for a contemporary audience as an encounter with a ghostly double, Ozick is simultaneously revoicing yet revising her literary "fathers." For thirteen years she was haunted by the "master," Henry James. From the age of twenty-two to the age of thirty-five, she was held in thrall by James, having first succumbed to his spell when, as a graduate student, she wrote her thesis on him. So absolute was her apprenticeship that she felt herself becoming transformed into "the elderly bald-headed Henry James" (Ozick, "Lesson" 294). She wrote, in "The Lesson of the Master": "You could see the light glancing off my pate; you could see my heavy chin, my watch chain, my walking stick, my tender paunch" (294). Under his domination she determined to craft a Jamesian masterpiece. Her immense novel, *Trust*, which ran more than eight hundred manuscript pages, was begun in 1957 and finally finished in 1963. To her disappointment, it "did not speak to the Gentiles, for whom it had been begun, nor to the Jews, for whom it had been finished" ("Lesson" 158). Significantly, what "judaized" her style was thinking through the novel's only Jewish character. By formulating the question, "What is it to think as a Jew?" ("Lesson" 157), she succeeded in freeing herself from her long indenture to the "religion of art." The offerings laid on its altar began to seem increasingly idolatrous to her in the light of the second commandment, and she began to think of that prohibition as requiring a perceptual shift. Were her essays indexed, the longest entry would no doubt appear under the term "idolatry." The Mosaic injunction against images freed Ozick from the Jamesian stress on a visual center of consciousness that sees all, the perceiving eye upon which nothing is lost.

Ozick has often mentioned that Judaism begins with the "Shema," meaning "hear." The devout Jew listens to the word of God. Jean-François Lyotard writes: "In Hebraic ethics, representation is forbidden; the eye closes; the ear opens" (Lyotard 402). To underscore Rabbi Kornfeld's transgression, the author literally underlined his narcissistic wish: "To *see* the soul, to confront it—that is divine wisdom" (Ozick, "Pagan Rabbi" 21). When his blasphemous desire is granted and his soul, disengaged from his body, faces him, he rejects it. "Didn't you wish to see me with your own eyes?" it asks (35). Rabbi Kornfeld's body shrieks, "It is not mine!" (35). This scenario may be a conscious reworking of Edith Wharton's famous story, "The Eyes," in which a man is periodically confronted with a pair of supernatural eyes that reflect his own dissolution but which he does not identify as his own. As in Ozick's story, a supernatural apparition dramatizes the extreme state of the viewer's soul, but the rabbi sees not what he has become but what he has lost.

The loss is rendered, however, in aural, not visual, terms, specifically Jewish terms. The soul tells him, "If you had not contrived to be rid of me, I would have stayed with you till the end . . . In your grave beside you, I would have sung you David's songs, I would have moaned Solomon's voice to your last grain of bone. But you expelled me" (36). Rabbi Kornfeld could have been comforted throughout eternity by the Psalms and the Song of Songs. Instead, through his own insistence on specular reflection, he will be deaf to the Word of the invisible God who manifests Himself only as a voice and has banned the making of images. Having carefully laid the ground that, for the pious, the truth is heard, Ozick shows the extent of his breach of the Covenant by depriving the Rabbi of the participation in the communal "Hear O Israel."

For Ozick, finding an authentically Jewish narrative strategy that encompassed this shift of emphasis from the eye to the ear liberated her from James's influence and allowed her to serve as a cultural ambassador in her own right. Invited to speak in Israel in 1970, she advocated a turning away from the "aestheticized, paganized, parodistic forms of fiction" toward a "centrally Jewish" genre ("New Yiddish" 164, 169).

What Ozick proposed specifically was a return to parable, in Hebrew "Aggada," rabbinic narrative. Aggada comprises one-quarter of the Talmud; the rest is called "Halacha," and consists of legal material. According to Susan Handelman, these narratives are so highly regarded that "a lesson derived from a story where the principle was applied has greater substantiality than a direct statement of the principle!" (66). Furthermore, she continues, "a law derived from a *story* in the Talmud has greater validity than a law directly stated in the Talmud" (66). So Aggada was valued over Halacha. Ozick urged other American-Jewish writers to experiment with the form "utilizing every innovative device," every possible linguistic technique, every available authorial strategy, even those developed by Romantic aestheticism, so long as they were adapted to the Jewish worldview ("New Yiddish" 175). Such aggadic fictions could prove, in her words, "significant literature capable of every conceivable resonance" (174).

Because aggadic fiction conveys its meaning implicitly, however, rather than didactically, those who miss the generic clues will misunderstand. Two examples from critics who misread "The Pagan Rabbi" by misunderstanding its genre illustrate such skewed responses. Catherine Rainwater and William Scheick read the story within the genre conventions of "popular romance" and find it to be "about metamorphosis and enchantment" (72). Victor Strandberg approaches it from the conventions of Frazer's *The Golden Bough* and finds it to be an instance of ritual magic in the sacred grove, going so far as to assert: "It is Pan who prevails over Moses in this encounter. Death here becomes (as Walt Whitman called it) a promotion rather than a punishment" (103). Both responses miss the story's parabolic nature, overlooking the epigraph and the significance of its echo in the climax, when the pagan rabbi confronts his soul.

An even more egregious example of misreading is Ruth Wisse's. Wisse ignores all of Ozick's denunciations of "aestheticism" and reads "The Pagan Rabbi" as the externalization of an inner, suppressed "aestheticist longing." To compound this misattribution, the critic then categorizes it as sentimental ghetto fiction.

> Into the mouth of the errant rabbi the author has put part of her own aestheticist longings, raising worship of the beautiful to the highest philosophic and religious pitch, but only to oppose it finally, almost pitilessly, in the name of religious values . . . One of the most pervasive subjects of the modern Yiddish and Hebrew literary tradition is the rediscovery of those natural human instincts which would free the dust-choked ghetto Jew from the stifling repression of "halakhah" and religious inhibitions. In the works of Mendele, Sholem Aleichem, Peretz, Bialik, Feierberg, and Tchernikovsky, the physical world of sun, storm, trees, and rivers provides a model of freedom counterposed to the self-denial of shtetl culture. (Wisse 41)

Yet Ozick goes out of her way to make Rabbi Kornfeld's "aestheticist longings" appear ludicrous, utterly unfounded on reality. He has gone from park to park, looking for the right setting in which to contemplate the beauties of nature. What he finds is a waste land, as the narrator describes it: "The tree was almost alone in a long rough meadow, which sloped down to a bay filled with sickly clams and a bad smell. The place was called Trilham's Inlet, and I knew what the smell meant: that cold brown water covered half the city's turds" ("Pagan Rabbi" 4). Where is that lyrically evoked world of sunshine? The weather in Ozick's text is "bleary with fog" (4), a beating rain falls (5), flattening decaying leaves. Where are the fresh air and the green grass luring scholars away from the ghetto? Ozick shows us an abandoned plastic wreath on the "rusting grasses" (4) and bulldozers biting "into the park" where "the rolled carcasses of trees" are stacked (4). Far from an enticement, the landscape emits "a stench of sewage" (5). No fresh breezes blow, only "a wind blowing out a braid of excremental malodor into the heated air" (29). By relying upon the eyes that feed his "aestheticist longings," Rabbi Kornfeld is duped into seeing what is not there.

The point being illuminated in the parable could not have been more tellingly made than by these critical commentaries. One's expectations are conditioned by what one has read. If one comes to a tale of oreads, nymphs, and dryads from a familiarity with Ovid's *Metamorphoses*, one will see it as an example of romance. If one approaches it from the perspective of the ritual slaughter of the king, then one focuses on the archetypal tree. If one's frame of reference is the shtetl culture, then one ignores all the cues that invalidate its appropriation into that tradition. The details fail to fall into place until the appropriate schema has been selected.

The danger, as the epigraph suggests, lies in lifting one's eyes from the appropriate book. The claim being made in this passage from "The Ethics of the Fathers" is that study of the Halacha has absolute priority. This is borne out by a pun. The Hebrew word derives from a root meaning "to walk" or "the way." Talmudic scholars studying Halacha as they walk figure prominently in the prefatory opening and in the closure of the story. Therefore, to interrupt one's concentration on scripture is to lose one's way. Furthermore, implicit in the epigraph are the defenses against so going astray. In the same tractate of the Mishnah as the quotation from Rabbi Jacob are the discussions of the "Fences around the Law." These safeguards against transgressions are called "takkanot" (enactments) and "gezerot" (decrees) in "The Ethics of the Fathers" (1:1).

To guard against being misled and losing the path, all the characters allude frequently to these fences. The most tragic such allusion is tattooed on Sheindel's cheek. The barb of the electrified fence around the concentration camp where she had been born and orphaned cut an asterisk-shaped scar into her face. Only seventeen when she married Isaac, the widow who bore him seven daughters asked why God had spared her from the Holocaust only to let her wed a transgressor: "I was that man's wife, he scaled the Fence of the Law. For this God preserved me from the electric fence" ("Pagan Rabbi" 24). More than a visual detail, Sheindel's scar carries the symbolic weight of individual and cultural history.

The secularized narrator, who has become a bookseller and therefore a reader of and trafficker in the wrong books, reads Sheindel's scar accordingly, as an "asterisk" that pointed to "certain dry footnotes" (7), namely, that for a woman, she is "astonishingly learned" (7). Thus even with the help of footnotes he cannot interpret the meaning of Rabbi Kornfeld's death or the rage and bitterness of his widow. The narrator further demonstrates his own lack of midrashic exegesis by his inability to interpret Isaac's notebook. He has lost the rabbinic method for making inferences from conjoined passages or "smuchin." The juxtaposed Greek, Hebrew, and English verses are dismissed by him as meaningless; but to the pious widow, they record her husband's growing paganism. She taunts the narrator for his incomprehension by telling him he "can't follow" (18, 37).

Scornfully, Sheindel begins to read him the letter in which her husband had argued that animism had a "continuous, but covert expression, even within the Fence of the Law" (20). Shortly afterward, the narrator reads Rabbi Kornfeld's account of an incident in which he saw a ghostly figure save his daughter from drowning. Sheindel "maliciously" accuses her husband of going out of his way to find "proofs" for what he saw (25), in other words, of attempting to alter the shape of the Fence of the Law to suit his convenience. When the narrator wonders at such skepticism in a woman so pious, Sheindel tells him: "Only an atheist could ask such a question" (25). She continues: "The more piety, the more skepticism. A religious man comprehends this. Superfluity, excess of custom, and superstition would climb like a choking vine on the Fence of the Law if skepticism did not continually hack them away to make freedom for purity" (25). Adherence to the Law does not imply blindness but rather a reasoned observation from the perspective of the Law, from within the Fence of the Law.

Since Ozick has characterized herself repeatedly as a rationalist, Sheindel's defense of her skepticism might well denote her status as authorial persona. To one interviewer, Ozick said: "I myself am hostile to the whole mystical enterprise. I'm a rationalist, and

I'm a skeptic" (Ottenberg 65). To another she said: "Ancestrally, I stem from the Mitnagged tradition, which is superrational and super-skeptical. That's the part of me that writes the essays and has no patience with anything mystical" (Blake 66).

This last comment suggests that the traditions of Judaism are multiple and distinct. On the basis of an onomastic link between Rabbi Kornfeld's legal wife and his illicit consort, one could argue a connection between the normative and covert traditions of Judaism. The spirit with whom Isaac coupled is repeatedly addressed by him as "Loveliness" (20, 23, 24, 32, 36). The Yiddish word for "Loveliness" is "Sheindel." This would suggest that the Rabbi's nocturnal search for manifestations of animism, or the secrets of the Zohar and of other "hidden" texts that had been suppressed in the interests of normative Judaism, was an effort to recover those censored heresies that ran counter to the official religion. In short, he was turning from the embraces of legitimate Judaism to embrace its forbidden doctrines. Gershom Scholem, whom Ozick visited in Israel, had made the recovery of this suppressed religion his lifelong project. In "The Magisterial Reach of Gershom Scholem," Ozick described his search as having sprung from a desire to revitalize religion for assimilated German-Jewish intellectuals like his friend, Walter Benjamin.

The counterargument to legitimizing Kabbala, however, is the most compellingly significant way of regarding Sheindel's scar. It gathers resonance when one weighs all the accumulated references to the Fence of the Law. If the mark of the Holocaust on Sheindel's cheek is taken as a sign that only a remnant of European Jewry escaped the furnaces, then the issue being raised in Ozick's parable is the survival of Judaism itself. Against the six million slaughtered and the thousands assimilated in the diaspora, where are those to inherit and to transmit the Covenant?

The story privileges Sheindel's survival, and indicates that hers is the appropriate form of "loveliness"—the beauty of the Law, the mark of which she carries on her cheek. Yet in linguistic citations, an asterisk denotes an anomalous form. Such an unattested entity is a pious and learned woman in the eyes of a patriarchal religion. Better qualified by virtue of her understanding than either of the former rabbinical students to transmit the Law, she cannot. And the narrator proposes to perpetuate her limited role as wife and mother by marrying her after a suitable period has elapsed. Yet the scar and the learning it represents to him make her inaccessible to him. Her command of the intricacies of the Law is a wasted resource to an orthodox community where women are consigned, in the synagogue, to a place behind the curtain. Therefore, the narrator's dilemma comes to stand for a historical impasse. The very intellectual gifts that render her incomprehensible to Gentiles are, by virtue of her gender, unavailable to those most urgently in need of them. This situation acquires further resonance against suggestions that she is the authorial persona.

An exploration of the layers of possible meaning for Sheindel's scar is typical of the reading required by Hebraic narrative. Robert Alter has said of Talmudic scholarship: "Meaning was conceived as a *process,* requiring continual revision—both in the ordinary sense and in the etymological sense of seeing-again— continual suspension of judgment, weighing of multiple possibilities, brooding over gaps in the information provided" (12). Alter's visual metaphor interrogates Rabbi Kornfeld's scholarly credentials; unlike the skeptical Sheindel, he does not question what he sees. He is not sufficiently critical. To the extent to which he is pursuing a hidden or suppressed truth, however, Rabbi Kornfeld is another Talmudic exegete in pursuit of endlessly deferred meanings. His quest is paralleled by that of the narrator, who is looking for the meaning of the rabbi's death but frustrated by the complexities of the meanings he encounters.

A further footnote to which Sheindel's scar may allude would involve Ozick's views of the Romantics, especially Wordsworth. Lionel Trilling asserted in "Wordsworth and the Rabbis" that Rabbi Jacob's warnings against nature implied four latent affinities between "the Law, as the Rabbis understood it, and Nature, as Wordsworth understood that" (125). Ozick's indignation at this equation spilled out in fiery polemics in three essays published in *Art and Ardor*. She considers "Tintern Abbey" a step away from the Nazi furnaces. The rationale for this denunciation derives from the view that nature-worship is idolatrous, a pantheism that assaults monotheism. The very worship of inert matter, for which Trilling had praised Wordsworth—"when sentience was like a rock or a stone or a tree . . . then existence was blessed" (131)—makes the poet blasphemous. And all Romantic quests for the muses in bushes or brooks are similar violations. For Ozick, such mystical impulses are sinister, decadent, diabolical, insidious, demonic, destructive forces. She condemns magic as the dark death-drive, as the "yetzer ha-ra" (evil impulse). To her, Wordsworth's contemplation of his own mind as it reflected back to him from a benign landscape is a profanity in its narcissistic, self-reflexive deification of his own creativity.

The author's attitudes, made so explicit in her essays, align her stance to the moral posture assumed by her fictive counterpart, Sheindel. They both depict themselves as wielding pruning shears, or sheathed in heavy garden gloves, tearing away the choking vines that are "excrescences" on the Fence. Their vehement energy scarcely enables them to keep pace with the unhealthy growths choking its "purity." It consumes all their strength to rip away these weeds that sprout up and strangle. They hack, and slash, and rip out, and still the Fence is entangled. The task Ozick set herself in her aggadic fiction is to represent this struggle with every literary device available. The olfactory imagery alone should have indicated her attitude toward nature-worship. But for those readers who, because of their own preoccupations, missed the fetid stench, the ghost is there to remind them that reality resides only in the text from out of which the universe was created. "To understand creation, one looks, *not to nature*, but to the Torah," Handelman writes (38). The possibilities of the ghost story form, a form favored by Ozick's old master Henry James, to warn against the purely visual by exploiting the visual supernatural were recognized by Ozick in "The Pagan Rabbi."

The centrality of the Torah is lyrically envisioned in the epiphanic ending of Ozick's aggadic rendition of "The Ethics of the Fathers." Isaac Kornfeld beholds his soul as "a dusty old man" with "a matted beard" who is "walking on the road" and "reading as he goes" (34). He "reads the Law" and "passes indifferent through the beauty of the field" (35); "his nostrils sniff his book as if flowers lay on the clotted page" (35): " 'I will walk here alone always, in my garden'—he scratched his page—'with my precious birds'—he scratched at the letters—'and my darling trees'—he scratched at the tall side-column of commentary. . . . 'The sound of the Law,' he said, 'is more beautiful than the crickets. The smell of the Law is more radiant than the moss. The taste of the Law exceeds clear water' " (36).

Works Cited

Alter, Robert. *The Art of Biblical Narrative.* New York: Basic Books, 1981.

Auerbach, Erich. *Mimesis: The Representation of Reality in Western Literature.* Trans. Willard Trask. Garden City, NY: Doubleday, 1953.

Blake, Patricia. "A New Triumph for Idiosyncrasy." *Time* 5 Sept. 1983: 64–66.

Cole, Diane. "Ozick, Cynthia." *Dictionary of Literary Biography.* Ed. Daniel Walden. Detroit: Gale Research, 1984, Vol. 28.

Handelman, Susan A. *The Slayers of Moses: The Emergence of Rabbinic Interpretation in Modern Literary Theory.* Albany: State U of New York P, 1982.

Lyotard, Jean-François. "Jewish Oedipus." *Genre* 10 (1977): 395–411.

Ottenberg, Eve. "The Rich Visions of Cynthia Ozick." *New York Times Magazine* 10 April 1983: 47–65.

Ozick, Cynthia. "The Lesson of the Master." *Art and Ardor*. New York: Knopf, 1971. 291–305.

———. "The Pagan Rabbi." *The Pagan Rabbi and Other Stories*. New York: Knopf, 1971. 3–37.

———. "Toward a New Yiddish." *Art and Ardor*. New York: Knopf, 1983. 151–77.

———. "We are the Crazy Lady and Other Feisty Feminist Fables." *Ms. Magazine* Spring 1982: 40–44.

Pollitt, Katha. "The Three Selves of Cynthia Ozick." *New York Times Book Review* 22 May 1983: 7, 35.

Rainwater, Catherine and William J. Scheick. "The Unsurprise of Surprise." *Cynthia Ozick*. Ed. Harold Bloom. Modern Critical Views. New York: Chelsea House, 1986. 69–78.

Strandberg, Victor. "The Art of Cynthia Ozick." *Cynthia Ozick*. Ed. Harold Bloom. Modern Critical Views. New York: Chelsea House, 1986. 79–120.

Trilling, Lionel. "Wordsworth and the Rabbis." *The Opposing Self: Nine Essays in Criticism*. London: Secker & Warburg, 1955. 118–50.

Wisse, Ruth R. "American Jewish Writing Act II." *Commentary* June 1976: 40–45.

Barbara Hill Rigney

"A Story to Pass On"

Ghosts and the Significance of History in Toni Morrison's *Beloved*

"NOT A HOUSE IN THE COUNTRY ain't packed to its rafters with some dead Negro's grief," says the wise woman in Toni Morrison's *Beloved* (5). Morrison's historic world is so unnatural, so horrific and brutal, that the only "natural" element is the supernatural. The spirit world is everywhere—in the houses, in the trees, in the rivers, manifested in hellish light or in hands that reach out to caress or to strangle—and it represents, finally, the ultimate Black revolution against slavery: the insistence on the link with Africa, the insistence on a myth beyond history and on an identity that is both racial and individual.

"History," for Morrison and for the characters in *Beloved*, most of whom are Black, is the reality of slavery. The "rememories" are a catalogue of atrocities, gross sexual indignities, a denial of human rights on every level. From "Sweet Home" in Kentucky to the chain gangs of Georgia, the Black experience in the American South is, as Margaret Atwood says in her *New York Times* review of *Beloved*, "as bad as can be imagined" (49). So terrible are her memories that Sethe, who is the focus of the novel and Morrison's re-creation of an actual historical figure, has killed her own infant daughter to protect her from the violations of slavery. Sethe spends her present "beating back the past" (73), her eyes blank and expressionless, "two open wells that did not reflect firelight" (9). Black history, thus, is fragmented into symbols, objects the color of blood: a piece of red ribbon with the black hair and chunk of scalp still attached, the chokecherry tree scars on Sethe's back, and Paul D's "loss of a red, red heart" (235). Morrison's novel is about "the people of broken necks, of fire-cooked blood and black girls who had lost their ribbons. What a roaring" (182).

Among slavery's crimes is the theft of identity, the inflicted loss of a name and of a culture. Paul D, "the last of the Sweet Home Men" (6), is one in a series of Pauls. Baby Suggs was called "Jenny" most of her enslaved life. People have no last names, having had no identifiable fathers and very little claim to their mothers. Sethe's own mother is nameless and faceless, a straw hat seen from a distance in a field, a mark beneath the breast the only identification: "Here. Look here. This is your ma'am. If you can't tell me by my face, look here" (176). Names, in fact, are often replaced in Morrison's works by brands, marks of Cain that both distinguish and protect: Sula's roselike birthmark in *Sula*, Pilate's smooth navel-less stomach in *Song of Solomon*, Sethe's chokecherry tree, the scar like a smile on the throat of Beloved left by her mother's gift of death. This is Beloved's only mark, for, coming from the spirit world, even her palms are without lines. Beloved's single name is taken from her tombstone, the engraving paid for by her mother with ten minutes of sex. Like that of Stamp Paid, Beloved's name represents a claim to freedom, a debt paid with the highest of prices: "Everybody knew what she was called, but nobody anywhere knew her name. . . . how can they call her if they don't know her name?" (174).

The disintegration of family, the denial of a mother's right to love her daughter, Morrison reiterates, is also part of the horror of the Black experience under slavery. Like Sethe, Baby Suggs also did not have an identifiable mother and so considers that she does not know herself, "having never had the map to discover what she was like. Could she sing? . . . Was she pretty?" (140). The final insult, the ultimate cruelty, which causes Sethe to flee Sweet Home is not the beating that results in the chokecherry tree scars, but that act of School Teacher's nephews "taking her milk," holding her down and sucking milk from her breasts, thus violating the sacred state of motherhood. Both Sethe and Baby Suggs, who has lost all her daughters and cannot even remember "the fingers, nor their nails" (176), are symbolic of violated motherhood and of the African spiritual values that state represents. According to Karla F. C. Holloway in *New Dimensions of Spirituality*, much of Morrison's work embodies "a celebration of African archetypes" (160), the most important of which is the Great Mother, the giver of both life and wisdom. The mother represents *nommo*, the creative potential, which is the sacred aspect of nature itself. Sethe recounts her love for her children, her sense of herself as Great Mother: "It felt good. Good and right. I was big . . . and deep and wide and when I stretched out my arms all my children could get in between" (162).

Sethe, and all the other women in Morrison's novels, are representatives of the powers of nature, no matter how subverted those powers might be by circumstance or the realities of history. Like Sula, who can change the weather and identifies herself with the redwood tree, and like Pilate, who can defy gravity and teach men to fly, and like the mystical women who hang from the trees in *Tar Baby*, Sethe is one with nature as she is one with her chokecherry tree. Baby Suggs, too, is holy, able to feed hundreds with a single bucket of blackberries, able to summon the spirits that pervade the forest clearing where she preaches. Hers is "the heart that pumped out love, the mouth that spoke the Word" (180). Beloved, too, is as much an incarnation of nature as she is of the supernatural, coming back from dark waters in search of Sethe, who is the map of her self.

Also like nature, the African Great Mother can kill as well

as create; she is Kali as well as Demeter. Holloway writes of *Sula*, "Morrison has shown us the incredible potential invested in creative power by noting that the extreme of creativity is destruction" (24). As Eva Peace sets fire to her own son in *Sula*, as Pilate Dead almost literally loves her granddaughter Hagar to death in *Song of Solomon*, so Sethe kills her daughter because "the best thing she was, was her children. Whites might dirty *her* all right, but not her best thing, her beautiful, magical best thing—that part of her that was clean" (151). Sethe's mother-love is so strong that, like Demeter, she can also resurrect that daughter, bring her back as tall and "thunder-black and glistening" (261), an image of Africa itself. Beloved is a ghost, but she is also part of Sethe's lost African self and that African view of nature as imbued with spirits and life. According to Wilfred Cartey in "Africa of My Grandmother's Singing," within the African view of nature, "nothing is dead, no voice is still. An essential continuity is preserved between earth-mother and child" (qtd. by Holloway and Demetrokopoulos 118). Denver, Sethe's remaining daughter, asks her mother about the ghost who haunts them: "If it's still there, waiting, that must mean that nothing ever dies." And Sethe responds, "Nothing ever does" (36).

If the continuity between earth-mother and child is broken, as it is so violently broken under slavery, then it cannot be restored without further violence. Beloved is not a benign spirit, and she does demand retribution. She is, as Denver describes her, not evil, just "rebuked. Lonely and rebuked" (13). Beloved, in her turn, will love Sethe almost to death, drinking her life as she once drank her milk, alienating her from Denver and from Paul D, who does not deserve it, because he has the "blessedness" that has made him "the kind of man who could walk into a house and make the women cry. Because with him, in his presence, they could" (17). Paul D is blessed, not only because he too has suffered, but also because he reverences the Great Mother in Sethe, worshipping every line of her chokecherry tree and loving her with respect.

However, in the kind of pre-Oedipal bonding that occurs between mothers and daughters in the absence of fathers, which also characterizes the female families in *Sula* and *Song of Solomon*, there is no room for men in Sethe's world. Rather, there is the merging of female personalities, even to the point of the disintegration of the boundaries of identity. Denver immediately recognizes her sisterhood with Beloved, having taken her sister's blood along with her mother's milk. Sethe and Beloved finally become one voice in the novel: "I am Beloved and she is mine. . . . I am not separate from her there is no place where I stop her face is my own and I want to be there in the place where her face is and to be looking at it too" (210).

Paul D's arrival can disperse the red light and end the antics of the baby ghost, but he cannot dislodge the spirit that is the grown Beloved manifested in the flesh. Nor can any single woman stop the destruction of Sethe by her spirit daughter; such magic requires a crowd of women, strong Black women who march together to Sethe's house to perform the necessary exorcism, searching "for the right combination, the key, the code, the sound that broke the back of words. Building voice upon voice until they found it, and when they did it was a wave of sound wide enough to sound deep water and knock the pods off chestnut trees. It broke over Sethe and she trembled like the baptized in its wash" (261).

The spirit of Beloved, thus, is relegated to the fringes of consciousness, to the watery essence from which she came, and to the world of myth that is the lost African identity. She remains there, where "her footprints come and go, come and go. They are so familiar. Should a child, and adult place his feet in them, they will fit" (275). Paul D can return to complete the separation, which is also the reintegration, the rebirth, of Sethe: "You your best thing, Sethe. You are" (273). Denver can also leave her mother and her house, find herself an identity that is not a dream, and make a place for herself in the world.

Obviously, *Beloved* is not an ordinary ghost story, certainly not the Henry James kind of psychological thriller that depends upon the psychopathology of the protagonist. Sethe's burnt-out eyes, Baby Suggs's depression before she dies, Paul D's uncontrollably trembling hands are all sane reactions to an insane world. Sethe asks herself, "Other people went crazy, why couldn't she? Other people's brains stopped, turned around and went on to something new." (70). But Morrison's characters are survivors, condemned to life and to sanity, and the spirits they see are as real as the history they endure. Ghosts are more real even than God; finally the spirit world is part of that form of grace that baby Suggs promises her followers: "She told them that the only grace they could have was the grace they could imagine. That if they could not see it, they would not have it" (88).

Morrison says again and again that the story of Beloved is "not a story to pass on" (275). But Sethe has told it, and Paul D and Stamp Paid and Baby Suggs and finally, Denver has told it. Like Baby Suggs, Sethe also speaks the "Word," recounting her "re-memories" in ritualized detail, singing them in made-up songs to her children, just as Paul D sang his passion in Georgia in songs that were "flat-headed nails for pounding and pounding and pounding" (40). Inherent in the songs, which are subversive and unintelligible to white listeners, is the lost language of Africa and of Sethe's mother, "which would never come back" (62). But, of course, it does. Holloway writes, "Black women carry the voice of the mother—they are the progenitors. . . . Women, as carriers of the *voice,* carry wisdom—mother-wit" (Holloway and Demetrokopoulos 123). The crime of history is that the mother-voice of memory and wisdom was silenced, however briefly, whether by the iron bit in the mouth—"how offended the tongue is, held down by iron" (71)—or by the creation of memories too traumatic to recall. But *Beloved* is full of wisdom and speaks the unspeakable; it is "a story to pass on."

Works Cited

Atwood, Margaret. Review of *Beloved. The New York Times Book Review* 13 Sept. 1987: 1, 49–50.

Holloway, Karla F. C., and Stephanie A. Demetrokopoulos. *New Dimensions of Spirituality: A Biracial and Bicultural Reading of the Novels of Toni Morrison.* Westport, CT: Greenwood, 1987.

Morrison, Toni. *Beloved.* New York: Knopf, 1987.

Wendy K. Kolmar

"Dialectics of Connectedness"

Supernatural Elements
in Novels by
Bambara, Cisneros, Grahn, and Erdrich

DURING THE SEVEN YEARS I have worked with women's ghost stories, I have been troubled by what seems to be an epistemological problem—at least for those of us who want to talk about women's writing—inherent in the way we define the genre of supernatural literature or perhaps inherent in the worldview propounded by the literature itself. Supernatural literature, traditionally, describes a world of dualisms: rational/irrational; human/ghostly; known world/unknown; natural/supernatural. As readers we are vested in the natural, knowable, rational, and human. Whether the story ultimately affirms this worldview, banishing the unknowable thing, or challenges its stability, the affect of the classic supernatural story seems to be to make us cling more closely to the rational side of those dichotomies, to reinforce the readers' sense that the world is in fact dualistic, that the present is distinct from the past, the living from the dead, the natural from the supernatural.

What troubles me then is that so often this is not the epistemology of women's stories. As feminist critics have repeatedly observed for other genres, women's work in this genre does not seem to fit; many women's ghost stories—not all, of course, for many are written as formulaic popular stories and seek to replicate the expected structures of the genre—seem to challenge this dualistic view of the universe. These supernatural stories seem to be one more place where women writers and thinkers explore the doubled or multiple vision that their insider/outsider status forces upon them.[1]

Rachel Duplessis, in her 1979 essay "For the Etruscans," suggests that this insider/outsider position is reflected in the literary forms women create. Duplessis writes:

> Insider/outsider social status will also help dissolve an either-or dualism. For the woman finds she is irreconcilable things: an outsider by her gender position, by her relation to power; maybe an insider by her social position, her class. She can be both. Her ontological, her psychic, her class position all cause doubleness. Doubled consciousness. Doubled understandings. How then could she neglect to invent a form which produces this incessant, critical, splitting motion. (278)

Women create, suggests Duplessis, forms which reflect a "both/ and vision. This is the end of the either-or, dichotomized universe." They propose forms and visions that are "in opposition to dualism, a dualism pernicious because it valorizes one side above another, and makes a hierarchy where there were simply twain" (276). Women, then, suggests Duplessis, "will produce art works that incorporate contradiction and nonlinear movement into the heart of the text" (278). In many women's supernatural stories we find, I think, just such texts.

To attempt to explore this idea briefly in relation to several par-

ticular texts, I have chosen four novels by contemporary American
women: Toni Cade Bambara's *The Salt Eaters*, the story of the
healing of Velma Henry after an attempted suicide and of the
healing through her of the Black community she inhabits; Sandra
Cisneros's *The House on Mango Street*, the story of Esperanza,
a Chicana girl growing up in her community; Louise Erdrich's
Tracks, the story of Fleur Pillager and the struggle of her Chippewa family to retain their beliefs and their land in the face of
the encroachment of Christianity, the government and the logging
companies; and Judy Grahn's *Mundane's World*, the story of the
initiation into womanhood of five young women in a matriarchal,
possibly prehistoric world.[2] In each of these texts that sense of
insider/outsider status, which Duplessis sees as inherent in being
a woman, is compounded by the marginalizing effects of race and
sexual preference, by the divided identity of living within and
between two cultures or two identities. The novels all draw, in
part, for their understanding of the supernatural on non-Western
traditions: Erdrich draws on Native American traditions passed
down to her through the stories of her grandfather; Bambara
draws on the voodoo and Yoruba strands of African religion;
Cisneros on the voodoo traditions in hispanic culture; and Grahn
on both African and Native American mythology, which she ex-
amines in her research for *Another Mother Tongue: Gay Words,
Gay Worlds*.[3]

These novels are not "ghost stories" in quite the same way as
other stories discussed in this collection; an encounter between
the story's protagonist and a ghost is not the central or even a
central part of their plot. In fact, it is, in a way, the absence of such
confrontations that I want to discuss. In each novel, the supernatural elements exist undifferentiated from the "present," "the
real," "the natural." Characters and readers do not confront them
as *other*, they are simply part of the experience of life and of the
text. As Gloria Hull suggests of the characters in *The Salt Eaters*:
"Some are quietly dead; others are roaming spirits. In many ways,

these distinctions are false and immaterial, for everyone we meet takes up essential space, and there is no meaningful difference between various states of corporeality/being/presence" (219). Each of these texts sets out to make "essential space" for creatures in "various states of corporeality/being/presence." In doing so, these texts become multilayered narratives that challenge dualistic categories and condemn the drawing of rigid boundaries between states of being, between moments in time, or even between species.

So, for example, in *The House on Mango Street*, "los espiritus" (60) visit the kitchen of the wise woman Elenita. Holy candles burn on the top of her refrigerator; "a plaster saint and a dusty Palm Sunday cross" adorn the kitchen walls along with a "picture of a voodoo hand." Elenita, the "witch woman" who "knows many thing" tells the protagonist's fortune with the tarot, while in the next room Elenita's children watch Bugs Bunny cartoons and drink Kool-Aid on the plastic slipcovered furniture. Esperanza sees her "whole life on that kitchen table: past, present, future" (60) and tries to feel on her hand the cold of the spirits, while a part of her mind is tuned to the favorite cartoon she hears from the other room. Waiting for the spirits at the kitchen table is made no stranger nor more unfamiliar here than sitting in the living room drinking Kool-Aid.

In *Salt Eaters*, a joke between two main characters, one human, one spirit, makes this same elision. In the midst of grappling with Velma Henry's illness and resistance to help, Minnie Ransom, the wise woman and healer who runs a clinic in Claybourne, Georgia's Black community, goes out to walk in her garden. There she seeks advice from her old friend and mentor, Old Wife, dead for several years, but no less present in Minnie's life. In the course of their conversation, Old Wife makes a joke about Oshun and Oye, sister spirits of the West African Yoruba tradition, that shows how little she differentiates the supposedly concrete world of the present from some other world of spirits. "Leastways, I know," says Old Wife, the spirit guide, to Minnie Ransom: "the Oshun ain't studyin this problem, Min, cause I hear Oshun and Oye prettyin up to hop a bus to New Orleans. Carnival in this town ain't fancy enough for them. Town gettin too small for some other proud spirits I could name too" (43). Clearly, the pun of "proud spirits" conflates Oshun and Oye with uppity folks who think they are too good for their neighbors. When Minnie objects to this joke, Old Wife continues: "I'm talking about them haints [i.e., ghosts, spirits] that're always up to some trickified business. They ride buses just the same's they ride brooms, peoples, carnival floats, whatever. All the same to them. What they care about scarin' people with they ghostly selves?" (43). Old Wife's summary comment, "I strictly do not mess with haints, Min," makes a double joke since she, not only imagines them on the bus to Mardi Gras, but is herself a spirit while she jokes. Minnie looks at her and makes "a full appraisal of this woman friend who'd been with her for most of her life, one way and then another. Nothing much had changed since she'd passed. Old Wife's complexion was still like mutton suet and brown gravy" (51). The powerful alliance of these two wise women and healers is unchanged by the death of the older one. They share and remember a history that connects them across the boundaries of time and death, and it is natural to them to see no distinction, to see spirits present throughout the ordinary experience of human life.

In Louise Erdrich's *Tracks*, too, the presence of ghosts and other nonrational elements is simply part of the experience and is also associated with history and memory. In this novel, the ghosts of members of the Pillager family roam the forest near Lake Matchimanito, the land that has always belonged to this Chippewa family: "The water was surrounded by the highest oaks and the woods inhabited by ghosts and by Pillagers who knew the secret ways to cure and kill, until their art deserted them" (2). When their art deserted them, the majority of the family perished in an epidemic, leaving only Fleur and her cousin Moses alive.

Nanapush, the narrator of half the novel and an elder of the tribe, imagines the spirits of the dead: "They would sit in the snow outside the door, waiting until from longing we joined them. We would all be together on the journey then, our destination the village at the end of the road where people gamble day and night but never lose money, eat but never fill their stomachs, drink but never leave their minds" (5). Fleur and her family ghosts are believed to have so harassed the local government agent that he is now "living in the woods and eating roots, gambling with ghosts" (5). Fleur herself is believed to have some extraordinary powers; she is said to have drowned three times and to be desired by the monster lake spirit, Mishepeshu.

Though Nanapush speaks with them, and others gamble with them, in this novel—unlike the other three—the ghosts inhabiting Fleur's wood are viewed with some fear, in part because they are the unsatisfied spirits of the unburied dead. The presence of these spirits identifies the wood Fleur inhabits as a place of powers and strangeness, but mainly for those in the community who are of mixed blood or are not Indian at all.

In *Mundane's World*, all states of being are comparable; there is distinction between them but no difference in this community governed by four matriarchal clans. One state is not valorized over another, not the living over the dead, nor the spirit over the body, nor the human over the plant or animal. Early in the novel, the permeability of the boundaries between states of being becomes clear in the situation of Lillian, a dead woman of the Bee clan, who moves from living woman to dead flesh to buzzard meat and free spirit: "The problem of a dead woman is too much property encasing the spirit because a wise buzzard does not care for hard surfaces and difficult entanglements. . . . A dead woman and her useless flesh that laid so heavy now that it could not move of its own volition has no other volition but to release her spirit. . . . As a body strives to release its spirit from the stuff of its former existence, it becomes more placid and unfeeling on the outside, but more moving on the inside" (20). Lillian's "free life spirit," freed from the burden of flesh by the buzzards, remains an essential being. In the description of this process, there are many perspectives—that of the buzzards, of Lillian, of her children, of her sister, Sophia—all perspectives given equal weight in the narrative. The human perspective is not valorized over that of spirit, tree, or animal. Later in the novel, Ernesta, one of the five girls initiated at the end of the novel is taken by her mother, Donna, to meet the "scheming weed," a twisted plant on the mountainside outside of town, whose spirit is her "spirit mate." This weed schemes for "a release from her confinement . . . for an animal who will take an interest in her berries" (68–69). The genius or spirit double of this plant "had for several years been reaching out to find the woman Donna's genius reaching back." Ultimately, Donna's spirit joins with the spirit of the nightshade; and Ernesta nurtures the plant they become and names it/them "Belladonna." From experiences such as this one, Ernesta learns to "see on two levels at once" (154), the mode of vision that is critical to a life in Mundane's world.

In part through the presence of the supernatural in these novels, the characters come to inhabit and to value liminal spaces, the spaces between, because they are the material of connection rather than separation; they, like the novels that describe them, are the spaces where many modes of experience meet. "Space ties everything altogether," says Mother Mundane in Grahn's novel. She teaches the girls to make nets "because in a net the spaces are as important throughout as the cord" (158). Fleur's spirit-inhabited wood at the end of *Tracks* is such a space, for a moment before its destruction. The Monkey Garden of *Mango Street* is such a space, a space in which the community's children disappear, a space that they imagine "could hide things for a thousand years." There Esperanza goes to hide herself from the ugliness of adult sexuality, where she tries to "will my blood to stop," where she hopes to "turn into the rain, my eyes melt into the ground like two black snails" (90). In *The Salt Eaters*, the town itself, poised for its spring festival, becomes such a space/place by the end of the novel.

In these novels, separation, self-involvement, isolation are problematic denials of connection. They mean an abandonment of the double or multiple vision crucial to the novel, for a perspective that is monofocal, for a life that is locked into one plane of experience. It is symptomatic of Velma's illness in *The Salt Eaters* that she covets separateness; she wishes to be the sand sealed in the hour glass. She longs "to be that sealed—sound, taste, air, nothing seeping in. To be that unavailable at last, sealed in and the noise of the world, the garbage locked out" (19). In *Mundane's World*, too, a refusal of interconnection is the cause of disruption in the society. Part of the explanation of Lillian's death is to be found in her own failures, her daughter learns. Lillian has been "doing her living in one straight line" (180); "she is trapped in a singularity of partial time" (181); "she does not trust interconnection" (180). In *Tracks*, Pauline, a mixed-blood whose narrative is set up against that of the Chippewa elder Nanapush, also distrusts connection and becomes an isolate. She joins an order of nuns and subjects herself to inordinate physical abuse at the same time trying to disrupt the lives and beliefs of Fleur's family. Pauline's image in the book is of the solitary watcher at the bedsides of the dying. Her laying out of the dead, her seeing them out of the world through Christian offices, seems in direct opposition to Fleur's spirit-inhabited wood and Nanapush's spirit-inhabited narrative.

Their supernatural elements are crucial to establishing these novels, both in form and content, as narratives of multiplicity and connection. They might all be defined as what Gloria Hull in her essay on *Salt Eaters* calls "a dialectic of connectedness." Each text proposes interconnection—between beings, between times— as the critical mode of organization—of human life and of narrative. Bambara herself, in an interview, describes *The Salt Eaters* as a novel that seeks "to bridge the gap, to merge . . . frames of reference, to fuse . . . camps" (Tate 16). In the same interview, she says that one basic perception offered by the novel is that "the universe is elegantly simple." We "blind ourselves and bind ourselves," she says, to avoid perceiving "the simple realities like the fact that everything is one in this place, on this planet. We and everything here are extensions of the same consciousness, and we are co-creators of that mind, will, thought" (24). This co-creation is clear in Minnie Ransom. Connections across space are the source of Minnie Ransom's and Old Wife's cooperative healing. Minnie heals by making mind and spirit contact with her patients; "she could dance their dance and match their beat and echo their pitch and know their frequency as if her own" (48). She "touch[es] mind to mind from across the room from cross town or the map linked by telephone cables" (48–49). Minnie is like a radio receiver, linked to a web of healing connection, "available to waves from the source" (54).

For Grahn, the basis for this web of connection is conversation and gossip. It is gossip that is the network of the community. "Dialogue, dialogue, dialogue," says one of the wise Aunts in *Mundane's World*: "talk to them [other beings, plants, animals] all the time, everyday, don't take it for granted. Once they lose interest in speaking to us, they will no longer tell us their healing secrets, . . . and we will fall down a pit of stupidity and loneliness, we will lose our powers, and our intelligence, and rightly so" (179).

One might say, I think, that conversation, or "dialogue," is not only a key metaphor for interconnectedness but it is also the structural principal of these narratives. Each is a narrative of many voices, of many perspectives. Through Velma's spirit, wandering from her body in time and space, many voices gain utterance in *Salt Eaters*—the voices of James Lee, her husband, Palma, her sister, and the other women of the Ida B. Wells Club, of Fred Holt the bus driver, and Porter, another bus driver who dies inexplicably, of the watchers in Minnie Ransom's clinic, and of many other inhabitants of the Black community of Claybourne, Georgia. Bambara describes her mode of narration here as "narrator as medium through whom the people unfold their stories, and the town telling as much of its story as can be told in the space of one book" (Tate 32).

In *House on Mango Street*, Esperanza herself is the narrative medium and the bridge. The narrative itself is a series of vignettes joined by the consciousness of Esperanza, whose role as medium and go-between is signaled by her doubled name: "In English it means hope. In Spanish it means too many letters. It means sadness, it means waiting" (12). The very titles of the vignettes suggest the conversation of voices the narrative represents: "Cathy Queen of Cats"; "Alicia Who Sees Mice"; "Edna's Ruthie"; "Elenita, Cards, Palms, Water"; "Rafaela Who Drinks Coconut and Papaya Juice on Tuesdays." Esperanza becomes a writer who will tell these stories: "I put it down on paper and then the ghost does not ache so much" (101). Esperanza can tell these stories because she is the one between, the one who has "gone away to come back. For the ones I left behind. For the ones who cannot out" (102).

In *Tracks*, Nanapush is the narrative medium. His story, rich with dreams and spirits, is a narrative of connection. Unlike Pauline, the novel's other narrator, he has a specific audience for his story—Fleur's daughter, Lulu, who has just been retrieved from the clutches of a government school and returned to her Chippewa community. The intention of Nanapush's narrative is connection, specifically to make a connection between Lulu and Fleur, her absent mother. Through his evocation of Fleur and her history, he recements the broken connection between mother and daughter, and returns to the daughter the power and multilayered experience of her Chippewa history. Without this story, Lulu would be stuck in the flat present that government bureaucracy has created for her tribe. With the story, the possibility of an alternate vision is at least opened for her.

Mundane's World, too, is a narrative dialogue of continually

shifting perspectives, perhaps best epitomized by the final scenes
of the five girls' initiation rite in which Mother Mundane cooks
the "girls up into women" (169). The five girls dream in a large
womblike pot. In dreaming, each enters the perspective of one
participant in Lillian's death: one becomes the cliff, another the
river, another the wind, another the buzzard, another the lion.
"Perspective," reads the title of one of these sections "is watching
yourself from the sky" (180). Through these multiplied perspectives, the death of Lillian, a partial version of which opened the
novel, is played over and over until the narrative is complete. But it
is only through these several perspectives that the full story can be
formed. The initiation rite and the novel end together as the girls,
now women, know that "the five of them together would now be
lifelong peers, ruling together. . . . They were woven together in
the images and events of each others' dream minds" (190).

Each of these three novels, Grahn's, Bambara's and Cisneros's,
ends with a vision of interconnectedness: the weaving together
of the five girls at the end of *Mundane's World*; the healing of
Velma's fragmented consciousness, the bursting of her cocoon at
the end of *The Salt Eaters*; the bridging of separateness and the
knitting together of the women of the community by Esperanza's
writing at the end of *Mango Street*. These visions can only be
achieved by the narrative's resistance of boundaries, separations,
and dualisms, by its refusal to "live in a straight line," by its
multiple voices, by its erosion of distinctions like natural/super-
natural. Each novel leaves us as readers in a liminal place like
the park at the end of *Salt Eaters*: "Slate rained clean, a blessing.
At least twenty-four hours delay, a respite. At least twenty-four
hours to try and pull more closely together. . . . New possibilities
in formation, a new configuration to move with" (295).

At the end of Erdrich's *Tracks*, however, we hover in such a
place of possibility for a moment, but we are not allowed to
remain. Through the doubled narrative of Erdrich's novel, the
understanding represented in Nanapush's tale is set up against two

other forces: the fanatical and isolating Christianity of Pauline, and the bureaucratic and dehumanizing encroachment of the government and the logging companies. The government forecloses on the Chippewa who cannot pay the taxes on their land allotments and then sells the allotments to logging companies, whose loggers, wagons, and equipment invade Fleur's land at the end of the novel. Just as Pauline sees in the Indian ways of the spirits, of healing, of dream, knowing only the monotonous darkness of sin, the loggers and the government see in Fleur's land, rich with spirits and family history, only the single possibility of profit.

As the loggers surround her woods, the last left standing, Fleur stages a final act of resistance. She has worked for weeks to saw through every tree so that, at a touch they fall, crushing loggers, wagons and equipment as they fall. But for one moment the "forest was suspended, lightly held. . . . The powerful throats, the columns of trunks and splayed twigs, all substance was illusion" (223). In this illusion of a forest, Nanapush realizes, all of the ghosts of the wood gather: "Not only the birds and small animals, but the spirits of the western stands had been forced together. The shadows of the trees were crowded with their forms. The twigs spun independently of the wind, vibrating like small voices. I stopped, stood among these trees whose flesh was so much older than ours, and it was then that my relatives and friends took final leave, abandoned me to the living" (221). Among these ghosts, Nanapush knows his wives and family, his dead child and Fleur's; he feels the snows of past winters and smells the ghost of its springs. The moment when the trees fall, marks the end of a worldview that has included all things, natural and supernatural, within the net of essential experience. Fleur leaves, and Nanapush, narrator of the tales of spirits and dreams, abandons his tale and becomes a bureaucrat to try to protect his tribe. And another kind of written narrative now takes over. "Once the bureaucrats sink their barbed pens into the lives of Indians," says Nanapush at the end of the novel, "the paper starts flying, a blizzard of legal forms, a waste of ink by the gallon, a correspondence to which there is no reason" (225).

But in one essential way the possibilities of Nanapush's narrative are not lost. Since the story has been told to Lulu, Fleur's daughter, its possibilities, its ghosts, become hers. Fleur's history and the history that has persisted around her in the ghost-inhabited forest go on in Lulu. Then Lulu, like Ernesta in *Mundane's World*, like Esperanza in *House on Mango Street*, will "see on two levels at once."

My final example from *Tracks* makes explicit what, for me, is one more critical function of supernatural elements in contemporary women's texts. Not only does the supernatural emphasize the importance of connection and of a multiple rather than a dualistic view, but it is also closely associated with the telling of stories. The use of the supernatural is one essential way in which these texts recover the past. Through the supernatural, Bambara, Erdrich, Cisneros, and Grahn create texts whose landscapes are rich with the presence of many stories; each ghost is a recovered story, and ghost seeing is story telling. These ghosts, these stories, are claimed and embraced. If we reject and fear these ghosts, which—to return to my original point—most traditional supernatural stories do, if we choose the natural, present, and knowable only, we choose to live in a flat plane, to "live in a straight line," rather than to inhabit those liminal, ghost-filled spaces of possibility that are the worlds of these texts.

Notes

1. This idea has been central to much feminist analysis from Simone de Beauvoir's *The Second Sex* to more recent works like Bell Hook's *Feminist Theory From Margin to Center* and Audre Lorde's *Sister/Outsider*.

2. Many other novels by contemporary women writers of color contain supernatural elements and might have been included in this

essay. Among them, Toni Morrison's *Beloved* and *Tar Baby*; Gloria Naylor's *Mama Day*; Paule Marshall's *Praisesong for the Widow*.

3. In her acknowledgments Grahn mentions particularly both Audre Lorde for *Black Unicorn*, a volume of poetry permeated with Yoruba mythology, and Paula Gunn Allen for her research and thinking on Native American women in *The Sacred Hoop*. *Another Mother Tongue* is dedicated to, among others, "Paula Gunn Allen who gave me a place to stand on 'the other side' so I could have the mirror image necessary for true vision."

Works Cited

Bambara, Toni Cade. *The Salt Eaters*. New York: Random House, 1980.

Cisneros, Sandra. *The House on Mango Street*. Houston: Arte Publico, 1984.

Duplessis, Rachel Blau. "For the Etruscans." *The New Feminist Criticism*. Ed. Elaine Showalter. London: Pantheon 1985.

Erdrich, Louise. *Tracks*. New York: Holt, 1988.

Grahn, Judy. *Another Mother Tongue: Gay Words, Gay Worlds*. Boston: Beacon, 1984.

———. *Mundane's World*. Trumansburg, NY: Crossings, 1988.

Tate, Claudia, ed. *Black Women Writers at Work*. New York: Continuum, 1984.

Relevant Criticism

THE FOLLOWING BIBLIOGRAPHY lists works cited in the Introduction and in many of the essays in this collection. It includes major
studies of British ghost stories as well as studies of the ghost story's
generic predecessor, the Gothic.

Auerbach, Nina. *Woman and the Demon: The Life of a Victorian
Myth.* Cambridge: Harvard UP, 1982.

Bendixen, Alfred, ed. *Haunted Women: The Best Supernatural Tales
by American Women.* New York: Ungar, 1985.

Birkhead, Edith. *The Tale of Terror: A Study of the Gothic Romance.*
1921. New York: Russell, 1963.

Bleiler, Everett F. *The Guide to Supernatural Fiction.* Kent, OH:
Kent State UP, 1983.

Briggs, Julia. *Night Visitors: The Rise and Fall of the English Ghost
Story.* London: Faber, 1977.

Cixous, Hélène. "Fiction and Its Phantoms: A Reading of Freud's
Das Unheimliche." *New Literary History* 7 (1976): 525–48.

Day, William Patrick. *In the Circles of Fear and Desire: A Study of
Gothic Fantasy.* Chicago: U of Chicago P, 1985.

Ellis, Kate Ferguson. *The Contested Castle: Gothic Novels and the
Subversion of Domestic Ideology.* Urbana: U of Illinois P, 1989.

Fleenor, Juliann E., ed. *The Female Gothic.* Montreal: Eden, 1983.

Freud, Sigmund. "The 'Uncanny.'" *The Standard Edition of the
Complete Psychological Works of Sigmund Freud.* 24 vols. Ed.
James Strachey. 1919. London: Hogarth, 1955. Vol. 17.

Gilbert, Sandra M., and Susan Gubar. *The Madwoman in the Attic:
The Woman Writer and the Nineteenth-Century Literary Imagination.* New Haven: Yale UP, 1979.

Hughes, Winifred. *The Maniac in the Cellar: Sensation Novels of
the 1860s.* Princeton: Princeton UP, 1980.

Hume, Robert D. "Gothic Versus Romantic: A Revaluation of the
Gothic Novel." *PMLA* 84 (1969): 282–90.

Kahane, Claire. "The Gothic Mirror." *The (M)Other Tongue: Essays
in Feminist Psychoanalytic Interpretation.* Ed. Shirley Nelson Gar-

ner, Claire Kahane, and Madelon Sprengnether. Ithaca: Cornell UP, 1985.

Kerr, Howard. *Mediums, and Spirit-Rappers, and Roaring Radicals: Spiritualism in American Literature, 1850–1900*. Urbana: U of Illinois P, 1972.

Kerr, Howard, John W. Crowley, and Charles L. Crow, eds. *The Haunted Dusk: American Supernatural Fiction, 1820–1920*. Athens, GA: U of Georgia P, 1983.

Lovecraft, H[oward] P[hillips]. *Supernatural Horror in Literature*. 1927. New York: Dover, 1973.

MacAndrew, Elizabeth. *The Gothic Tradition in Fiction*. New York: Columbia UP, 1979.

Messent, Peter B., ed. *Literature of the Occult*. Twentieth Century Views. Englewood Cliffs, NJ: Prentice-Hall, 1981.

Moers, Ellen. *Literary Women*. Garden City, NY: Doubleday, 1977.

Mussell, Kay. *Women's Gothic and Romantic Fiction: A Reference Guide*. Westport, CT: Greenwood, 1981.

Peel, Ellen. "Psychoanalysis and the Uncanny." *Comparative Literature Studies* 17.4 (1980): 410–17.

Penzoldt, Peter. *The Supernatural in Fiction*. 1952. New York: Humanities Press, 1965.

Punter, David. *The Literature of Terror: A History of Gothic Fictions from 1765 to the Present Day*. New York: Longman, 1980.

Railo, Eino. *The Haunted Castle: A Study of the Elements of English Romanticism*. New York: Dutton, 1927.

Ringe, Donald. *American Gothic: Imagination and Reason in Nineteenth-Century Fiction*. Lexington: U of Kentucky P, 1982.

Roberts, Bette B. *The Gothic Romance: Its Appeal to Women Writers and Readers in Late Eighteenth-Century England*. Gothic Studies and Dissertations. New York: Arno, 1980.

Salmonson, Jessica Amanda, ed. *What Did Miss Darrington See?* New York: Feminist Press, 1989.

Scarborough, Dorothy. *The Supernatural in Modern English Fiction*. New York: Putnam, 1917.

Summers, Montague. *The Gothic Quest: A History of the Gothic Novel*. 1938. New York: Russell, 1964.

Thompson, G. R., ed. *The Gothic Imagination: Essays in Dark Romanticism*. Pullman: Washington State UP, 1974.

Todd, Janet Marie. "The Veiled Woman in Freud's 'Das Unheimliche.'" *Signs* 11 (1986): 519–28.

Todorov, Tzvetan. *The Fantastic: A Structural Approach to a Literary Genre.* Trans. Richard Howard. Cleveland, OH: Case Western Reserve UP, 1973.

Tompkins, J. M. S. *The Popular Novel in England 1770–1800.* London: Constable, 1932.

Varma, Devendra. *The Gothic Flame.* London: Barker, 1957.

Wagenknecht, Edward. *Cavalcade of the English Novel: From Elizabeth to George VI.* New York: Holt, 1943.

Weiss, Frederic. *The Antic Spectre: Satire in Early Gothic Novels.* Gothic Studies and Dissertations. New York: Arno, 1980.

Woolf, Virginia. "Henry James's Ghost Stories." *Collected Essays.* 4 vols. London: Hogarth, 1966. Vol. 1.

———. "The Supernatural in Fiction." *Collected Essays.* 4 vols. London: Hogarth. Vol. 1.

Selected Bibliography

The following bibliography covers works discussed in this book and other significant collections of ghost stories by women, including American women. In the case of individual authors, we have included all major collections of their ghost stories. We have also completed a more extensive annotated bibliography of women's ghost stories due to be published by Garland Publishing, Inc.

Andrews, Mary Raymond Shipman. *The Eternal Feminine and Other Stories*. New York: Scribner, 1916.

Atherton, Gertrude. *The Bell in the Fog and Other Stories*. New York: Harper, 1905.

————. *The Foghorn*. Boston: Houghton, 1934.

Austin, Mary. *Lost Borders*. New York: Harper, 1909.

Bacon, Josephine Daskam. *The Strange Cases of Dr. Stanchon*. New York: Appleton, 1913.

Bambara, Toni Cade. *The Salt Eaters*. New York: Random House, 1980.

Beck, L. Adams [E. Barrington]. *The Openers of the Gate: Stories of the Occult*. New York: Cosmopolitan, 1930.

Bendixen, Alfred, ed. *Haunted Women: The Best Supernatural Tales by American Women Writers*. New York: Ungar, 1985.

Bowen, Marjorie [Margaret Campbell]. *Kecksies and Other Twilight Tales*. Sauk City, WI: Arkham House, 1976.

Cisneros, Sandra. *The House on Mango Street*. 2nd ed. Houston: Arte Público Press, 1988.

Counselman, Mary Elizabeth. *Half in Shadow*. Sauk City, WI: Arkham House, 1978.

Dalby, Richard, ed. *Victorian Ghost Stories by Eminent Women Writers*. New York: Carroll & Graf, 1988. (Includes both British and American writers.)

Dawson, Emma Frances. *An Itinerant House and Other Stories*. San Francisco: Doxey, 1897.

Erdrich, Louise. *Tracks*. New York: Holt, 1988.

Freeman, Mary E. Wilkins. *The Wind in the Rose-bush and Other Stories of the Supernatural*. New York: Doubleday, 1903.

——. *Collected Ghost Stories*. Sauk City, WI: Arkham House, 1974.

Gilman, Charlotte Perkins. *The Yellow Wallpaper*. 1892. New York: Feminist Press, 1973.

Glasgow, Ellen. *The Shadowy Third and Other Stories*. Garden City, NY: Doubleday, 1923.

Grahn, Judy. *Mundane's World*. Trumansburg, NY: Crossing, 1988.

Hawthorne, Hildegarde. *Faded Garden: The Collected Ghost Stories of Hildegarde Hawthorne*. Ed. Jessica Amanda Salmonson. Madison, WI: Strange, 1985.

Hurston, Zora Neale. *Spunk: The Selected Stories of Zora Neale Hurston*. Berkeley, CA: Turtle Island Foundation, 1985.

Jackson, Shirley. *The Haunting of Hill House*. New York: Viking, 1959.

Jewett, Sarah Orne. *The Country of the Pointed Firs*. Boston: Houghton, 1896.

Kingston, Maxine Hong. *The Woman Warrior: Memoirs of a Girlhood Among Ghosts*. New York: Random House, 1976.

Lavigne, Jeanne de. *Ghost Stories of Old New Orleans*. New York: Rinehart, 1946.

Morrison, Toni. *Beloved*. New York: Knopf, 1987.

——. *Song of Solomon*. New York: Knopf, 1978.

——. *Tar Baby*. New York: Knopf, 1981.

Muller, Marcia and Bill Pronzini, eds. *Witches' Brew: Horror and Supernatural Stories by Women*. New York: Macmillan, 1984. (Includes both British and American writers.)

Naylor, Gloria. *Mama Day*. New York: Ticknor, 1988.

Ozick, Cynthia. *The Pagan Rabbi and Other Stories*. New York: Knopf, 1971.

Peattie, Elia Wilkinson. *The Shape of Fear and Other Ghostly Tales*. 1898. Freeport, NY: Books for Libraries Press, 1969.

Petry, Ann. *Miss Muriel and Other Stories*. Boston: Beacon, 1989.

Phelps [Ward], Elizabeth Stuart. *Men, Women, and Ghosts*. Boston: Fields & Osgood, 1869.

Salmonson, Jessica Amanda, ed. *The Haunted Wherry and Other Rare Ghost Stories*. Madison, WI: Strange, 1985.

——. *What Did Miss Darrington See?* New York: Feminist Press, 1989. (Includes British and Canadian stories as well as American.)

Slosson, Annie Trumbull. *Puzzled Souls*. Philadelphia: Sunday School Times, 1915.

———. *Seven Dreamers*. New York: Harper, 1891.

Southworth, [Mrs. Emma] E. D. E. N. *The Haunted Homestead: And Other Nouvelettes*. Philadelphia: Peterson, 1860.

Spofford, Harriet Elizabeth Prescott. *The Amber Gods and Other Stories*. Boston: Ticknor, 1863.

———. *Sir Rohan's Ghost*. Boston: Tilton, 1860.

Rives [Troubetzkoy], Amélie. *The Ghost Garden*. New York: Stokes, 1918.

Wharton, Edith. *Ghosts*. New York: D. Appleton-Century, 1937.

———. *The Ghost Stories of Edith Wharton*. New York: Scribner, 1973. (Reproduces the contents of *Ghosts*, but replaces "A Bottle of Perrier" with "The Looking Glass"; not a complete collection of Wharton's ghost stories.)

Contributors

Lynette Carpenter is a former women's studies administrator who teaches English and women's studies at Ohio Wesleyan University. Her essays on literature and film have appeared in such journals as *Film History, Film Criticism, Studies in Short Fiction*, and *Legacy*.

Kathy A. Fedorko is a professor of English at Middlesex County College in Edison, NJ, where she teaches "Women in Literature" in addition to other courses in literature and writing. In 1984 she received a Woodrow Wilson Research Grant in Women's Studies for her dissertation on Edith Wharton. She is assistant editor of *The Edith Wharton Newsletter*, published by the Edith Wharton Society, and she is currently working on a book about Edith Wharton's Gothic.

Beth Wynne Fisken is currently a part-time lecturer in the English department at Rutgers University. She has previously published an essay on Freeman in the *Colby Library Quarterly*, and an essay on Alice Brown in *Legacy*, the latter based on a paper presented to the Northeast Modern Language Association. She has recently completed a biographical and critical profile of Alice Brown.

Wendy K. Kolmar teaches women's studies and Victorian literature and directs the women's studies program at Drew University. Her work on Victorian literature and culture has been presented at numerous area conferences. She is also the associate director of the New Jersey Project to Integrate Women and Gender Into the Curriculum, and has served as a women's studies consultant on many university campuses.

Priscilla Leder has taught American literature at the University of Oklahoma, Louisiana State University at Eunice, and presently at Southwest Texas State University. In addition to her work on Jewett, she has written on Kate Chopin for *Southern Studies* and on Alice Walker for the *Journal of the American Studies Association of Texas*. Her current research focuses on Flannery O'Connor.

Tricia Lootens is an assistant professor of English at the University of Georgia. She received a Woodrow Wilson Women's Studies Research Grant for her dissertation on the mythification of Elizabeth Barrett Browning. She is a regular contributor to the feminist newspaper *off our backs* (Washington, D.C.).

E. Suzanne Owens has previously been a member of the English faculties at Ohio State University, Winthrop College, the University of Florida, and Ursuline College. She has published and lectured widely on nineteenth-century American literature and fine arts, focusing on such figures as Edith Wharton, Charlotte Perkins Gilman, and Mary Cassatt. She serves as an Ohio Humanities Council Scholar and a reviewer for *Small Press*.

Barbara Hill Rigney is a professor of English at Ohio State University. She has written numerous articles on feminist critical theory and is the author of three books: *Margaret Atwood* (Macmillan, 1987); *Lilith's Daughters* (U of Wisconsin P, 1979); and *Madness and Sexual Politics in the Feminist Novel: Studies in Bronte, Woolf, Lessing, and Atwood* (U of Wisconsin P, 1978).

Ruth Rosenberg teaches writing at the City University of New York. She recently completed a dissertation on a text-mapping strategy for composing argumentative essays.

Gayle K. Fujita Sato, previously a faculty member at the University of Hawaii at Manoa, is presently associate professor of English at Keio University in Yokohama, Japan. Her research field is Asian-American literature.

Geraldine Smith-Wright teaches American literature and women's studies at Drew University, and chairs the American studies program. Her current research and writing are focused on African-American women writers and particularly on Zora Neale Hurston's short fiction and nonfiction.

Jennice G. Thomas, a former English instructor, is currently an editor and advertising consultant for *Catskill Country Magazine.* She is writing a book on utopia and the twenty-first century, as well as a novel. Her dissertation focused on feminist utopias.

Index

reading, 32, 34, 68, 101, 120, 217, 222–23, 227
Reeve, Clara, 3
religion, 26–29, 234; African, 19, 142–45, 162–64, 231–32, 238–39; Christianity, 11, 52, 238, 247; Judaism, 215–28
revenge, 18, 76, 127, 131
Riddell, Charlotte, 1, 6
Ringe, Donald, 3, 4, 5
Rives, Amélie, 15, 22
Romanticism, 32, 104, 220, 225

Salmonson, Jessica Amanda, 2, 7, 12, 20
Scarborough, Dorothy, 22
servants, 83–92, 130
sexuality, 82, 87–102, 112–16, 157, 167, 168–70, 177, 181–89, 198, 229, 230, 242
Showalter, Elaine, 1, 97
silence, 18, 90–92, 100–2, 103, 133–34
single women, spinsters, 20, 47–50, 54–58, 92–102, 108–16, 132–36, 166–92
sisters, 12, 43–44, 51, 55–57, 60, 61, 111–16, 118–19, 168–71, 179–82, 206, 233
slavery, 142–47, 153, 160–61, 164, 229, 230, 232
Slosson, Annie Trumbull, 8, 12
Southworth, E. D. E. N., 15, 21, 22
spiritualism, 6, 167
Spofford, Harriet E. Prescott, 5, 18
storytelling, 26–29, 32–38, 100, 101, 142–45, 195, 203, 205, 207, 234, 245, 247–48
Stowe, Harriet Beecher, 5, 8, 22
sympathy, 13–14, 19, 28, 46, 50, 58, 98, 117–32

terror. See horror
Twain, Mark, 9, 21, 29

Walpole, Horace, 3
Wharton, Edith, 2, 18, 64, 80–105, 108–16, 120, 219
women: as victims, 16, 18, 67, 81, 82, 87–105, 110–13, 120–32 (see also *domestic violence*); bonds between, 10, 14, 28, 45, 86, 90–92, 97, 98, 108–16, 117–38, 152–53, 172, 178–84, 191–92, 193–213, 233–34, 239–40
Woolf, Virginia, 120

Haunting the House of Fiction was designed by Deborah Wong, composed by Tseng Information Systems, Inc., and printed and bound by BookCrafters, Inc. The book is set in Linotron 202 Sabon and printed on 50–lb Glatfelter natural.